POPE BENEDICT XVI'S LEGAL THOUGHT

Throughout Pope Emeritus Benedict XVI's pontificate he spoke to a range of political, civil, academic, and other cultural authorities. The speeches he delivered in these contexts reveal a striking sensitivity to the fundamental problems of law, justice, and democracy. His contribution goes well beyond the community of Catholic believers, since he didn't rely on moral or doctrinal arguments, but on what all humans have in common: reason.

This book takes on Benedict XVI's pivotal question "How do we recognize what is right?" in contemporary democratic and pluralistic constitutional contexts, and discusses five speeches in which the Pope Emeritus reflected most explicitly on this issue along with the commentary from a number of distinguished legal scholars from different cultural and religious backgrounds. It responds to Benedict's invitations to re-open a public conversation on the limits of positivist reason; to leave the windowless "bunker" in which positivism has confined human reason; and to reach out for a wider understanding of human possibilities, in the name of the "whole breadth of reason." Although the topics of each address vary, they nevertheless are grounded on a series of core ideas, which Benedict sketches, unpacks, and develops in an organic and coherent way to formulate a "public teaching" on the topic of justice and law.

Marta Cartabia, full professor of constitutional law, is currently a member of the Italian Constitutional Court. She has taught in a number of Italian and foreign universities.

Andrea Simoncini is full professor of constitutional law at the University of Florence, Italy. In 2009 he was Fulbright Distinguished Lecturer at Notre Dame University where he was also a visiting professor at the Law School.

LAW AND CHRISTIANITY

The Law and Christianity series publishes cutting-edge work on Catholic, Protestant, and Orthodox Christian contributions to public, private, penal, and procedural law and legal theory. The series aims to promote deep Christian reflection by leading scholars on the fundamentals of law and politics, to build further ecumenical legal understanding across Christian denominations, and to link and amplify the diverse and sometimes isolated Christian legal voices and visions at work in the academy. Works collected by the series include groundbreaking monographs, historical and thematic anthologies, and translations by leading scholars around the globe.

Pope Benedict XVI's Legal Thought

A DIALOGUE ON THE FOUNDATION OF LAW

Edited by

Marta Cartabia

Constitutional Court of Italy

Andrea Simoncini

University of Florence

CAMBRIDGE
UNIVERSITY PRESS

CAMBRIDGE
UNIVERSITY PRESS

32 Avenue of the Americas, New York, NY 10013-2473, USA

Cambridge University Press is part of the University of Cambridge.

It furthers the University's mission by disseminating knowledge in the pursuit of education, learning, and research at the highest international levels of excellence.

www.cambridge.org
Information on this title: www.cambridge.org/9781107090200

First published 2015

A catalog record for this publication is available from the British Library.

Library of Congress Cataloging in Publication Data
Pope Benedict XVI's legal thought : a dialogue on the foundation of law / edited by Marta Cartabia, Andrea Simoncini.
pages cm
ISBN 978-1-107-09020-0 (Hardback)
1. Benedict XVI, Pope, 1927–Political and social views. 2. Law–Philosophy 3. Catholic Church–Doctrines. 4. Canon law. 5. Christian sociology–Catholic Church I. Cartabia, Marta, editor. II. Simoncini, Andrea (Law professor) editor.
K230.B463P67 2015
340′.115–dc23 2014042926

ISBN 978-1-107-09020-0 Hardback

English translations from foreign languages were provided by Mariangela Crema.

CONTENTS

FOREWORD

During the pivotal years of his papacy, Benedict XVI offered a body of legal–political thought characterized by such a breadth and wealth of sources that it both merits and inspires highly qualified study, reflection, and discussion of the kind collected here at the behest of Marta Cartabia and Andrea Simoncini.

I am delighted with this project, and pleased to draw on it in order to understand better and clarify – for myself, first of all – the unique relationship I had with the Holy Father Benedict XVI as President of the Republic of Italy.

Our relationship was unique in the intensity and naturalness, harmony and trust, which characterized it from the start, perhaps in some ways surprising even ourselves. I would say that this reflected a personal affinity, including particularly a shared preference for quiet, free, and respectful dialogue, as well as a generational affinity. The latter was manifest, above all, in our common background: both of us have lived out our lives in the historical context of the twentieth century, with its magnificent and terrible intertwining of light and shadow, which our two countries experienced more than all the others, in both dramatic and traumatic terms until the middle of the last century. This experience motivates our shared personal identification with the project of a new Europe, united at last in freedom and peace.

In one of his most recent speeches, delivered at the Bundestag of Berlin in December 2011, Benedict masterfully diagnosed the precondition for this achievement as the "culture of Europe," that culture born of "the encounter between Jerusalem, Athens and Rome." In the same speech I found the most explicit reference to the legal and political development that culminated in the German Fundamental Law and in contemporary democratic constitutions of other Western European countries, Italy's among them.

This implicit identification of both of us with the foundations of a form of politics that is illuminated by history and supported by reason formed the backdrop of the ongoing dialogue that Benedict XVI and I carried forward in a spirit of active collaboration, without any rifts, as Heads of the State of Italy and of the Catholic Church.

And there is no doubt that another factor played a role in making richer and more consistent both our relationship and that of the two institutions we represented – "independent and sovereign" and "each within its own sphere" as the Italian Constitution prescribes. This other factor is the characteristic practice, long-established in Italy, of non-exclusion of the religious element from the public sphere, "the conviction" – at the contrary – "that the social and public dimension of the religious fact must be objectively recognized." I uttered these words before the Italian Parliament when I took the oath of office as President on May 15, 2006. This conviction enabled and continues to enable me to contribute to the dialogue between religious believers and non-believers, to represent them together as citizens, and to strive always to bring them closer to unity.

Giorgio Napolitano

1 A JOURNEY WITH BENEDICT XVI THROUGH THE SPIRIT OF CONSTITUTIONALISM

Marta Cartabia and Andrea Simoncini

INTRODUCTION

In this book legal scholars from many different places and cultural backgrounds discuss the legal thought of Pope Benedict XVI.

Where did the idea for this project come from? Benedict XVI is neither a jurist nor a legal scholar, and probably never intended to be. Yet, throughout his pontificate he was invited to dialogue with political, civil, academic, and cultural authorities, and the speeches he delivered in these contexts reveal a striking sensitivity to the fundamental problems of law, justice, and democracy. This book collects some of the speeches in which the Pope Emeritus reflected most explicitly on these issues along with the comments of a number of legal scholars: it means to respond to the invitation to engage in public discussion on the limits of positivist reason in the domain of law that Benedict launched in his address to the Bundestag.

Each of the speeches considered here was intended for a particular audience, and their contents are framed according to their respective contexts. For example, the lecture at Regensburg took place in an academic environment; there, Benedict focused on the relationship between faith and reason. The speech to the Collège des Bernardins in Paris was addressed the cultural elites of France, a country that, since its foundation, has cultivated a secular culture that distrusts religion; in that context, Benedict described the historical contribution of the Christian faith to the development of European civilization, pointing to the work done by Benedictine Monasteries after the fall of the Roman Empire and the Barbarian devastation. At Westminster Hall in London, Benedict found himself before the oldest Parliament in all the western democracies, and in the place where Sir Thomas More was condemned to a cruel death in the name of religious discord; there he expressed enthusiastic appreciation for the liberal democratic tradition, without downplaying his concern for an authentic protection of religious freedom in the West, even today, from any form of subtle threat. When he was invited to the United Nations in New York, Benedict praised the project of human rights, which developed particularly in the post-World War II period with the approval of the Universal Declaration of Human Rights (UDHR) in 1948, and yet did not spare observations that were critical of the contemporary practices of international institutions in protecting rights. And, in his speech before the Bundestag of Berlin, he went straight to the heart of the matter, addressing the foundation of the legal order and the limits of legal positivism, which has dominated the European continent throughout the twentieth century.

The topics vary, as they were designed for and addressed to different audiences; nevertheless, they are joined by a series of core ideas, which Benedict sketches, unpacks, and develops in a coherent way, in the end nearly formulating a sort of organic "public teaching" on the topic of justice and law. None of them is about the so-called nonnegotiable values. Although he was invited to talk to legislators and other civil authorities of western secular democracies, Pope Benedict XVI did not touch upon issues of family, gender, life, abortion, and so on. He rather goes to the foundation of the law, and addresses a set of methodological questions.

The speeches have another common characteristic as well: all were addressed to institutions rooted in the legal and political principles of the western liberal democracies.

In a variety of his writings, Benedict has demonstrated that he is well aware of the phenomenon he calls the "intercultural dimension" of human existence today[1] – the fact that today's world is host to cultural and anthropological traditions that are radically different from those derived from the encounter between Jewish, Greco-Roman, and Christian thought, which we tend to classify as

[1] J. Habermas, J. Ratzinger, The Dialectics of Secularization: On Reason and Religion, San Francisco: Ignatius Press, 2005, 73 ff.

"western." These include Islam; Indian culture, or more precisely, the Hindu and Buddhist cultures; and the great tribal cultures of Africa and South America. "In many ways, these seem to call Western rationality into question; and this means that they also call into question the universal claim of Christian revelation."[2] For this reason, it is still more important to return to the question of the foundation of legal thought as it has developed in the context of liberal democracies; only a clear awareness of one's own identity allows for a true openness to dialogue with the various "other" cultures. This dialogue represents the pivotal challenge of the new, globalized millennium.

LAW, REASON, AND REVELATION

"In history, systems of law have almost always been based on religion: decisions regarding what was to be lawful among men were taken with reference to the divinity. Unlike other great religions, Christianity has never proposed a revealed law to the State and to society, that is to say a juridical order derived from revelation. Instead, it has pointed to nature and reason as the true sources of law – and to the harmony of objective and subjective reason, which naturally presupposes that both spheres are rooted in the creative reason of God."[3]

This excerpt is among the best-known passages from the speech delivered before the Bundestag of Berlin on September 22, 2011, and with good reason. It captures the heart of Benedict XVI's thought on religion's contribution to public debate and, in particular, to the construction of the legal juridical order.

The originality of Christianity with respect to other religions is self-evident in this thought – an originality that is often overlooked, not only by secular commentators, but by Christians themselves: it is not revelation, but "reason and nature in their interrelation" that form "the universally valid source of law," as Benedict says a few lines later in the same speech.

[2] Id., at 75.

[3] Pope Benedict XVI, Visit to the Bundestag, Reichstag Building, Berlin, September 22, 2011.

On September 17, 2010, at Westminster Hall, he had proposed a similar concept in these terms: "The Catholic tradition maintains that the objective norms governing right action are accessible to reason, prescinding from the content of revelation. According to this understanding, the role of religion in political debate is not so much to supply these norms, as if they could not be known by non-believers – still less to propose concrete political solutions, which would lie altogether outside the competence of religion."[4]

With these statements, Benedict clears up a persistent misunderstanding in contemporary culture, which has influenced and continues to influence the debate on the relationship between religion and public reason. Benedict XVI overturns the assumption that the contribution of Christianity to the public debates derives from the command of an authority – *ipse dixit.* In political and legal disputes he does not rely on the statements of the religious authority, but on the authority of reason.

Most people believe, to this day, that religious people intervene in democratic discourse on the basis of authoritative dogmas. Therefore they would violate the fundamental rule of every deliberative democracy – *dialogos* among the different positions – and would act as discussion stoppers, irreparably distorting the democratic dynamic[5]. There is a fear that religious authority may contend with the democratically constituted civil authority for the power to set legal norms, leading to an irremediable incompatibility between the two sources of authority. The inevitable conclusion is that "it is precisely the exile of any *Ipse dixit* from the realm of public discussion, the ostracism of all faiths, which guarantees the common ground of the *dialogos* and the mutual equality of all as co-citizens," with the resulting requirement that "The entire public sphere be emptied of God," so that a neutral ground for dialogue is preserved.[6]

[4] Pope Benedict XVI, Meeting with the representatives of British society, Westminster Hall, Westminster, September 17, 2010.

[5] See, among many, P. Flores D'Arcais, "Laicità tout court, laicità debole, laicità tradita," MicroMega, 1, 2013, 49–59; G. Zagrebelsky, Imparare democrazia, Turin: Einaudi, 2007.

[6] D'Arcais, "Laicità tout court," 55, 59.

The case for God's exile from the public square comes from the belief that religious groups' intervention in the democratic dialectic would take the form of a series of prescriptions or commandments derived from a higher will, eternal and unquestionable: indeed, an *ipse dixit*. But nothing seems more alien to Benedict's thinking. He demands that Catholic people engage in a thorough use of reason; he does not allow them to deprive themselves of the beauty and the appeal of using their own reason nor does he permit them to hide behind the authority of the Church, or of the commandments, or of religious precepts. He requires Christians to take part in the democratic *dialogos* using arguments open to everybody, believers and nonbelievers alike: reason and nature, in their interconnection. Because of his certainty that the divine, as *logos*, may be reached through the rational search for truth, Benedict does not hesitate to require the faithful to enter public democratic dialogue with tools that are universal and accessible to all: reason and nature in their interrelation. From this point of view, contrary to a widespread bias, admitting religion into the public square is not tantamount to introducing a fideistic principle into democratic dialogue; nor does it imply relying mechanically on religious precepts as the source of regulation for social, political, and legal problems. Benedict's primary, fundamental point is to remind us that the ultimate sources of law are found in reason and nature and not in a command, no matter what its source.

In the Pope Emeritus' thought we find praise of human reason that is rooted in an understanding of Christianity as the religion of the *logos*, linked since the Old Testament – and more precisely since the translation of the Septuagint into Greek – with Greek culture, with philosophy, and with the "devout enlightenment" of Socrates, who was at once enlightened and in search of God.[7]

[7] On Socrates, see Joseph Ratzinger, Truth and Tolerance: Christian Belief and World Religions, San Francisco: Ignatius Press, 2004. See also the speech that Benedict XVI intended to give in the course of his visit to the Università degli Studi "La Sapienza" in Rome, which was scheduled for January 17, 2008, and then canceled.

The originality of Benedict's view on Christians in the public square derives from a vision of Christianity as a universal religion, oriented toward everyone, which trusts in the possibility that reason can transcend reason's own abilities.[8] Benedict makes this point in the words of Saint Paul: "[W]hen the Gentiles who do not have the law [the Torah of Israel] by nature observe the prescriptions of the law, they are a law for themselves even though they do not have the law. They show that the demands of the law are written on their hearts, while their conscience also bears witness" (Romans 2:14).[9]

Because he holds in high regard the value of reason, Benedict offers an interesting response to the dilemma that has persistently dogged contemporary culture in recent decades: that of the role of religion in public democratic discourse. There have been two significant developments in this debate in our contemporary, post-secular era: first, there is a push to rehabilitate religion as a presence in civil life after years of ostracism, which recognizes the contribution religion makes to public dialogue and social life. At the same time, this openness to religions' participation opens up new issues that must be addressed. Indeed, the second prominent aspect is that those who are most sympathetic to the religious phenomenon run into the challenge of communicating doctrines of religious origins to all citizens through a universal language.

The first aspect represents a significant evolution in the debate, which was for decades dominated by a secularist culture that was openly suspicious – if not hostile – to any public expression of religion. This secularist culture sprang from the early theories of John Rawls, who famously believed it is necessary to exclude all "comprehensive conceptions of the good," especially religious ones, from public discourse.[10] Rawlsian theories, although soon mitigated

[8] For more thorough treatment of the idea of reason freed from positivist reduction and the relationship between religion and reason, see Ratzinger, *Truth and Tolerance*.

[9] English Biblical quotations were taken from *The New American Bible*, Wichita: Fireside Bible Publishers, 1998.

[10] J. Rawls, Political Liberalism, New York: Columbia University Press, 1993.

by the author himself,[11] have deeply influenced the cultural mindset of the western liberal democracies, at both the theoretical and the practical levels. More recent developments, however, reveal a new attitude – one that is decidedly more sensitive to the contribution of religious traditions to public decision making. This openness – which can be found even in the more recent thought of Rawls himself – has been developed further by such scholars as Jürgen Habermas and Charles Taylor[12] For Habermas "as long as religious communities play a vital role in civil society and the public sphere, deliberative politics is as much a product of the public use of reason on the part of *religious* citizens as that of *nonreligious* citizens."[13] Similarly, Taylor holds that "the general principle is that religious groups must be seen as much as interlocutors and as little as menace as the situation allows."[14] Both authors, beginning with a realistic consideration of the fact that "vibrant religious communities" or "spiritual families" are present in social life, underline the urgent need of every regime wishing to remain democratic to include them in the decision-making process, given that they are, in fact, components of the social fabric.

The reduction of religion to the private sphere and its exclusion from public debate, propagated by the earliest theorists of the secular state, appear to have now been overcome on the basis of the same fundamental principles of liberal democracy, which originally seemed to lead to the opposite conclusions. Nevertheless – and this is the second significant aspect of the recent debate – this dramatic change generates new issues that must be addressed. If public life opens itself

[11] J. Rawls, "The Idea of Public Reason Revisited," *The University of Chicago Law Review*, 64, 765–807.

[12] See the debate that took place at New York University in October 2009, now published in E. Mendieta, J. VanAntwerpen (eds.), with contributions of J. Butler, J. Habermas, C. Taylor, C. West, The Power of Religion in the Public Sphere, New York: Columbia University Press, 2011.

[13] J. Habermas, "The Political – The Rational Meaning of a Questionable Inheritance of Political Theology," in E. Mendieta and J. Vanantwerpen (eds.), *The Power of Religion in the Public Sphere*, 23.

[14] Ch. Taylor, "Why We Need a Radical Redefinition of Secularism," in E. Mendieta and J. Vanantwerpen (eds.), *The Power of Religion in the Public Sphere*, 36.

up to the religions, how can the "neutrality" of the state be preserved with respect to each creed, be it Christian, Muslim, Jewish, Marxist, Kantian, Utilitarian, and so on? By the same token, how can the possibility of dialogue between citizen believers and nonbelievers be maintained?

Habermas responds to these concerns by proposing a "translation proviso": on the one hand, he asserts that "all citizens should be free to decide whether they want to use religious language in the public sphere"; on the other, however, he holds that "the potential truth contents of religious utterances must be translated into a generally accessible language before they can find their way onto the agendas of parliaments, courts, or administrative bodies and influence their decisions"[15] For Taylor there is, in principle, no difference between religious and secular discourse, both being legitimate modes of participation in public debate, even in parliaments and courts. But he, too, finally comes to recognize that the formal acts of public organs, such as enacting laws, passing administrative regulations, or pronouncing judicial decisions, should be formulated in a neutral language, common to the various faiths and traditions, because these measures express "the official language of the State." Although the two authors differ in where they draw the borders of the "free zone," they agree on the requirement that arguments inspired by religion, once allowed into the public debate, must divest themselves of their religiousness in order to become accessible to all and usable in the official language of the state.

Benedict XVI resolves this difficulty at its root by asserting that the source of legal norms is not revelation, but reason and nature in their interrelation; that is, as the then-Cardinal Ratzinger had explained in many places prior to his election to the pontificate, "History is, so to speak, the kingdom of reason; politics does not establish the Kingdom of God, but it certainly ought to be concerned about the just kingdom of man," in order to remind Catholics engaged in politics that "politics is the sphere of reason."[16] From this perspective, the issue of translating religion-based arguments

[15] J. Habermas, "The Political," 25.

[16] J. Ratzinger, *Europe: Today and Tomorrow*, San Francisco: Ignatius Press, 59–60.

into comprehensible language, or the neutral language of official acts of the state, is a question that does not even need to be asked.

Benedict's thought, free from all epistemic discrepancy between knowledge and belief, reason and faith, offers a simple and truly persuasive response to one of the most complicated problems faced by contemporary democracies, which are called on to govern over a social fabric that is highly complex and diverse. He invites Christians to make their contribution to political and legal life on the basis of what they share with all humankind, "but never forgetting that the contribution of Christians can be effective only if knowledge of faith becomes knowledge of reality, the key to judgment and transformation."[17]

DEMOCRATIC RELATIVISM AND PRINCIPLES OF JUSTICE

This understanding of the Christian presence in civil life, that relies on reason rather than revelation, has unexpected consequences. Pope Benedict, who was presented to the public as a conservative theologian, the enemy of cultural relativism, and the Pope of nonnegotiable values, surprised many people when, in the speech he delivered to the Bundestag, he asserted that "[f]or most of the matters that need to be regulated by law, the support of the majority can serve as a sufficient criterion." In essence, this statement expresses an appreciation (a realistic appreciation!) for democracy, with its processes based on the principle of the majority and the method of consensus, which – abstractly speaking – are traditionally ascribed to precisely the relativistic culture that Cardinal Ratzinger firmly opposed. From the time of Hans Kelsen on, western legal culture has explicitly asserted that "relativism is the *Weltanschauung* that the *democratic idea* presumes."[18]

[17] Benedict XVI, Address to the 24th plenary session of the pontifical council for the laity, Consistory Hall, May 21, 2010.

[18] H. Kelsen, "Vom Wesen und Wert der Demokratie," Mohr, Tübingen, 1929; "Democracy and Weltanschauung," in A. Jacobson and B. Schlink, Weimar: A Jurisprudence of Crisis, 2000, 108.

There is something unexpected in Benedict's esteem for a political doctrine that contains the seeds of relativism. And yet, there is nothing at all surprising about this conclusion, in light of the premises laid out in the preceding paragraph. In reality, Ratzinger's thought is much richer and more articulate than it would seem from reductionist media portrayals. There are two essential cornerstones of his vision of civil life and politics: the first is rooted in the idea that the legal and political order belongs to the realm of what is human, and as such is not an absolute. In the original Christian tradition a distinction is drawn between the *Civitas Dei* and the *civitas mundi*.[19] This supports a "healthy relativism" when it comes to secular choices, which concern politics and law, and an appreciation for the rule of the majority in the ordinary functioning of governments. On the other hand, and this is the second cornerstone, this relativism cannot, in itself, be absolute without becoming the uncontrollable province of the majority: "Yet it is evident that for the fundamental issues of law, in which the dignity of man and of humanity is at stake, the majority principle is not enough: everyone in a position of responsibility must personally seek out the criteria to be followed when framing laws."[20]

The drift toward totalitarianism that took place, particularly in Germany and Italy, between the two World Wars, of which Benedict is constantly aware, including from life experience, attests to how the rule of the majority can easily turn into brute force, which does not hesitate to order or consent to the most atrocious acts. In this awareness, Benedict's thought bears a striking similarity to certain recent developments within contemporary European constitutionalism, which arose during the post-World War II period in response to the atrocities that were brought about by uncontested domination by pure majority rule.

Constitutionalism emerged on the European continent in France in the late eighteenth century, with the "sovereignty" of Parliament, as

[19] We refer here to St. Augustin, Civitas Dei; the relationship between politics and theology and its evolution over time has recently been revisited by M. Borghesi, Critica della teologica politica – Da Agostino a Peterson: la fine dell'era costantiniana, Marietti, Milano, 2013.

[20] Pope Benedict XVI, Visit to the Bundestag.

the representative organ of the people, and of legislation, as the appropriate *expression de la volonté générale* (expression of the general will). The exercise of power was entrusted to it, on the assumption that the people and their representatives would use it well/properly. They were even entrusted with the power to guarantee the fundamental rights of the person, which in the meantime, and for the first time, were "codified" in constitutional charters. Many of the dispositions of the Declaration of the Rights of Man and of the Citizen of 1789, the symbol of that epoch, testify to the centrality of formal legislation and of Parliaments. This mindset dominated continental culture unchallenged until the end of the Second World War. Then, during the rewriting of the constitutions after the catastrophe of war,[21] the weakness of that system became evident along with the urge to amend the limits of eighteenth century legal positivism, which had focused on the sacredness of the Parliamentary legislation and popular will.

Indeed, the Nazi and Fascist regimes not only ushered in the terrible realities of racial discrimination and unprecedented brutality against human dignity, but, even worse, did so with the support of legislation: for example, the 1935 laws of Nuremberg in Germany and the racial legislation in Italy that began in 1938, which provided legal cover for the regimes. At that time, racial persecution and the oppression of the individual had become part of the law of the land. Legislation itself, which liberal constitutionalism held to be the best tool for safeguarding the rights of citizens, turned into a tool of oppression, disastrous for people's dignity and for their very existence. This accounts for the banality of evil of that era, conveyed to us in Hannah Arendt's unforgettable pages on the trial of Adolf Eichmann:[22] evil had become the law of the land and, as such, the citizens had to obey it. In this way even the most horrendous acts could be easily "digested" by the state's legislative machine, therefore assuming the characteristics of an appalling banality which, because imposed by law, came to be considered the rule that everyone must follow.

[21] G. Capograssi, Il diritto dopo la catastrofe, Padova: Cedam, 1950.

[22] Hannah Arendt, Eichmann in Jerusalem: A Report on the Banality of Evil, New York: Penguin Books, 2006.

The "statutory lawlessness" of those years, to use the effective expression of Gustav Radbruch,[23] revealed the drawbacks of legal positivism and the urgency of overcoming it. In the face of the atrocities of the totalitarian regimes the response was to create "the age of rights" (Norberto Bobbio): the new constitutional wave after World War II brought about a number of declarations of rights or charters of rights, starting with the UDHR of 1948, the European Convention on Human Rights, and all the new national constitutions. Both at the international level and at the national level these documents were meant to impose rigid limits on the floating majorities. In order to secure the protection of the human person and of his or her rights, a number of "rigid" bills of rights were proclaimed, with the purpose of taking those basic rights out of the hands of the legislators. New and higher principles were added to the legal system, in order to set up intangible limits to legislation.

There is significant overlap between these evolutions of contemporary constitutionalism and Pope Benedict's call for limits on democratic procedures based merely on majority rule. Recalling the words of Saint Augustine, Benedict, in the speech delivered before the Bundestag, began with a reflection on the totalitarian state: "'Without justice – what else is the State but a great band of robbers?' as Saint Augustine once said. We Germans . . . have seen how power became divorced from right, how power opposed right and crushed it, so that the State became an instrument for destroying right – a highly organized band of robbers, capable of threatening the whole world and driving it to the edge of the abyss."[24] He praised the resistance fighters who in every totalitarian regime have opposed the enacted law that was, in reality, an injustice, "thereby doing a great service to justice and to humanity as a whole."[25]

Benedict leaves room for a twofold construction of the legal system, also typical of contemporary constitutionalism, that

[23] G. Radbruch, "Gesetzliches Unrecht und übergesetliches Rect, Süddeutsche Juristen-Zeitung I (1946), Statutory Lawlessness and Supra-Statutory Law," trans. B. Litschewki Paulson, St. L. Paulson, Oxford Journal of Legal Studies, 26/1, 2006, p. 7.

[24] Pope Benedict XVI, Visit to the Bundestag. [25] Id.

encompasses, on the one hand, legislation produced by the majority will and democratic consensus and, on the other, the safeguard of certain principles of justice that cannot be left at the mercy of the unpredictable outcomes of the sometimes fickle game of democracy. This twofold construction reminds us of the need to preserve a conceptual difference between the enacted (positive) legislation and the right (or justice) and to maintain constant dialogue within this dualism, resisting the temptation to resolve it in favor of either of its two poles, a need that has been reiterated recently by distinguished secular voices as well, including Gustavo Zagrebelsky.[26]

In a memorable passage from his book *Truth and Tolerance*, then-Cardinal Ratzinger had already stated that

> A free society is said to be a relativistic society; only on this condition can it remain free and open-ended. In the realm of politics this view is to a great extent true. The one single correct political option does not exist . . . – thinking that it could be was precisely the error of Marxism and of the political theologies. Even in the realm of politics, of course, one cannot always manage with absolute relativism: there are things that are wrong and can never become right (killing innocent people, for instance; denying individuals the right to be treated as humans and to a way of life appropriate to that); there are things that are right and can never become wrong.[27]

Social life is the domain of history, is the "City of man," and therefore leaves ample room for the decisions of the majority as the ordinary method of governance; nevertheless, we cannot forget that "majorities, too, can be blind or unjust, as history teaches us very plainly."[28] What Ratzinger considers unacceptable about positivistic and relativistic culture – and he has addressed Hans Kelsen's ideas on this point several times – is that, under that view, "[t]ruth is

[26] G. Zagrebelsky, La legge e la sua giustizia: tre capitoli di giustizia costituzionale, Bologna: Il Mulino, 2008.

[27] J. Ratzinger, Truth and Tolerance: Christian Belief and World Religions, San Francisco: Ignatius Press, 2004, 118.

[28] Ratzinger, *Europe*, 70.

replaced by the decision of the majority," so that "[t]he chance occurrence of a majority becomes an absolute."[29]

So far, we have taken note of the correspondence that exists between Pope Benedict XVI's legal approach and the spirit of constitutionalism. However these similarities go hand in hand with some important differences that are worth pointing out.

Constitutionalism tends to codify the limits that should be placed on the majority in written constitutions, perhaps ascribing them superior value to other laws, making them higher laws so that certain undebatable points of the legal order are secured. This is the *raison d'être* of constitutions, and also of the declarations and international agreements where the rights of the person and other universal principles are "consecrated." The guardianship of these principles is then entrusted, for the most part, to judicial authorities, often to special tribunals – the constitutional courts – endowed with the power to enforce these principles against parliamentary legislation and even to annul it. Where the constitutional narrative imposes limits on majoritarian rule, it is by means of a "superior law," a "higher" codification, the guardianship of which is entrusted to the judiciary, from which to draw the criteria for validating legislation. Essentially, a further "layer" is added to the legal order, to contain democracy's deviations.

The Pope Emeritus sees a great value in this framework, as he made clear in his speech to the United Nations in 2008.[30] That speech praises the UN Declaration of 1948 for the contribution that it has given to the "common good of the human family." Nevertheless, as Mary Ann Glendon pointed out in one of her articles,[31] in that speech the expressions of appreciation for the UDHR "are accompanied by a set of warnings" and she singles out no fewer than nine dilemmas that have beset the human rights project from the beginning and which are referred to by Pope Benedict. One of the

[29] Ratzinger, *Truth and Tolerance*, 72, 190.

[30] See M.A. Glendon, "Justice and Human Rights: Reflections on the Address of Pope Benedict to the UN," in European Journal of International Law, n. 5, November 2008, 925–930.

[31] Id.

most relevant is his critique of legal positivism: "Experience shows that legality often prevails over justice when the insistence upon rights makes them appear as the exclusive result of legislative enactments or normative decisions taken by the various agencies of those in power. When presented purely in terms of legality, rights risk becoming weak propositions divorced from the ethical and rational dimension which is their foundation and their goal. The Universal Declaration, rather, has reinforced the conviction that respect for human rights is principally rooted in unchanging justice, on which the binding force of international proclamations is also based.... Since rights and the resulting duties follow naturally from human interaction, it is easy to forget that they are the fruit of a commonly held sense of justice built primarily upon solidarity among the members of society, and hence valid at all times and for all peoples.... Human rights, then, must be respected as an expression of justice, and not merely because they are enforceable through the will of the legislators."[32]

Neither the will of the majority – not even that special, qualified majority required to approve a constitutional amendment – nor the divine will, nor that of a religious authority is an appropriate foundation for the legal order. In other words, good legal texts, fair rules, and procedures are useful tools, but are not sufficient in themselves to guarantee that legislation does not turn into an instrument of wrongdoing. New charters of rights and declarations might be extremely important – and actually have been extremely important – for the protection of human freedom and dignity, but they cannot do the whole job.

Paradoxical as it may sound, the mere setting of human rights and principles of justice into a worded text is no guarantee of their observation in practice. That is why Ratzinger's critique of legislation as the expression of a mere act of power does not envisage replacing the popular will with the will of a superior authority. Rather Ratzinger trusts the inexhaustible process of reason, open to the progressive recognition of what is just or unjust, true or false. As such, it is an ever-unfinished work, always in need of renewal and always alive.

[32] Benedict XVI, Meeting with the Members of the General Assembly of the United Nations Organization, New York, April 18, 2008.

Proof of the wisdom of this position can be found, among the many other examples, in the historical events surrounding the first, glorious constitutional experiment in the West, the United States of America, which was solidly founded on an admirable text, the Declaration of Independence of 1776: "We hold these truths to be self-evident, that all men are created equal, that they are endowed by their Creator with certain unalienable Rights, that among these are Life, Liberty and the pursuit of Happiness."

Seeing this proclamation, who would have imagined that the first and largest constitutional democracy would have to undergo a bloody civil war less than a century later, then await the approval of the Thirteenth Amendment to its Constitution, paid for with the life of President Abraham Lincoln, and then overcome many other political, social, and legal obstacles (lasting through recent years), before the scars of slavery and racial discrimination were finally somewhat healed? A document – even an exemplary one – did not suffice to ward off the shameful reality of slavery.

Myriad examples throughout history may be recalled in order to confirm the wisdom of Pope Benedict XVI's insight, which stresses the need for every legal and political decision to be open to the language of truth, and for public decision making to be always "sensitive to the truth."[33] According to Benedict, human laws must remain constantly attentive to nature and reason, as the true sources of law, and to which every legal command is subject. Texts may help. Nevertheless Benedict does not rely on texts alone. Justice cannot be achieved once and forever simply by establishing a set of written principles. Striving against injustice is rather a dynamic task, an ongoing and endless drama. And in the never-ending, inexhaustible struggle against injustice the protagonist is a living person, a subject. It is each of us.

No legal system, even the most perfect, can do without the tireless energy of each human person, that springs from the ineradicable human longing for justice. "[T]he kingdom of good will never be

[33] Benedict XVI, quoting Habermas, in the speech he intended to give during his visit to the Università degli Studi "La Sapienza" di Roma, scheduled for Janurary 17, 2008, and later canceled.

definitively established in this world. Anyone who promises the better world that is guaranteed to last for ever is making a false promise.... If there were structures which could irrevocably guarantee a determined – good – state of the world, man's freedom would be denied, and hence they would not be good structures at all. What this means is that every generation has the task of engaging anew in the arduous search for the right way to order human affairs; this task is never simply completed."[34] Described as a "conservative Pope," from the legal point of view, Benedict XVI is in fact a great reformer calling for each citizen to use his or her critical reason and his or her conscience; a great reformer, as he proved to be in the life of the Catholic Church, with the unexpected final act of his pontificate.

Like other great humanists, Benedict XVI knows very well that no matter how perfect a set of rules is, it is always exposed to the danger that *summum ius* become *summa iniuria* – that the most perfect law become the most perfect injustice. And in order to prevent this inevitable decline he summons the conscience of the individual. In a previous age, Sophocles described the importance of the individual conscience in the character of Antigone, who accepted the sacrifice of her own life in opposition to an unjust law applied by Creonte. Or, in a lighter comedy, *The Merchant of Venice*, Shakespeare shows us Portia's ability to elaborate a subtle and creative interpretation of legislation, which saves Antonio from an unjust death for outstanding debts.

Throughout Western culture the reason and the conscience of the individual, and therefore of the peoples, are presented as the last citadel against injustice.

Here is one of the most interesting paradoxes of human nature as understood by Pope Benedict XVI: the antidote to moral relativism is the conscience of the individual. He does not juxtapose an objective truth – or objective moral values – to the individual conscience. In line with John Henry Newman, he trusts that the "way of conscience is everything except a way of self-sufficient subjectivity: it is a way of

[34] Benedict XVI, "Spe Salvi, Encyclical Letter to the Bishops, Priests, and Deacons, men and women religious, and all the lay faithful on Christian Hope," November 30, 2007, 24, 25.

obedience to objective truth."[35] He trusts that the *logos*, the objective truth, can be recognized within the human heart. In fact, the Pope Emeritus referred to individual conscience in the speech delivered before the Bundestag: "everyone in a position of responsibility must personally seek out the criteria to be followed when framing laws."[36] It is always the individual conscience that refuses to surrender and manages to prevent formal legislation from generating injustice.

POSITIVIST REASON AND OPEN REASON

But what kind of reason is so open to justice and truth that it cannot be satisfied with the laws in force? We cannot avoid this question. The crucial question, from which all the others derive, and which reveals the extraordinary power and pertinence of Benedict's position, is "what are reason and nature?" rather than "what are law and politics?" Benedict was perfectly aware of this when he took the podium before the members of the Bundestag:

> If nature – in the words of Hans Kelsen – is viewed as "an aggregate of objective data linked together in terms of cause and effect," then indeed no ethical indication of any kind can be derived from it.... The same also applies to reason, according to the positivist understanding that is widely held to be the only genuinely scientific one. Anything that is not verifiable or falsifiable, according to this understanding, does not belong to the realm of reason strictly understood. Hence ethics and religion must be assigned to the subjective field, and they remain extraneous to the realm of reason in the strict sense of the word. Where positivist reason dominates the field to the exclusion of all else – and that is broadly the case in our public mindset – then the classical sources of knowledge for ethics and law are excluded. This is a dramatic situation which affects everyone, and on which

[35] Presentation by His Eminence Card. Joseph Ratzinger on the Occasion of the First Centenary of the Death of Card. John Henry Newman, April 28, 1990, available at www.vatican.va (last visit: January 7, 2014).

[36] Emphasis added.

> a public debate is necessary. Indeed, an essential goal of this address is to issue an urgent invitation to launch one.[37]

A wide-open, thorough, and unbiased public discussion must be opened to address this question. What is *reason*? What is *nature*? Is a relationship between the two possible? And if so, under what conditions? The destiny of our institutions depends on these questions, and so does their ability to contribute the common good – that is, on the one hand, to decide by majority rule "most of the matters that need to be regulated by law," and, on the other hand, to continuously recognize and reaffirm those things that cannot be subjected to a vote. Deprived of this continuous, tireless search for the foundational and constitutive elements that undergird the political community,[38] the state itself degenerates into a "band of robbers" (*magna latrocinia*). What can make this daunting task possible? What can trigger that tireless twofold construction described here? Only an open reason, that is, one that is open to reality and to nature, and which is not closed.

For Benedict, closed means "reduced." A certain "scientistic" mentality is the greatest contributor to this reduction today ("scientistic" and not *scientific*, you will notice): "The positivist approach to nature and reason, the positivist world view in general, is a most important dimension of human knowledge and capacity that we may in no way dispense with. But in and of itself it is not a sufficient culture corresponding to the full breadth of the human condition."[39] This is clearly not an a priori attack on positivism, which he calls a "a most important dimension of human knowledge." But Benedict rejects the idea that this vision of nature and reason can explain everything about the person. The positivist approach is not wrong, per se, but it is simply partial; therefore it falls into error whenever it is believed to be the only possibility, or is imposed as "the only secular vision" or "the only public reason" endowed with objectivity. "In its

[37] Benedict XVI, Visit to the Bundestag

[38] A. Rosmini, Filosofia della politica, ed. by S. Cotta, Milano: Rusconi, 1985, 105.

[39] Benedict XVI, Visit to the Bundestag.

self-proclaimed exclusivity, the positivist reason... recognizes nothing beyond mere functionality."[40] Positivist reason has a certain sphere of validity, but it cannot explain all of reality.

Interestingly, substantial support for Benedict's ideas on this topic comes from decidedly secular thinkers who denounce the limits of "materialist reductionism," which they consider inadequate to explain even scientific phenomena in their entirety.[41] Thus the following paradox: just as a growing part of the scientific world – the world that originally gave rise to rational positivism – perceives the inadequacy of a merely reductionist approach for explaining nature and the cosmos,[42] that same approach, imported into the social and human sciences, has become the indisputable, universal paradigm.

In all his speeches collected in this book, Pope Benedict openly condemns the permanent, terrible temptation to confine reason to what is measurable – of conceiving a reason that is debased, humiliated, and, therefore, no longer humble. One of the most dangerous characteristics of the scientistic reduction is its claim to be the only way. The Pope Emeritus uses a wonderful image (a masterpiece, even from a purely literary point of view) to illustrate this core idea. A reason that is so closed "resembles a concrete bunker with no windows, in which we ourselves provide lighting and atmospheric conditions, being no longer willing to obtain either from God's wide world.... The windows must be flung open again, we must see the wide world, the sky and the earth once more and learn to make proper use of all this."[43] It is finally time, once again, to deal with reality as a whole, without assuming that the only way to effectively understand it is to reduce it into preconceived frameworks.

But what are the alternatives to this scientistic reduction? Are we left with no choice but to abandon the dominant idea of reason

[40] Id.

[41] T. Nagel, Mind and Cosmos: Why the Materialist Neo-Darwinian Conception of Nature Is Almost Certainly False, New York–London: Oxford University Press, 2012.

[42] C. Di Martino, "La conoscenza è sempre un avvenimento," in Aa. Vv., La conoscenza è sempre un avvenimento, Milan: Mondadori Università, 2009.

[43] Pope Benedict XVI, Visit to the Bundestag.

and take refuge in irrationalism or subjective emotionalism? Nothing could be further from Benedict's intentions.

Pope Benedict, who, as a former professor, pays careful attention to the accessibility of his thought, used another example to suggest to his countrymen where we might begin to "fling open" the "windows of our reason": the green movement. This movement arose in the 1970s out of a feeling of unease and that "something is wrong in our relationship with nature; that matter is not just raw material for us to shape at will, but that the earth has a dignity of its own and that we must follow its directives."[44] It rekindled a crucial element of human reasoning: the perception of a "datum." There is something in nature that humanity cannot subjugate to its every whim – the value (the structure) of the earth, air, water, and living beings, and the equilibrium between them all. Nature and its equilibrium have an intangible dignity that exceeds the technical capacity of humankind. The environmentalist movement concretely demonstrates that, in reality, human will run up against objective limits. If reason is to be true to itself, and not lose its ability to grasp the many aspects of reality in dealing with nature and the world (the very ability that defines reason), it must acknowledge the existence of something greater, which exceeds its capacity for calculation and domination, and which eludes its control.

Here it is as though Benedict was saying: "why stop here?" Why confine this new impulse, this breath of fresh air brought in by the green movement, to the consideration of nature, as if – paradox of paradoxes – the human being were not also included in its scope? "The importance of ecology is no longer disputed. We must listen to the language of nature and we must answer accordingly. Yet I would like to underline a point that seems to me to be neglected, today as in the past: there is also *an ecology of man*. Man too has a nature that he must respect and that he cannot manipulate at will."[45]

This is the great challenge that Benedict XVI lays down for those involved in culture and in public institutions: that reason come back to an openness without limits or prejudgments, once again capable of

[44] Id. [45] Id. (emphasis added).

recognizing what eludes our decision making and manipulation, not only in the environment, but also in the human person itself.

Here, in essence, are the dialectical poles of Benedict's thought: on the one hand we see a reduced reason, which is restricted by the positivist paradigm and fails to acknowledge anything that cannot be subjected to its capacity for calculation and control. This form of reason is structurally incapable of perceiving the tension between the law and the common good – the perpetual, ever-unresolved strain between justice and law, which is the proper purview of a true political institution. Under such a paradigm, a "reasonable" political approach is one that limits itself to equating what is just with the enacted legislation of the state, at the very most referring to constitutional, rather than ordinary, law, but always deriving the good from an abstract rule, imposed by the will of an authority, be it a sovereign, a parliament, a court, or a religious authority.

On the other hand is an open reason, able to admit that reality holds more than reason itself can fathom. Using the image of the closed "bunker" and the windows flung open to let in the fresh air, Benedict suggests a correction to modern rationalism that restores reason and reality to their proper relationship. A reason that is self-sufficient and absolute lacks the capacity to lift itself out of the mire of uncertainty. Something must come to its rescue. Something must happen – a real event, which, by exceeding what is already known, invites reason to open itself to newness, to what lies beyond itself.

The limit of modernity – from Descartes' *cogito ergo sum* (I think, therefore I am) on – is its focus on the subjective dimension of reason. Trapped within the limits of a purely subjective reason, it overlooks the fact that the interaction with reality constantly stimulates knowledge. Knowledge entails a polarity, or an encounter, between a subject and a real event, between human energy and a presence. Both components are necessary because, while reality always exceeds the grasp of subjective reason, at the same time, reality can only be grasped if it is perceived by a subject. In the dynamic of human experience, new aspects of reality continually stimulate reason: scientific evidence, historical facts, personal relationships, assumptions, and events of every kind. These provoke its interest and curiosity, inviting it to reopen the windows and face new dimensions that broaden its view. Reality, with all its natural, historical, social, and personal events, is a formidable ally for reason. Unforeseen factors impact, disturb, at times even traumatize human experience and constantly, with an incessant dynamism, invite it to open itself up to transcendence.

The more the person loyally enters into the knowledge of reality – be it physical or social – the more he or she glimpses the outline of "objective reason" (as the Pope Emeritus calls it), that is, that underlying structure that inevitably begs the question that Benedict used to close his speech in Berlin: "Is it really pointless to wonder whether the objective reason that manifests itself in nature does not presuppose a creative reason, a Creator Spiritus?"

For the Pope Emeritus the very heart of reason precisely coincides with this question, and not with an apodictic conclusion.

OPEN REASON AND RELIGION

Pope Benedict's spectacular relaunch of reason presents one last issue to be considered. One last, lingering doubt may remain, which undermines the universality of Benedict's proposal: is this view of reason and nature – and therefore of law and justice – an exclusively Christian or, generally speaking, religious view? That is, does this approach to law and politics require prior adherence to some particular religious hypothesis, or to beliefs of some other kind? When the Pope Emeritus addressed these public institutions, was he speaking only to a particular audience: Catholics, or Christians, or believers in particular religious creeds? The answer is certainly no. The idea that the very fabric of the physical and social world is made up of "reasonable" threads is far older than Christianity. As Benedict puts it, the legal culture of Europe was born of the encounter between three great pre-Christian streams of thought: "The culture of Europe arose from the encounter between Jerusalem, Athens and Rome – from the encounter between Israel's monotheism, the philosophical reason of the Greeks and Roman law. This three-way encounter has shaped the inner identity of Europe."[46] First, there is the idea of a single God who created and orders the universe, belonging to Judaism and differing so strikingly from the contemporary Mesopotamian cosmogonies; second, the philosophical inquiry about the true source of the law, which was rendered immortal by the first lines of Plato's *Laws* ("Tell me, Strangers, is a god or some man supposed to be the author of your laws?"); and finally, the idea of the law as *recta ratio* (right reason), typical of Roman legal thought.

All three of these great, pre-Christian schools of thought share the recognition that, in reality and in society, there is an order that exceeds human measure, and this fact confers a dramatic character (the bipolar tension described above) on any political power that is not satisfied with ruling by force, but aspires to establish a fair social order. What quality did the great King Solomon ask for from the God of Israel? "Give your servant, therefore, an understanding heart to judge your people and to distinguish right from wrong" (1 Kings 3:9). Justice resides in the heavens, and the king's mind is the place where this eternal justice interacts with the issues of this world. Antigone, as we mentioned earlier, serves as an immortal symbol for all places and times of the struggle between human laws and the *agrafoi nomoi* (unwritten laws) written on each person's heart. *Summum ius summa iniuria* (absolute application of the law makes for absolute injustice) is the maxim that best expresses the heart of Rome's legal realism (at least of the Republic).

Europe's cultural patrimony, conceived in this tripartite encounter between Jerusalem, Athens, and Rome that occurred well before the time of Christ, constitutes the fertile ground that gave rise to Christian theology which, as we have already explained, has entrusted the construction of a fair legal-political order to "reason and nature in their interrelation," and not to revealed rules. At base, Benedict's call to reenlarge the boundaries of reason is a call to reclaim the very origins of the philosophical and legal culture that produced Europe with exceptional results.

> The conviction that there is a Creator God is what gave rise to the idea of human rights, the idea of the equality of all people before

[46] Pope Benedict XVI, Visit to the Bundestag.

> the law, the recognition of the inviolability of human dignity in every single person and the awareness of people's responsibility for their actions. Our cultural memory is shaped by these rational insights. To ignore it or dismiss it as a thing of the past would be to dismember our culture totally and to rob it of its completeness.[47]

Here we find ourselves at the heart of the cultural challenge that the Pope Emeritus intends to lay down in these speeches. If reason closes itself within positivism's narrow schemes, it loses its ability to investigate the physical and social reality with the kind of openness necessary to understand it in depth, that is, to grasp its ultimate substance, in its totality. When it is thus diminished, reason ends up excluding from its scope the most "specifically human questions about our origin and destiny; the questions raised by religion and ethics, then, have no place within the purview of common reason as defined by 'science,' and must thus be relegated to the realm of the subjective."[48]

Altering the structure of human reason in this way has a devastating effect on the legal–political order. The will to power is left with no limits save those imposed by an even more powerful will. Justice is reduced to legislation alone, understood as a majority decision; therefore, it becomes extremely difficult to find areas of true agreement on ethical issues, which are not simply reciprocal, utilitarian exchanges. Majority dictatorship has become, once again, "a spectre that is haunting Europe." What, then, can restore the fullness of reason? How can reason be once more flung open to reality?

Joseph Ratzinger, in a book published before he became Pope, observed that reason that attempts on its own to extract itself from the slough of uncertainties recalls the famous Baron Munchhausen, who tried to pull himself out of a swamp by his own hair.[49] What can come to its aid? Contemporary reason needs to get out of the bunker, and go back to breathing the fresh air. As we alluded to briefly earlier, *reality* is reason's closest ally in this continual reopening, with its constant chain of troubling events that force reason to ask questions,

[47] Id.

[48] Pope Benedict XVI, Meeting with the representatives of science, Aula Magna of the University of Regensburg, September 12, 2006.

[49] Ratzinger, *Truth and Tolerance*, 136.

preventing it from collapsing in on itself. The positive value of religious experiences in the public square is linked to this dynamic.

The role of faith is not to antagonize reason; on the contrary, it is a formidable ally. To borrow the wonderful image from Pope John Paul II's *Fides et Ratio*: "Faith and reason are like two wings on which the human spirit rises to the contemplation of truth."[50] In the same vein, Cardinal Ratzinger writes: "By no means the least important practical function of faith is to offer healing for the reason as reason… to bring it to itself again. Faith, as a historical instrument, can set reason itself free again, so that – now that faith has set it on the right path again – reason can once more see properly for itself.… Without faith, philosophy cannot be whole, but faith without reason cannot be human."[51]

Benedict's conception of faith can be interesting for understanding how faith can be an instrument of healing for reason, rather than obscuring it as is generally believed: "Being Christian is not the result of an ethical choice or a lofty idea, but the encounter with an event, a person, which gives life a new horizon and a decisive direction."[52] Faith can heal reason to the extent that it does not belong to sentimentality, irrationality, or morality. Faith, as an event, belongs to reality and to human history: it originates in a real encounter. In human experience, among the many elements of reality that continually provoke reason and invite it to grow, we find the encounter with a presence, with a human experience renewed by faith, which pushes reason beyond its limits.

History provides countless examples of how the event of faith serves reason, even in the public sphere, and therefore also serves politics.[53] To exclude it would be to eliminate from political discourse a voice like that of Ambrose, a bishop of Milan and former Roman

[50] Pope John Paul II, "Fides et Ratio, Encyclical letter to the Bishops of the Catholic Church on the relationship between faith and reason," Libreria Editrice Vaticana, 1998.

[51] Ratzinger, *Truth and Tolerance*, 136.

[52] Pope Benedict XVI, "Deus Caritas Est, Encyclical Letter to the bishops, priests, and deacons, men and women religious, and all the lay faithful on Christian love," Libreria Editrice Vaticana, 2005, para. 1.

[53] On the relation between faith and political theories in a philosophical and historical perspective, see Borghesi, *Critica della teologia politica*.

prefect, who spoke out single-handedly against the Emperor Theodosius, who had just killed thousands of men in a legitimate act of power (*quod principi placuit habet legis vigorem*: the will of the prince has the force of law):

> Surely your majesty is not aware of the heinousness of the slaughter which has taken place. Passion is over; yet reason does not yet estimate the crime. Perchance kingly rule is an obstacle to repentance, and sovereignty prevents reflection. Yet it is as well for a man to feel his perishable nature, and remember that dust is his beginning and his end, in spite of that gorgeous purple which may beguile the heart, but cannot reverse the feebleness of the frame it covers. Your subjects, emperor, are your fellow-creatures; I should rather say, your fellow-servants, – servants of one universal Lord and King, the Maker of the universe.[54]

The great bishop of Milan did not employ moral arguments or religious prescriptions against the Emperor, but rather objected to the fact that rage had so clouded his reason that he failed to recognize his true nature, which was equal to that of every other person ("perishable"); the only thing that distinguishes the Emperor from any other man is the fact that he governs, not an intrinsic quality, since both are "subjects" of their creator, the one true sovereign. Once again we see "reason" and "nature" in their interrelation – these are the bases of Ambrose's dialogue with the Emperor, not religious values or precepts.

THE PRODUCTIVE ENCOUNTER BETWEEN FAITH AND REASON

Over the centuries, faith has not only played a deciding role in defending reason against power, which constantly attempts to blind it, but has also contributed significantly to reason's growth and development. Pope Benedict's speech at the Collège des Bernardins in Paris provides a broad and fascinating account of how Christianity

[54] Quoted in J.H. Newman, The Church of the Fathers, London: G.J.F. &. J. Rivington, 1840, 50–51.

contributed to the healing of reason, to its progress, and to the rebirth of an entire civilization, which had been buried under the rubble of the barbarian devastation of Europe, which destroyed the old order and overthrew ancient certainties. The Pope used the example of Western monasticism: the monks, religious men, were captivated by and engaged in a continuous quest for God: *Quaerere Deum*. But how did they carry out this quest? God himself had blazed a trail, placing signs along the way through his Word, which lay open to human eyes in the books of sacred scripture.[55] So, the secular sciences that reveal the way through language became important because of the quest for God: writing, the study of grammar, libraries, schools – all are components of Benedictine Monasticism.

Quaerere Deum: the prayer demanded expression not by words alone, but also in music. Thus,

> This intrinsic requirement of speaking with God and singing of him with words he himself has given, is what gave rise to the great tradition of Western music. It was not a form of private "creativity", in which the individual leaves a memorial to himself and makes self-representation his essential criterion. Rather it is about vigilantly recognizing with the "ears of the heart" the inner laws of the music of creation, the archetypes of music that the Creator built into his world and into men, and thus discovering music that is worthy of God, and at the same time truly worthy of man, music whose worthiness resounds in purity.[56]

Quaerere Deum:

> In the Greek world, manual labour was considered something for slaves.... The Jewish tradition was quite different: all the great rabbis practised at the same time some form of handcraft.... Monasticism took up this tradition; manual work is a constitutive element of Christian monasticism. In his Regula, Saint Benedict ... does speak explicitly about work (cf. Chap. 48). And so does Augustine, who dedicated a book of his own to monastic

[55] Cfr. J. Leclerq, L'amour des lettres et le desir de Dieu, Paris: Les éditions du Cerf, 1963, 14.

[56] Pope Benedict XVI, Meeting with representatives from the world of culture, Collège des Bernardins, Paris, September 12, 2008.

> work. Christians, who thus continued in the tradition previously established by Judaism, must have felt further vindicated by Jesus's saying in Saint John's Gospel, in defence of his activity on the Sabbath: "My Father is working still, and I am working" (5:17).... God is working; he continues working in and on human history. In Christ, he enters personally into the laborious work of history. "My Father is working still, and I am working." ... Monasticism involves not only a culture of the word, but also a culture of work, without which the emergence of Europe, its ethos and its influence on the world would be unthinkable.[57]

Language, writing, grammar, music, community, school, craftsmanship: an entire civilization was reborn from the energy of people who, "Amid the confusion of the times, in which nothing seemed permanent, ... wanted to do the essential – to make an effort to find what was perennially valid and lasting, life itself. They were searching for God. They wanted to go from the inessential to the essential, to the only truly important and reliable thing there is.... [T]hey were seeking the definitive behind the provisional."[58]

In Benedict's view, reason and faith are linked by a deep and fruitful friendship, in which neither of the two friends wants to subjugate the other, recognizing and appreciating its otherness, but in which each one needs the other in order to live well. As with true friendships, encounter is fundamental: that moment in which something unexpected occurs and leaves the other changed; in which new, previously ignored perspectives open up, and different personalities become attuned in a way that a person becomes aware of the richness of his/her own identity, but also aware of his/her need of the other, without whom such an awareness would be impossible.

The history of European civilization is covered with indelible signs of this vibrant, fruitful encounter between faith and reason, and in his speech at the Collège des Bernardins, the Pope painted an elaborate picture of many of the wonderful fruits of this encounter. Because of this, considering the future of our political institutions, Benedict's trajectory, which started as a real cultural and anthropological challenge, ends with a heartfelt offer of friendship and cooperation.

[57] Id. [58] Id.

The solemn words uttered at Westminster Hall still clearly resound: "[T]he world of reason and the world of faith – the world of secular rationality and the world of religious belief – need one another and should not be afraid to enter into a profound and ongoing dialogue, for the good of our civilization. Religion, in other words, is not a problem for legislators to solve, but a vital contributor to the national conversation."[59]

The Pope Emeritus offers his outstretched hand to lawmakers and all political institutions; it is an offer of help and reciprocal correction (in the original meaning of *cum-regere*, to hold together), in which reason and religion need each other to face the new challenges posed by living side-by-side in human society today.

[59] Pope Benedict XVI, Meeting with the representatives of British society.

PART I Law, Reason, and Religion

2 REALITY AND TRANSCENDENCE

More Than a Religious Issue

Armin von Bogdandy and Sergio Dellavalle

In many different circumstances over the course of his pontificate, Pope Benedict XVI addressed a much broader community than that made up only of Catholic-Christian believers. In doing so, he dealt with topics that are equally important to the Roman Catholic faithful, to nonbelievers, and to believers in other religions, including the relationships between faith and reason, science and ethics, formal legality and substantive legitimacy, and natural reason and individual rights. In the speeches reproduced herein, these topics were presented (first to specific audiences in their respective venues, and later to the general public) with scholarly acumen, but also with an ability to go beyond the frontiers of theology. This Benedict did with the conviction of faith, but no less with the desire to arouse interest and debate even among those whose reflections are not habitually of a religious bent.

Joyfully accepting the proposal of dialogue, in the following pages we will discuss certain points that Benedict touched on in his speeches – in particular those points that most correspond to our backgrounds as legal philosophers.

We will begin by attempting to reconstruct Benedict's statements that most directly address issues of a philosophical and legal nature, tying them into what seems to us to be a critical diagnosis of the excessive *positivity* – or *positivism* – of the contemporary world.[1]

[1] The term "positivity" is used here as it was used by Hegel in many of his early works. In that context, it is employed negatively, to indicate rigid adherence to a reality, be it material or cultural, that is "positive" in the sense that it is taken as given, immutable, charged with an incontrovertible authority,

We will then outline the proposed cure that emerges from Benedict's speeches, which repeatedly focus on the necessity for a renewed osmosis between faith and reason. We will conclude by presenting our perspective, which, while sharing in a good number of Benedict's critiques of certain distortions in contemporary culture, nevertheless ends in a different proposal, in which reason and faith, while maintaining dialogue, remain ontologically, epistemologically, and axiologically distinct.

THE DIAGNOSIS: A CRITIQUE OF THE POSITIVITY OF THE CONTEMPORARY WORLD

Benedict focuses his critical attention on certain aspects of contemporary culture which he views – even if he never explicitly uses the term – as akin to authentic pathologies.

The first of these is the disconnect between natural science and ethics. The field of scientific knowledge is separated from that of ethical reflection to the extent that nature is reduced to a collection of objective data united by a causal relationship.[2] This is the dominant, value-neutral positivism of contemporary science, which, in Benedict's view, corresponds to legal positivism (not by accident, he uses Hans Kelsen as the critical point of reference for both positions). For both, scientific and legal positivism, only knowledge that reflects the positivity of reality can be regarded as true, and only judgments that refrain from ethical considerations are rationally grounded and legally legitimate.

indifferent to the dialectic and communicative complexity of the lifeworld, and impenetrable by the quest for what is "other" and "yet to come," that is, to what we call "transcendence." See G.W.F. Hegel, Frühe Schriften (Early Writings), in Id., *Werke in zwanzig Bänden* (Work in twenty volumes), Suhrkamp: Frankfurt am Main 1970 sgg., vol. I. Keeping in mind this definition of positivity, positivism is the doctrine which limits scientific knowledge to the study – in various disciplines – of "positive" reality, without leaving space for any dialectic with counter-factual rationalities.

2 Pope Benedict XVI, "The Listening Heart: Reflections on the Foundations of Law," Visit to the Bundestag, Reichstag Building, Berlin, September 22, 2011.

Against such a constricted cognitive and normative view, Benedict repeatedly emphasizes the centrality of interpretation in approaching the Scriptures.[3] Although he only stresses the fundamental importance of interpretation in reference to biblical exegesis, it is not a stretch to extend its application to the other discipline that constantly and inevitably hangs in the balance between the authority of a written text and the need to interpret it, namely the law. Therefore, leaving behind textualism – the already epistemologically doomed attempt to interpret a written text literally – the real understanding of what is given to us as positive rule and norm (that is, given through the medium of the written language) requires the involvement not only of the intellect, but also of love – of that *agape* that refers to the paramount importance of communication within the epistemic community, be it legal or religious.

From this critique of positivity and from the importance of interpretation Benedict derives a series of reflections and admonitions that deal with faith, ethics, law, and politics. First of all, he clearly distances himself from the usual solipsism in issues of faith and ethics: it is not enough that each of us, alone and independent of any contact with other individuals, constructs his or her own idea of the meaning of the biblical text, or of how he or she should behave in a given situation. In order to obtain valid results in both cases it is necessary to refer to the community of our peers and to share with them the results of our inquiry.[4]

Just as it is crucial to overcome the mere "textuality" of the Scriptures, or of ethical codes of conduct, in favor of an interpretation that involves the wider context of community, rights too, in their juridical dimension, should not be understood in a merely legalistic sense.[5] Only interpretation can put them into proper

[3] Pope Benedict XVI, Meeting with Representatives from the World of Culture, Collège des Bernardins, Paris, September 12, 2008.

[4] Pope Benedict XVI, "Faith, Reason and the University: Memories and Reflections," Meeting with the representatives of science, Aula Magna of the University of Regensburg, Regensburg, September 12, 2006.

[5] Pope Benedict XVI, Meeting with the Members of the General Assembly of the United Nations Organization, New York, April 18, 2008.

relationship with their deeper rationale, with their underlying *logos*, and with the natural reason that makes up their most basic justification. If separated from natural reason and read only according to textual positivism, rights run the risk of undergoing two distortions of meaning that would seriously impoverish their content. First, they can be read, through a relativistic lens, not as necessary results of reason in its universalistic scope, but rather as products of a historical contingency that renders them different according to the cultural or religious context in which they are to be applied.[6] The second distortion is a purely legalistic idea of rights, which attributes them exclusively, and in abstract form, to the individual, without any reference to the overall social and natural equilibrium. This distortion favors the delirium of individual omnipotence: that *hybris* that can lead one to the wrong belief that anything is permissible and there is no limit to his or her freedom.[7]

On the political plane, the majority principle is a first expression of the positivistic approach that Benedict critiques. Albeit fundamental and, in general, sufficient to regulate most of the issues associated with civil coexistence in a satisfactory way, the majority principle nevertheless comes up short when faced with the "fundamental issues of law, in which the dignity of man and of humanity is at stake."[8] More generally – and here once again Kelsen serves as a critical point of reference – the Pope Emeritus fundamentally critiques the conception according to which politics is understood as a collection of formal rules of interaction between members of a community characterized by plural, nonhomogeneous ethical views.[9] In Benedict's view, political and civil coexistence must be founded on ethical principles which, in turn, are rooted in more solid ground than mere "social consensus."[10]

According to this diagnosis, the many problems which seem to emerge from a merely positivistic reading of the natural, ethical,

[6] Id. [7] Id. [8] Pope Benedict XVI, "The Listening Heart."

[9] Pope Benedict XVI, Meeting with the Representatives of British Society, including the Diplomatic Corps, Politicians, Academics and Business Leaders, Westminster Hall, London, September 17, 2010.

[10] Id.

political, and legal worlds – that is, according to Benedict, from the dominant contemporary reading of them – can be traced back to the fundamental defect gripping our society and thought: the rejection of transcendence. Indeed, only openness to transcendence allows us to overcome the positivity of the material world, basing science, politics, and law on just and ethical foundations. Ignoring transcendence, Benedict points out, leads to the violation of human liberty and dignity and, ultimately, to the most abominable crimes against humanity. What the United Nations have been in the fields of law and international politics, the rediscovery of transcendence has been in the realm of human consciousness: both respond to the one-dimensionality of positivity, emphasizing the need to cast human horizons toward principles and dimensions that transcend the "realistic"[11] logic of power and worldliness.[12]

According to Benedict, the treasured awareness of transcendence is best preserved in the chest of religion. Therefore, no antidote is stronger against the positivity of the contemporary world than religion and the intransigent defense of its freedom. Within religious freedom – understood not just as the private freedom of an individual or of a group, but, above all, as the freedom to give religion an explicit public dimension[13] – we find the most sure guarantee of the protection of human dignity and human rights.[14]

[11] By "realistic" logic here we mean the logic found at the basis of human, social, political, and legal relationships, as they were viewed by Thucydides in antiquity and Machiavelli in early modern ages (to cite perhaps the two most important names). Under this interpretation, social interaction is guided by a single rationale, that is, the struggle for power. Accordingly, whoever acts following to a different kind of rationality, dialectically opposed to the mere logic of power in the name of values, principles, or shared rights, has abandoned "reality," revealing him- or herself to be, at best, deluded, and at worst, a fool. In this view there is no room for a theory of transcending the existent (unless it is self-destructive or hypocritical), either in the name of a nonstrategic rationality, or in the name of faith.

[12] Pope Benedict XVI, Meeting with the Members of the General Assembly of the United Nations Organization.

[13] Id. [14] Id.

THE CURE: TOWARD A REASON NOT CUT OFF FROM FAITH

What remedy can be identified against the troubling diagnosis of the contemporary world's shortcomings, in particular its positivity, that is, its materialism, relativism, and its distance from the need for transcendence? Benedict, in his attempt to outline an exit strategy, turns his attention to one of the most thoroughly discussed *topoi* of western thought: the relationship between faith and reason.

Ever since Paul of Tarsus' famous words from the *Letter to the Romans*[15] – and, more generally, following the introduction of the stoic doctrine of natural reason[16] into nascent Christian philosophy and theology – Christianity has worked to forge a positive and constructive relationship between faith and reason. This is not to say that there have been no exceptions, but these have been largely on the Protestant side; it suffices to think of Martin Luther's defamation of reason as the "devil's greatest whore,"[17] or of the more elegant, but no less skeptical, Calvinist theological claim that through original sin the human being has lost the ability to fully grasp God with his reason alone, and is therefore limited to understanding only a *particula* of divine truth.[18] The autonomy of human reason, according to

15 "For when the Gentiles who do not have the law by nature observe the prescriptions of the law, they are law for themselves even though they do not have the law. They show that the demands of the law are written in their hearts, while their conscience also bears witness." Romans 2:14–15.

16 Regarding this it is worth recalling the definition of reason as described by Cicero: "There is a true law, a right reason, conformable to nature, universal, unchangeable, eternal, whose commands urge us to duty, and whose prohibitions restrain us from evil.... This law cannot be contradicted by any other law, and is not liable either to derogation or abrogation. Neither the senate nor the people can give us any dispensation for not obeying this universal law of justice" (Marcus Tullius Cicero, "Treatise on the Commonwealth," in Edmund Spettigue, Cicero, The Political Works, London 1841–42, Vol. 1, Book III).

17 M. Luther, Werke: Kritische Gesamtausgabe (Works: Complete edition), Weimar: Böhlau, 1914, vol. LI, 126.

18 A. Gentili, De jure belli libri tres (1612), Oxford: Clarendon Press, 1933, I, I, 10.

Calvinist thinkers, is purchased at the high price of distancing itself from God.[19] This is not so in Catholic thought, where reason has always been seen as an indispensable tool for growing closer to God, and where a theory of osmosis between faith and reason has generally prevailed, even while maintaining a scrupulous respect for the differing degrees of closeness to truth.

In this sense, the Pope Emeritus is fully in line with the prevalent Catholic tradition: "The Catholic tradition maintains that the objective norms governing right action are accessible to reason, prescinding from the content of revelation."[20] In other words, the ethical and moral norms that protect human dignity can be grasped with the help of reason alone, and therefore by any human being, including those who have not embraced the Christian message or adopted the doctrine of the Church. In dealing with this topic, Benedict also addresses the issue (a thornier one than most) of whether God can act outside of what we define as reason, maybe even contrary to it, not bound by anything but the own inscrutable preference; or whether he is instead part of an "objective" reason that coincides with his freedom and will (not understood in this case as radical arbitrariness). The Pope Emeritus assumed a clear position in responding to this question, and one that is more radical than it appears from a superficial reading. He explicitly rejects the voluntarism of Duns Scotus, for whom God is free in a dimension that is beyond our reason, with no bridge connecting the two spheres. In that view, God's will is ultimately not rational, but arbitrary, to the point that he "could have done the opposite of everything he has actually done."[21] At least implicitly, however, Benedict also distanced himself from the rationalism of the most moderate scholastic stream of thought, represented by Thomas Aquinas and, at least partially, by Francisco de Vitoria, according to which what we perceive as according to reason corresponds to the divine free will.[22]

[19] H. Grotius, De Jure Belli ac Pacis (1646), Buffalo, NY: William S. Hein & Co., 1995, I, I, X, 1–5, 4.

[20] Pope Benedict XVI, Meeting with the Representatives of British Society.

[21] Pope Benedict XVI, "Faith, Reason and the University."

[22] On this, see Vitoria's important passage, according to which "il diritto divino, anche quello positivo, ha la stessa forza del diritto naturale, poiché questo non

Under this understanding, God freely desires what we understand as rational. Reason, however, remains ontologically and axiologically subordinate to the divine will in that it belongs only to our perceived world and only binds us. Benedict, instead, assumes the most radically rationalistic position that can be found in Catholic theological thought. The approach was developed by the last and most "modern" of the great members of the School of Salamanca, Francisco Suárez. For Suárez rationality and the divine will coincide:[23] the existence of an "objective" reason is presupposed, representing the purest essence of the divine freedom and will. God's will remains completely free[24] (obviously, one might add, if one adopts the Christian perspective) but that freedom is coexistential with reason, which is not merely perceived as such by us, but also *is* such in God's very will. Starting from the most openly rationalistic positions in Catholic theology, Benedict stresses how the Catholic God is a *logos* God and not an arbitrary God. Although there is much more to God's love than to our reason, the "eternal Creator Spirit" and our reason are analogous, and not substantially different.[25] What distinguishes them is a matter of nuance, and not of opposition.

On the basis of these assumptions, Benedict defends Christian theology's Greek heritage[26] and the close relationship between faith and *logos*.[27] Against this background, he identifies religion's task as the "'corrective' role," which consists of helping "purify and shed light upon the application of reason to the discovery of objective

ha forza se non per il fatto che è stato stabilito dall'autorità divina. In caso contrario non sarebbe obbligatorio . . . dal momento che un obbligo non può esistere se non a partire da un'istanza superiore," De potestate papae et concilii, in F. De Vitoria, Relecciones Teológicas, ed. Luis G. Alonso Getino, Madrid: La Rafa, 1934, II, 216.

23 "The free acts of God . . . are ruled by the divine reason as by a natural law of God Himself. The proof of this statement is that God always acts according to right reason, not the reason of another, but His own; and therefore, the rectitude of the free acts of God's will is measured by the judgement of His own intellect" (F. Suárez, "De legibus, ac Deo legislatore," in Selections from Three Works, Oxford: Clarendon Press 1944, II, II, 152 f.).

24 Id., II, III, at 162.

25 Pope Benedict XVI, "Faith, Reason and the University."

26 Id.

27 Id.

moral principles."[28] Benedict links the universal mission of Christianity to the relatedness of Christian doctrine and the universal applicability and breadth of the rational *logos*.[29]

The assumption that an uninterrupted bridge unites faith and *logos* also has important consequences for the way in which reason itself is understood. If faith is indeed revealed, and therefore must be accepted as a given truth, reason too, which is claimed to be ontologically and axiologically bound to it, as well as the natural law, which is based on reason, with its laws valid for all human beings,[30] ought to be understood as present *in re*,[31] that is, as objects to be discovered in the external reality. Reason and faith, therefore, would not be faculties that allow us, through free argumentation, to arrive at a better understanding of the outside world and to correctly orient our actions. Joseph Ratzinger, before ascending to the papal seat, used the "objectivity" of reason in its essential relationship with revelation[32] as the basis for his severe criticism of relativistic rationalism, which he saw as a Pilate-like rejection of the search for truth,[33] and not as a tool for dialogue among different individuals or groups.

If revelation is connected to the *logos*, then the keeper of true revelation – at least what is considered as such – will also be the keeper of true reason. From this premise derives the conviction of Catholic exceptionalism and of the privileged position of the Roman Church, not only concerning matters of faith and theological truth, but also concerning rational truth.[34] Benedict also, in reference to the social and political plane, insists on the fact that, according to Christian doctrine correctly interpreted, the truth entrusted to the guardianship of faith should not be imposed on the political

[28] Pope Benedict XVI, Meeting with the Representatives of British Society.
[29] Pope Benedict XVI, Meeting with Representatives from the World of Culture.
[30] Pope Benedict XVI, "The Listening Heart."
[31] Pope Benedict XVI, "Faith, Reason and the University."
[32] J. Ratzinger and T. Bertone, Declaration "Dominus Iesus" On the Unicity and Salvific Universality of Jesus Christ and the Church, 6th August 2000, II, 9 et seq.
[33] J. Ratzinger, "L'Europa nella crisi delle culture," in Il Regno-Documenti, 9/2005, 214–219.
[34] Pope Benedict XVI, Meeting with Representatives from the World of Culture.

community by means of an insane commingling of religious and political authority, nor must the Church give in to theocratic nostalgia. Rather, the Church must make itself the champion of truth before the political authorities by passing through reason. That is, it must staunchly defend the natural law it feels was entrusted to it, but which is also always accessible to every reasonable human being.[35]

AN ALTERNATIVE PROPOSAL: A SECULAR TRANSCENDENCE

Despite our differences, which we will address shortly, we understand and share many of Pope Benedict XVI's critical remarks about contemporary culture. In general, we share his doubts concerning a merely and radically positivistic interpretation of science and law. We adopt his belief in the centrality of the interpretation of text (essentially legal text, in our case), in the nonrelativism of the rights universally ascribable to the human being, and in the essential importance of religion, not only in the sense of religious freedom, but also in the sense of the social function of religious discourse. Furthermore, we believe – although we must admit that, under a more analytical examination, different undertones may emerge in our positions here – that politics is more than a contractual relationship. That is, it must be based on common principles, or even promote shared values able to guide social action. Moreover, we are convinced that the reference to transcendence is an inevitable part of our relationship with our own existence: if we were inseparably bound only to the material reality, without finding plausible reasons even to think – or hope – of an "other" world, we would lose what is probably the highest and most distinctive human trait.

However, when we go on to examine the possible reasons for what we see as the potential deficits of certain influential trends in the contemporary scientific, political, and legal cultures, and attempt to sketch solutions, our trajectory deviates from the one Benedict

[35] Pope Benedict XVI, "The Listening Heart."

proposed. In particular, we maintain that it is possible to suggest strategies that respond to what we see as social and cultural "pathologies," without resorting to an "objective" concept of reason. This is accomplished by suggesting a relationship between reason and religion that does not depend on an express or implied relationship of subordination.

There are two alternative reflections: one concerns the concept of reason, and the other the relationship between reason and faith. Let us begin with the first. This, too, takes the form of two distinct considerations. First of all, it is interesting to briefly wonder about the relationship between reason and positivity. Benedict points to and criticizes a contemporary positivity, in which there is not only the hypostasis of the natural datum (in science) or the symbolic one (in legal or religious texts), which is considered complete in and of itself and cut off from interaction with rational interpretation; rather, there is also a specific idea of rationality, which, in the current usage, is generally defined as "systemic rationality." It deals with the kind of functional, value-neutral rationality that governs social subsystems and their *modus operandi*. Benedict presents this rationality in an almost exclusively negative light, so that it gives way to the superiority of objective natural reason inspired by the *lex divina*. This position risks unilaterally denying the advantages that can flow from developing the autonomy of systematic rationalities. Legal language, for example, owes much of its value precisely to its formalism. And science and economics – and the list could be much longer – best respond to human needs when they are respected and protected in the specificity of their unique ways of functioning. Does this mean that the kind of reason that underlies critical reasoning and ethical values must bow to the omnipotence of systemic rationality? Not at all. Respect for the specificity of systemic rationalities is not tantamount to the refusal to interact with them, even critically. Simply, in our view, value-based rationality does not claim to supplant systemic rationality, but instead enters into a dynamic of tension with it. This tension can give rise to the entire universe of thought that passes beyond the functional dimension. Transcendence reappears – in a secular way – as one of reason's needs, but this does not erase the best outcomes brought about by the positivistic culture.

Having clarified our view that axiopoietic reason (the creator and bearer of values of principles) should not ignore or deny systemic rationality, which is coessential with positivism, but should instead enter into dialogue with it and, when necessary, galvanize it with critiques, the next question is: what are the characteristics of such a reason? Benedict XVI proposes an objective reason illuminated by faith. In our view, there are two problems with this proposal. First of all, it is epistemologically difficult to identify an "objective" basis for reason: in all of modern culture – and even more so in recent decades – reason is identified with a process of reasoning, with the intelligent "I" (or "We"), and not with an object, a *res rationalis* that is in some way traceable in the outside world. It was precisely this antiobjectivist turn that allowed enlightenment thought to complete the universalization of human reason in a form and with a humanistic fullness never realized before. Second, if reason needs the light of faith, there is always the danger that it will be transformed into its maidservant, losing the freedom that defines it. Moreover, given the indispensable existence of religious pluralism, a reason that depends on faith will always and forever be merely *the* reason of *that specific* faith, distancing itself from a truly inclusive universalism. These criticisms implicitly reveal the notion of reason that we hold most dear: the reason of dialogue, debate, and argumentation, of a secular truth, exhaustively sought after and always provisional, never taken as given or deduced from superior truths.

But, if we accept the hypothesis that reason claims to find its ultimate justification in itself and in its procedures, might religion come to lose its relevance, at least in the public arena? Might it come to be marginalized, at best being reduced to something akin to a personal preference with no relevance to public discourse, and at worst being dismissed as a spiritual weakness in people who refuse to put their intellectual capacities to full use? And would we, under such circumstances, come to lose our ability to turn our gaze on high, to seek alternatives to what offends our humanity in the given reality and to find new reasons to hope? In our view, such deplorable developments are not at all the necessary result of a secular reason, but are rather the consequence of a reason that has lost contact with an important part of itself, with the communicative and normative dimension, trusting blindly only in the functional principle. From a secular-reasoning perspective, too – which originates from the communication that goes in search of knowledge, principles, or shared values, with mutual respect for other ways of reasoning and without prejudgment – the religious narrative (even in its pluralistic sense) is assigned an essential task for social life. Social communication focused on the search for the deeper meaning of our existence – a form of communication that, for many human beings, begins within a particular religious community and moves outward from there – is indispensable for rational discourse as well, since it pushes the latter to enrich its contents and enlarge its horizons. Therefore, although secular-rational discourse and religious discourse should be respected in their separateness, they should never be considered mutually indifferent. And by its contrast with religious discourse, secular reason will be reminded to turn its gaze upward – the prerogative that makes the human, with all its defects, a very special being.

3 HUMAN DIGNITY WITHOUT GOD? Reflections on Some Relevant Speeches of Benedict XVI

Rafael Domingo

"The conviction that there is a Creator God is what gave rise to ... the recognition of the inviolability of human dignity in every single person."[1] In my opinion, this statement is the common thread that unites the five speeches of Benedict XVI selected by the editors. Indeed, a comprehensive idea of human dignity cannot be atheistic; it must be theistic, open to God. Otherwise, the idea of dignity is thoroughly undermined, and when the idea of dignity is undermined, the human person is trivialized.

In these informal comments, I will refer, first, to the idea of dignity; second, to two important dimensions of human dignity – freedom of religion and ethical autonomy; and lastly, to the effective protection of the unity of the person as a requirement of dignity.

* * *

Dignity is the human being's most radical and intrinsic quality. It is more than a right, a basic good, a value, and a principle. It is the unique, absolute, irreplaceable, and permanent ontological status of the person and justifies the human person as an ultimate reality. All human beings have dignity, without exception. Thus, all human beings without exception are persons. Dignity and personhood are inseparable realities; they go hand in hand. Without the person, there is no dignity, and without dignity, there is no person. Personhood adds to dignity the idea of relation. Personhood is relational. Thanks to dignity, the human person can preserve his or her unity while living

[1] Benedict XVI, Address to the Bundestag, Berlin, September 22, 2011.

in various forms of harmony with others. In this way, dignity is the meeting point of the legal, the moral, the ethical, and the religious – indeed all the dimensions of the human person. Human dignity lies at the intersection of two core axes: the horizontal axis links persons among themselves (political community); and the vertical axis links the person (and communities of persons) with transcendent truth (traditional religion), that is, with God.

Dignity means the primacy of the particular over the universal;[2] it places the human person at the center of the universe. However, dignity also means plurality insofar as all persons have equal dignity. Because dignity is shared by all persons, it calls for an original model, for a supreme source of dignity. This model can be called God, the creative love, in whose "image and likeness" human beings have been created. However, dignity also places the human person at the heart of all political communities (local, national, and global) and teaches against making any political community total. In this sense, all political communities should be relative, not absolute. Indeed, because of dignity, plurality never becomes totality. Thus, the Absolute must be found outside the universe, as an uncaused entity.

The person cannot be considered a mere fragment that participates in the life or consciousness of an absolute universe. Additionally, if each person is not a part of the universe but a whole in him- or herself, the Absolute dwells outside the universe. Dignity offers the human being the capacity to transcend the universe by looking for absolute truth. In this deepest sense, dignity is self-determination in the search for truth that gives sense to human existence.

From a juridical perspective, dignity is the status of each person as a "bearer of rights" and "lawmaker." Because dignity is at the heart of the origin of law, the law has to protect dignity as a whole and not only its legal dimension. By protecting dignity as a whole, the law protects the person as an acting unity living in internal and external harmony and not as a mere subject of certain rights. Because religion is also an expression of human dignity, the law has to protect religion as a basic good. By protecting religion, the law is protecting dignity, and by

[2] Cf. Benedict XVI, Introduction to Christianity, San Francisco: Ignatius Press, 2004, 161.

protecting dignity, the law is protecting itself. The province of religion is different from the province of law, but they converge and have to act in harmony according to the unity of the person: "Refusal to recognize the contribution to society that is rooted in the religious dimension and in the quest for the Absolute – by its nature, expressing communion between persons – would effectively privilege an individualistic approach and would fragment the unity of the person."[3]

Just as a legal system or constitutional model should never be an obstacle to human dignity, so should it never be an obstacle to religion, for religion is an expression of human dignity. The religious dimension of life is, in James Madison's well-known words, "precedent, both in order of time and in degree of obligation, to the claims of civil society."[4] Indeed, religion precedes law as for the order of time because the relation between the creator and a creature predates the relation between and among creatures as members of a political community. The existence of religion also could precede the existence of the law because there could be religion in the world with only one human being (and its creator). However, the existence of law requires at least two persons. The reason is the essential otherness of the law. As for the degree of obligation, the vertical relation established between creator and creature is, by nature, different than the horizontal relation between equal creatures. However, this relation is not necessarily a matter of subordination or domination but can be a matter of freedom: the freedom to recognize God as creator and the ultimate source of morality.

* * *

Perhaps the most radical difference between the liberal secularist approach to religious freedom and the approach Benedict XVI defends arises with respect to the concept of ethical independence. Religious freedom should be supported not by *ethical independence* in the liberal sense but by *ethical autonomy*, a substantially different

[3] Benedict XVI, Address to United Nations, New York, April 18, 2008.
[4] Memorial and Remonstrance against Religious Assessments (1785), no. 1.

concept. This slight difference of nuance has many political implications. The most important implication is that, although ethical independence tries to resolve the religious question by privatizing religion entirely, ethical autonomy, in the much deeper sense, makes it possible to see religion as a common foundational good that any human person or political community can share. Ethical independence is, of its essence, individual; however, ethical autonomy can be applied in all the dimensions of the human person: individual, social, and transcendent.

According to the liberal approach to ethical independence, the government must not rely on any justification that directly, indirectly, or covertly supposes any ethical conviction about what is better or worse for a good life. Ethical independence means an absolute personal sovereignty in foundational matters, such that a person should never accept any judgment in place of his or her own.[5] Insofar as religion is a foundational matter, no government may constrain religion for any reason except when necessary to protect the life, security, or liberty of others. Moreover, in no case may a political community dictate ethical convictions to its citizens. A decision of the political community may force us to live in accordance with collective decisions only if it does so without imposing ethical convictions. Therefore, there is no place for any religious "ethical paternalism." Thus, ethical independence requires individuals to refrain from imposing ethical convictions by treating a particular religion as *sui generis* or considering religion as such as a special phenomenon.

Ethical autonomy, however, emphasizes the indispensable relation between human freedom and moral order in all dimensions of the human person: individual, social, and transcendent. According to the doctrine of ethical autonomy, it would be possible to harmonize law, truth, religion, and freedom. For ethical autonomy, the essence (and the end) of religious freedom is the search for truth, in accordance with which people can shape their own choices. From this point of view, freedom of religion is analogous to freedom of scientific research. The purpose of freedom of research is the research as such,

[5] Ronald Dworkin, Justice for Hedgehogs, Cambridge: Belknap Press of Harvard Press, 2011, 369.

not self-determination, although researchers need freedom to their fields of research. Freedom of research is valuable only as a means to high-quality research. However, for the ethical independence approach, religious freedom will be closer to freedom of thought (if it is not a species of it), in which the essence is the freedom, regardless of the quality of the resultant thought.

The fact that there are many religions does not mean that the truth in religious matters is not attainable or that religious relativism is the only reasonable position to take. The truth, like light, can be shared and varies in intensity. To affirm that there is a true religion, as Judaism, Christianity, and Islam (among others) do, does not mean that all others are necessarily false, as if religion were a matter of mathematics. What it does mean is that one religion has the fullness of the truth about the relationship of God and man (*plenitudo veritatis*), and other religions have only part of it (*pars veritatis*). This explains why interreligious dialogue is so fitting and precisely for religions that define themselves as true religions. It would be a mistake – a legal, moral, and political mistake – to try to universalize the liberal doctrine of ethical independence and its legal consequences as if it were the best theory to promote worldwide religious freedom.

The secularist approach exalts individual human freedom to the point of absolutizing it, even at the expense of dignity itself. The liberal secularist approach believes that an absolute libertarian freedom in foundational matters protects dignity. However, the libertarian absolutization of freedom replaces the search for ethical and moral truth with a criterion of personal authenticity that inescapably leads to a subjectivist conception of ethical or moral judgment without the possibility of an external rule. Ethical independence understands freedom as the absence of dependencies that restrict the self, without taking into account the fact that decisions about foundational matters can affect other human beings. Thus, for ethical independence, the only concern is that the personal decision be free, even if this decision objectively damages dignity.

Second, ethical independence creates a false conflict between freedom and the moral law. Objective moral rules are a limitation, but limitations are not always against human freedom. Sometimes they are simply a consequence of our own intrinsic interdependence. If human freedom is limited and interdependent, as it is, then each person's freedom must be ordered and balanced with the coexistence of others' freedoms. In this sense, a kind of moral order is an indispensable complement to personal decisions. Thus, freedom and moral law constitute a whole. The best way to practice freedom is to follow the objective moral law without any coercion. The moral law is a condition of individual freedom – a constitutive element of it, which reduces, at a minimum, the limitations of human freedom.[6] No conflict exists between the existence of God and our freedom or between the so-called laws of God and human freedom. The laws of God do not reduce or undermine human freedom; rather, they protect the very essence of freedom, illuminating it with the light of divine truth. Moral truth is not by itself a creation of human freedom. However, human freedom is an inescapable means of grasping moral truth.

Third, the application of the doctrine of ethical independence, rather than promoting freedom of religion, restricts it by imposing a nonpluralistic framework. Liberal secularists argue that no political community should dictate ethical convictions to its citizens. However, this requirement to avoid the imposition of ethical convictions is itself a dictate of an ethical conviction. It dictates the ethical conviction, an ethical restriction, that religion is, by definition, a *res privata*, a mere attitude. It therefore dictates an ethical conviction about the concept and end of religion itself.

Last, liberal secularist approach to religious freedom is discriminatory because it does not allow for collective pluralism or, therefore, collective self-determination in religious matters. The solution to the question of religious freedom is not just to strive to create a neutral individual environment far from the political arena in which individuals may define their ethical convictions. It is important also to promote political pluralism to recognize the possibility of the existence of different political communities based

[6] Joseph Ratzinger, Truth and Tolerance: Christian Belief and World Religions, San Francisco: Ignatius Press, 2003, 249.

on various religious and moral convictions, which are at the origin of the political community as such.

* * *

The right to religious freedom in Western culture was established as a right supported by a Protestant value of the world (which Catholics, Jews, and, increasingly, Muslims have come to share) in which each person may choose his or her religion, that is, how to worship God. At the core of the right was the duty to worship God, and religion was an instrument. Thus, the right also protected the option of believing in God apart from religion. An example of this was deism. The possibility of atheism or of religion without God was not especially protected by the right to religious freedom. The original approach to religious freedom was chiefly theistic.

Today, a wider and more multicultural concept of religion is making headway in the international realm – religion as a coherent system of beliefs, convictions, and worldviews, regardless of content. The terms *belief* and *religion* have been "broadly construed" to protect theistic, nontheistic, and atheistic beliefs, as well as the right not to profess any religion or belief. This new and wider pluralistic approach to religion does not necessarily imply either the existence of God or the transcendent nature of the human being, as it did originally, so that agnosticism and positive nonreligious beliefs, for instance, have been recognized as standards of "religious beliefs." In modern secular age, paradoxically, no longer are there nonreligious human beings because all human beings (e.g., theistic, nontheistic, agnostic, and skeptical) are legally religious (i.e., protected by freedom of religion), even if they are fervently opposed to religion.

I personally agree, and I think Benedict XVI also does, with this approach as an inexorable effect of multiculturalism and globalization. Indeed, there is no justification for a special right to protect exclusively theistic religions. Both types of "religion" should be protected. However, this does not mean that we must base the right to freedom of religion on ethical independence, as if God did not exist. Otherwise, the liberal secularist position would become mandatory.

Indeed, this recent and welcome international legal trend, which tries to avoid intolerance and discrimination against any kind of belief in religious matters, can never justify the exclusion of the Abrahamic God as such from the legal concept of religion. It is one thing to deny that the idea of God is constitutive of the legal concept of religion to protect under the umbrella of the right to religious freedom all kinds of convictions and beliefs; it is a very different thing positively to exclude God, in the Abrahamic sense of the term, from the idea of religion. The liberal atheistic approach to religious freedom is one option but is neither the only option nor, in some opinions, the best option.

A legal system open to transcendence is not necessarily closed to immanence; much less must it protect only transcendent religions and beliefs. As an essential expression of pluralism and a precious asset for believers and nonbelievers, a democratic constitutional model has to protect both transcendent and immanent religions and beliefs, with the only limit being imposed by public order. To regard religion only as an immanent phenomenon is a negative way to protect religious freedom; it protects only a part of religion, not religion in its fullness. This unjustified reductionism, which could be called the tyranny of legal secularism, would impose a unique secular religion. On its face, it seems to be broader and more open because it is presented as such, as a good alternative to the very narrow, old-fashioned view of religious freedom. However, on inspection, it is narrower than the previous view insofar as it excludes any openness to transcendence and any consideration of God as a source of morality.

What is happening to the legal concept of religion is similar to what has been happening to the legal concept of the family: it is being expanded so much that it is becoming difficult to limit at all. However, that does not mean that this concept can do without legal limitations or regulations. A legal system can admit that offspring are not a constitutive element of the family, but it should not positively exclude offspring from the legal concept of the family by regarding a couple with children as not a family. This example would be a discriminatory manipulation of the law to the extent that a mere part would be equated with the whole, with the result that some family relations that ought to enjoy legal protection would lack protection. Similarly, a legal system can admit, as international law does, that the idea of God is not a constitutive element of the idea of religion, but it should not positively exclude God from the legal concept of religion by rejecting transcendence. This also would be a discriminatory manipulation of the law.

* * *

The unity of the person, as Benedict XVI suggested in his address to the United Nations in New York, harmonically integrates the three essential dimensions of the human person: the individual, social, and transcendent. The individual dimension refers to the person as a self ("I"). The social dimension refers to the person in relation with other persons ("we"). Last, the transcendent dimension develops when a person embraces the ultimate sense of his or her own life, aware of his or her creaturely condition and searching for the divine plan of the creator ("He"). Therefore, without at least acknowledging the possibility of the existence of God, it is not possible to open the doors to this dimension. The individual dimension is supported by individual freedom, the social dimension by political freedom, and the transcendent dimension by religious freedom.

A religion closed to transcendence, and especially to the idea of God, can be easily integrated into the individual dimension ("I"), or into the "we," for instance, by considering humanity as an integrative part of the universe. However, Abrahamic religions require a transcendent dimension. Indeed, for Abrahamic religions, God is the creator and the ultimate source of morality, and therefore, religion is a source of both individual and collective value.

Dignity shapes the three-dimensional unity of the person. All human values operate to varying degrees in all three dimensions to support the unity of the person, although some play more prominent roles in some dimensions than in others. In other words, although a value might affect each dimension to different degrees, none should close the door to one of the three dimensions of the person. These dimensions are not watertight compartments. Legal values, and, therefore, legal systems, operate in the individual and social dimensions of the human person, but they should be open to transcendence. The openness to transcendence reinforces the individual and social dimension and strengthens human freedom, for nothing is mandatory in the realm of transcendence.

The right of religious freedom operates along the three dimensions of the human person. Dignity justifies its special status. The right to religious freedom operates in the individual dimension by protecting the human person in his or her personal search for the truth against any constraint by political authorities. Because freedom of religion is the inclusive patrimony of believers and nonbelievers, it fully protects from religion those who choose to have nothing to do with religion. In the social dimension, the right to religious freedom allows individual persons to live their faith in community and protects political communities against religious and secularist fundamentalisms as rejections of legitimate pluralism. Finally, in the transcendent dimension, the right to religious freedom operates by protecting religion as a basic good and also by opening the door to transcendent truths. However, it also works by scrupulously protecting those who freely decide not to have anything to do with God or religion. In this way, Joseph Weiler is correct that it is not possible to protect adequately "freedom of religion" without protecting first "freedom from religion."[7] In other words, the first step toward protecting religious freedom is to protect those who freely decide to say "no" to God.

The concrete way in which a constitutional model or legal system should be open to transcendence becomes one of its most important features. This openness to transcendence, that is, to the external light of religion, should be ordered according to legal justification, standards, and procedures (*ratio iuris*). Thus, openness to transcendence, instead of devaluing the science of law, dignifies it by contributing to the just development of a legal system and political community. By opening the door to transcendence, the legal system is not crossing from rationality into irrationality. On the contrary, it is approaching the very foundation of rationality itself, that is, of law itself.

Law, freedom, and religion operate in all three dimensions of the person with different degrees of intensity and dependence. Without freedom, there is neither law nor religion. So freedom is a constitutive and intrinsic element of both law and religion. Without the protection of the law, freedom and religion can hardly survive in a political

[7] "The Crucifix in the Classroom: On Freedom of Religion and Freedom from Religion," *Scripta Theologica*, 44, 2012, 187–199.

community: freedom becomes anarchy, and religion falls into mere spirituality. However, without religion, law and freedom could survive, at least at first glance. That is why religion is more vulnerable than freedom or law. Without religion, law and freedom do not fully develop. Religion strengthens freedom insofar as it provides human beings with truths that allow them to make more adequate decisions about how to live. Religion also strengthens law by illuminating the reason for protecting human rights and establishing links of solidarity among human beings and political communities. Law, freedom, and religion are three fundamental expressions of human dignity that all political communities must protect and promote. This is why Benedict XVI suggests that "the world of reason and the world of faith – the world of secular rationality and the world of religious belief – need one another and should not be afraid to enter into a profound and ongoing dialogue, for the good of our civilization."[8]

[8] Benedict XVI, Address at Westminster Hall, September 17, 2010.

4 THE WINDOWS OF BENEDICT XVI

Reason, Revelation, and Law

Wael Farouq

A PLURALISM THAT EXCLUDES

In the speech he delivered to the German Parliament in September 2011, Pope Benedict XVI used an eloquent metaphor to represent positivist reason, as he called it; that is, practical-scientific reason, as the context makes clear. The metaphor compared positivist reason to a concrete bunker without windows, in which the natural elements, such as light and air, are replaced with artificial substitutes.[1] This positivist reason is self-sufficient and autonomous. A form of reason so closed in on itself cannot avoid creating a world in its own image in its isolation. In the world, which, thanks to technology, has become a small village, individuals and societies have become "bunkers without windows." The sense of solitude grows; desire dwindles; curiosity fades; the fear of the other gets the upper hand; and the artificial chokes out the natural in every aspect of life so that the chasm between the *human being* and *humanity* grows ever larger.

Speaking at the University of Regensburg in September 2006, Pope Benedict alluded to the risk run by the West, which "has long been endangered by this aversion to the questions which underlie its rationality, and can only suffer great harm thereby."[2] The Pope

[1] Pope Benedict XVI, "The Listening Heart: Reflections on the Foundation of Law," Address to the German Parliament (Bundestag), September 22, 2011, available at www.vatican.va/holy_father/benedict_xvi/speeches/2011/september/documents/hf_ben-xvi_spe_20110922_reichstag-berlin_en.html.

[2] Pope Benedict XVI, "Faith, Reason and the University: Memories and Reflections," Meeting with the Representatives of Science, Aula Magna of the

Emeritus exposed the incapacity of this kind of reason to enter into dialogue with the other, because "In the Western world it is widely held that only positivistic reason and the forms of philosophy based on it are universally valid. Yet the world's profoundly religious cultures see this exclusion of the divine from the universality of reason as an attack on their most profound convictions. A reason which is deaf to the divine and which relegates religion into the realm of subcultures is incapable of entering into the dialogue of cultures."[3]

Pope Benedict pinpoints the danger of this way of reasoning, and the crisis it has engendered, by pointing to its tendency to categorize other cultural realities as culturally backward or antiquated. In this way, "it diminishes man, indeed it threatens his humanity."[4] Thus, Benedict confronts the *exclusion* that, in many different forms, dominates the contemporary world. In societies in which ideology prevails, or in which religion has become ideology, the exclusion of who is different is violent and, at times, bloody. And in societies founded on secular, democratic governments, in which "the questions raised by religion and ethics . . . must thus be relegated to the realm of the subjective,"[5] it is widely believed that peaceful coexistence between people belonging to different religions, traditions, and cultures can only succeed if religious and ethical experience are excluded from the public square. This implies exclusion of difference, and when religious experience is one of the most important elements of a person's identity, the exclusion of difference becomes exclusion of the self.

To counter the exclusion of the self and of the other, Pope Benedict says "the windows must be flung open again,"[6] so that reason can open itself to the language – or languages – of existence. These "windows" of Benedict's metaphor are bridges that, in the first place, unite contemporary rationality with "the classical sources of knowledge for ethics and law"[7] and with the values that God has

University of Regensburg, September 12, 2006, available at www.vatican.va/holy_father/benedict_xvi/speeches/2006/september/documents/hf_ben-xvi_spe_20060912_university-regensburg_en.html.

[3] Id. [4] Pope Benedict XVI, "The Listening Heart."

[5] Pope Benedict XVI, "Faith, Reason and the University."

[6] Pope Benedict XVI, "The Listening Heart." [7] Id.

impressed upon His creatures. These values, as a result, are within reach for everyone, since, in the words of Saint Paul, "they show that the demands of the law are written in their hearts, while their conscience also bears witness"(Romans 2:15). Benedict's windows, in the second place, connect the self – once he or she has become aware of his or her own vast human horizons – with the other. This is because at that point "we become capable of that genuine dialogue of cultures and religions so urgently needed today."[8]

Benedict is not speaking here of traditional dialogue, which insists on working toward the rapprochement of theological doctrines. In his encounters with Muslims, for example, the Pope always avoided the usual theme of adoration of the one God, choosing to focus instead on those values that derive from human nature and form the real basis of both peaceful coexistence and fruitful interreligious dialogue. This is an invitation to move beyond an illusory communion in faith to a true communion in life. And this communion in life opens the third window, or builds the third bridge: the one that joins reason with reality. In fact, in all his speeches, Benedict always links the "understanding of God" with the "practice of religion" and the concept of "reason" with its "use." The Pope Emeritus connects freedom from exclusion with the capacity for dialogue because if the violent imposition of faith amounts to exclusion of the other, then ignoring the long history of fruitful intersection between faith and reason amounts to exclusion of identity – just as the rejection of religious knowledge by scientific reason is the exclusion of the entire reality which religious knowledge is primarily responsible for shaping.

With each step taken to destroy exclusion, the characteristics of identity take shape more solidly, more completely, and their relationship with reality is revealed, finally reaching the clear and frank invitation to take part in an experience of true dialogue. True dialogue does not aspire to either agreement or disagreement, to reciprocal understanding or coexistence, because its object is a deeper understanding of the self in relation to the other, as part of a reality that results from a continuous encounter with God (in Islamic tradition,

[8] Pope Benedict XVI, "Faith, Reason and the University."

too, we meet and love one another in God). It is a brilliant, balancing formula between what is stable and what is changeable in human life. God, in himself, does not change, but each encounter with Him is a unique event, a new creation, a life renewed.

What Pope Benedict proposes is an invitation to productive pluralism, which guarantees interaction between and contribution from everyone in constructing the common good. This model contrasts starkly with what can be called negative pluralism, which claims, on the contrary, that, on the road of dialogue and coexistence, "it is necessary to overcome the differences and dissimilarities that distinguish one culture from another."[9] Productive pluralism does not impose concessions on the individual because it is aware that what distinguishes cultures one from the other is precisely the contribution they have to offer each other.

One could go so far as to say that many laws, by preferring the criterion of the majority to that of justice, enact the negative pluralism described above, which excludes difference. Indeed, France, one of the oldest Western democracies – and one of the most historically rich in its defense of rights and freedoms – effectively forbid the display of religious symbols in public spaces with its ratification of the so-called anti-veil law on April 11, 2011. By doing so, it became a state in which the Constitution vouchsafes difference and religious pluralism, while its legislation forbids the expression thereof.

Switzerland also offers a clear example of exclusion of diversity enshrined in law. On November 29, 2009, it passed a referendum in which the majority decided the architectural shape that all mosques must take in that country (though it is unclear what constitutional right allows the promulgation of laws that concern only one specific social group). In both cases, the justifications offered lead us to a single rule, which clearly illustrates the lengths to which rationality based on exclusion can go: the rule which affirms that *equality in injustice is just.*

Practices of exclusion touch every aspect of life – at times unintentionally – while the divisions and barriers between the different

[9] Interview with Koichiro Matsuura, Majallat al-Siyasa al-Dawliyya, January/February 2002, p. 95 n. 147, Al-Ahram Center for Strategic Studies, Cairo, Egypt.

"teams" within a single country remain entrenched. A Jewish professor at the Sorbonne once explained how the famed *saucisse*, the national dish of France, had become an expression of discrimination against Muslims and Jews, who do not eat pork. Members of the two religions were left with only two choices: abandon public feasts, or pretend to be vegetarians in order to avoid hearing the inevitable, "Look! They don't eat *saucisse*!"

In other societies, the various forms of religious expression have the benefit of greater protections, but only if their presence in the public square does not go beyond the practice of their own rituals. In such cases, religion is reduced to simple liturgies, emptied of any social significance. This results in profound divisions within societies whenever they are faced with the ultimate questions of life and death, for example with regard to issues such as abortion, euthanasia, and organ donation. In cases like these, the incapacity of scientific reason to formulate an ethical judgment is plain, and society's lack of experience with positive pluralism, which could at least offer a common language for debating such issues, becomes equally obvious. Instead, society always relies on the criterion of the majority, rather than that of justice.

Pope Benedict has said that one of the major goals of his talk at Regensburg was to urge debate of this tragic situation, and he proposes a model for doing so (at least as it is understood here): reason that does not exclude faith, faith that does not exclude the other, and law that does not exclude human nature. The need to discuss this proposal is undoubtedly even more urgent in Islamic societies, as is the need to be given the opportunity to respond. This is precisely what I will attempt to do in the following pages.

THE CODIFICATION OF REVELATION

Article 1 of the recently approved Egyptian Constitution[10] affirms that Egypt is a secular state; but Article 2, which follows, establishes *sharia* (Islamic law) as the primary source of legislation. An attached

[10] The Constitution referred to here is the one approved in a referendum held on December 15 and 22, 2012, which was later suspended by

article explains that authoritative references for the laws are no longer limited only to divine revelation – the Quran and the *hadith*[11] – but also include the interpretations of these texts developed by medieval Islamic jurists. Nor does the circle of reference stop there, for the Constitution also declares that a supreme board of *ulema*, experts of Islamic law, must examine all laws prior to their promulgation and evaluate their harmony or discord with the rulings of *sharia*. Then, in the same article that sanctions religious liberty and the freedom to practice religious rituals, the Constitution goes on to reserve the right to construct places of worship only to members of the three revealed religions (Jews, Christians, and Muslims), excluding all others.

These contradictions (and, sometimes, paradoxes) implicate all the articles of the Constitution, but our purpose in this chapter is not to enter into the details of the text, or to understand the conflict that led to its creation. What is relevant to the current topic is the incapacity of the drafters of the Constitution to perceive any contradiction between its articles – so much so that some of them have even dubbed it the best Constitution ever known to humankind. In the constitutional Charter, Islamists see a document that must express the collective national identity and safeguard the rights of the *umma* (the community of Muslim believers), and they see *sharia* as the incarnation of this identity. Individual rights and freedoms, in their view, do not exist outside the *umma*.

Already in the second half of the nineteenth century, Khedive Ismail invited the *ulema* of al-Azhar to codify *sharia*. As the historical record reveals, the Azharites refused to respond to the call of the khedive; that is, they refused to organize *sharia* into articles of a book, modeled after European legal volumes. Tareq al-Bishri, one of the greats of contemporary jurisprudence, has accused the Azharites of shirking their historical and cultural mission, therefore becoming "the cause of the institution of the civil tribunals and of the government's

Presidential decree on July 8, 2013, and is currently being amended by a new Constitutional Committee.

11 The corpus of prophetic traditions passed down orally from the first generations of Muslims, and today preserved in a series of collected writings.

dependence on French laws."[12] But Al-Bishri does not consider the possibility that the *ulema*'s refusal could be traced to fear for *sharia* itself – after all, codification would, by its very nature, have threatened the heterogeneity of *fiqh* (Islamic jurisprudence), destroying the plurality that distinguishes it, and which is the result of a long history of practice and of *ijtihad* (interpretative effort) in societies that were strongly culturally diverse, and which made up part of the immense geographic area governed by Muslims.

After this episode, attempts to codify *sharia* continued for more than a century. One of the most important of these took place at the end of the 1970s, when President Sadat, the self-dubbed "believer president," assigned the task to committees made up of dozens of jurists and religious men. The efforts of these committees produced a number of proposed laws, which codified the opinions of the Islamic legal scholars regarding the medieval age rather than the rulings of *sharia*. The majority of judges and legal scholars was against it, because they did not understand this new formulation of the laws (which, from a linguistic and structural perspective, dated back to the second century of hijra [ninth century A.D.]), and because most Egyptian laws did not conflict with *sharia*, even if *sharia* had not been their source. This was eventually recognized by the al-Azhar *sheykh* Abdel Moneim al-Nimr, who led the codification of *sharia* law, and who confirmed that more than 90 percent of Egyptian laws were not in conflict with Islamic law. As a result, the work of the committees was ultimately limited to the task of harmonizing the small percentage of conflicting laws with the rest of the Egyptian legal order. Notwithstanding this, all the movements of political Islam, such as Wahhabism in Saudi Arabia and the Muslim Brotherhood in Egypt, have focused all their energies, and all their slogans, on a single issue: the application of *sharia* as the Islamic legal order.

For the secular government, on the other hand, *sharia* provided a broad and generic framework that could be invoked as needed. In its dealings with the West, it would abandon this framework, adopting

[12] Tareq Al-Bishri, Al-Siyaq al-Thaqafi wa-l-Tarikhi li-Taqnin al-Sharia al-Islamiyya, Cairo: Dar al-Shorouq al-Dawliyya, 2011, p. 27.

liberal terminology; but when addressing national political forces within Egypt – the Nasserists or the Marxists, for example – it would return to *sharia* and religion, to legitimize its power through the religious devotion of the President and government elite. Given all this, it should come as no surprise that the 1984 campaign platform of the Communist Party al-Tagammu'included the phrase: "To draw inspiration from *sharia* as the main source of law, and to support mosques, churches, and places of worship."[13]

Political analyst Nabil Abdel Fattah, commenting on this long history, has said that the most dangerous aspect of the conflict between *sharia* law and positive law has been the inability to produce valuable change in the areas of *fiqh* and legal thought, because the driving political forces have always and only addressed the issue with generic slogans, unaccompanied by in-depth study of historical, judicial, and legislative problems.

Whenever Islamic law was adopted in place of the existing laws in territories conquered by Islam, the historical record shows no resulting conflicts (unlike when the same was done with doctrine) between the old, pre-Islamic era and the new one brought by Islam. Islamic law, in fact, adopted many of the preexisting customs that did not conflict with its principles, while ignoring others.

From this it can be understood that the conflict between reason, revelation, and law is a figment of the imagination. Its contradictions tend to be merely products of the interaction between traditional structures and values and modern structures and values. The result is a tremendous amount of contradiction and incongruity, which acts as a dead weight on society and exposes it to the constant risk of explosion, self-destruction, and self-"consumption." In light of this, modernity and traditional structures (Islam, first of all) do not seem to be truly in conflict. Instead, their relationship produces a culture that is neither modern, nor traditional, nor a mix of the two. Rather, it is a third, distinct culture: the culture of a people who receive modernity without creating it

[13] Nabil Abdel Fattah, Siyasat al-Adyan wa-Darurat al-Islah, Cairo: Dar al-Kutub, 2005, p. 133.

or, to be more precise, a people on whom modernity has been imposed by means not of their choosing, and by a history which they themselves did not generate.

This "third culture" is founded on principles antithetical to the ones that underlie modernity in the western sense of the word – principles that, nevertheless, do not necessarily derive from tradition either, since this false modernity distorts tradition in the same way that it distorts authentic expressions of modernity. There is no stronger proof of this than the fact that this third culture, in both cases, rejects reason (that same reason on which Islamic tradition and civilization are founded).

The third culture prefers to resort to the labyrinths of irrationality and to exalt innate instinct over reason. It reproduces itself through the growing contradictions in its fundamental components, that is, tradition and modernity. This implies that, over time, the contradictions within this third culture will become increasingly severe, while nevertheless remaining necessary for this culture to endure. At this point the culture becomes fuel for conflict, and the false project of modernity becomes the object of the disputes, whether they emerge from the ranks of the self-styled modernists or from those of the self-styled traditionalists. This perspective necessarily belies a dualistic analysis, since no one has an exclusive monopoly on modernity, and pure traditions do not exist: indeed, everything traditional is, to a certain extent, also modern, and everything modern is, likewise, somewhat traditional. At the same time, the modern and the traditional war with one another, each in an attempt to subjugate the other. This is the logic of the third culture, which attempts to meld them both in a single crucible.

If we wish to create a space where reason, revelation, and law can meet, this socio-cultural context forces us to return to the origins. The space/interpretation proposed in these pages may not reflect the current Islamic reality, but it is certainly built on its latent potential and expresses the future it yearns to achieve. It is a window opening on a generation of young people who rose up and eradicated tyrannical regimes, and whose struggle against the culture that remains in the wake of these regimes will go on for a long time to come.

REASON, REVELATION, AND LAW: AN ISLAMIC PERSPECTIVE

The Natural Religion

The prevailing translation of the word *sharia* is "Islamic law," which is adequate for the reality referred to in the preceding pages, but is an inaccurate account of the Arabic word itself, which means the "path through the desert that leads to water." The defining characteristic of this path is that it is trampled into existence by the feet of those who walk toward the water, the font of all life in the desert. In the same way, *sharia* is a road toward life that we – humanity – have participated in, and continue to participate in tracing and paving with each step we take along it. It is not a predesignated road imposed on us from above; it is our action and our choice.

In the Quran, the term *sharia* appears five times, as a noun, a verb, or another derivative. In none of these instances, according to Quranic commentators, is the word ever used to mean "law," but rather signifies "way" or "road." For example: "Then we put you [O Mohammad] on an ordained way concerning the matter [of religion]; so follow it" (Quran 45:18).[14]

It is clear that the word *sharia* in the Quran does not mean law, but rather religion, method, and so on. In the context of the Quran, *sharia* is the same eloquent metaphor of religion as a divine road toward eternal life, traced by human beings endowed with free will who have chosen to follow it. *Sharia*, therefore, is not a divine law to be applied to the letter. The verses dealing with social relationships and commercial transactions (*mu'amalat*), to which the narrow interpretation of political Islam has reduced *sharia*, make up only 80 of the 6,000 verses contained in the Quranic text. In reality, *sharia* is a place of encounter between divine will and human action. In its broadest and deepest meaning, *sharia* is the all-encompassing law of Creation, which includes not only the planets, plants, animals, and so on, but which also extends to the evolving relationships that govern the connections between all these different things. These relationships

[14] The Noble Quran, Sahih International Translation, found at quran.com.

are also part of Creation and the divine will. They are the laws of nature, through which the Universe can work – the laws of chemistry and physics, which the Universe cannot avoid to obey and submit to. This means that Creation is "Muslim," and, by the same token, every human being is "Muslim" because his or her biological functions are subject to nature and nature's laws. Human beings are, nevertheless, distinct from the rest of Creation, because they are free in some ways to choose whether to accept or reject the divine will. *Sharia*, in the final analysis, is God's will for humanity, achieved through the actions of the human being.

> But how can humanity know the will of God?
> The Quran tells us about the "*fitrah* [first nature] of Allah upon which he has created [*fatara*] [all] people" (Quran 30:30), the beauty of which God has placed within the human intellect, together with a revulsion for all things other than itself. Thus has God instilled in the hearts of all creatures the propensity to follow the rulings of *sharia* along with a love of truth. The Quran says of Adam: "And [mention] when your Lord took from the children of Adam – from their loins – their descendants and made them testify of themselves, [saying to them], "Am I not your Lord?" They said, "Yes, we have testified." [This] – lest you should say on the day of Resurrection, "Indeed, we were of this unaware" (Quran 7:172). Indeed, at the very moment in which God created Adam, he revealed to him His will. Thus, Adam became the first of God's prophets, and humanity, from its very beginnings, possessed the necessary knowledge to conform to His desires, as well as an instrument able to guide humanity forward when it happened to lose the road or forget what God had instilled in the hearts of His children. Therefore, one can never be a *mukallaf* Muslim (one who receives divine orders and obeys them) if he or she lacks *reason*, because reason guarantees that knowledge, and the encounter between the divine will and human action, will endure.

The Arabic root *'ql* (from which derives the word *'aql*, reason) appears forty-nine times in the Quran. In all except one, it takes the form of a verb in the present tense, usually in the second or third person plural, as in: *ta 'qiluna* (you are endowed with reason) and *ya 'qiluna* (they are endowed with reason). The verb *ta 'qiluna* is repeated twenty-four times and *ya 'qiluna* twenty-two times, while the verbs *'aqala, na 'aqilu,* and *ya 'qilu* each appear once.

In every verse in which they are found, these verbs are always presented in the context of an invitation to employ reason to understand nature and the human being, and in so doing to connect with God. For example: "Indeed the worst of living creatures in the sight of Allah are the deaf and dumb who do not use reason" (Quran 8:22); "So have they not traveled through the earth and have hearts by which to reason (*ya 'qiluna biha*) and ears by which to hear? For indeed, it is not eyes that are blinded, but blinded are the hearts which are within the breasts." (Quran 22:46).

The word reason as a noun (*'aql*) does not appear in the Quran, because it is not a concept or a fixed and complete entity unto itself. Rather it is a *becoming*, a journey, an action and practice that happens in the present; and it appears as a verb in the present tense because its most important feature is its fulfillment in the *now* (neither in the past nor in the future). And, moreover, the verb is plural, because reason is our common language, the unifying element that vouchsafes and protects plurality.

In the context of the Quran, reason is a bridge connecting the human being with nature and with God, the *self* with the *other*. For this reason, every time the verb *'aqala* and its derivatives appear with a negation, they are also accompanied by a metaphor that alludes to the breakage of this connection (deafness, muteness, blindness). God says: "Do they not then meditate (*yatadabbaruna*) on the Quran, or are there locks upon their hearts?" (Quran 47:24).

The verb *yatadabbaruna* is synonymous with *yata'aqqaluna* (they are endowed with reason). Without reason, the heart (where the spirit abides) is a prisoner; the human being is not free, but remains imprisoned by prejudices, stereotypes, and rigid traditions that prevent him or her from living a true life, which is the encounter with God, creatures, and other people.

Therefore, reason in the context of the Quran is an act of continuous connection with God and others, here and now. Reason is freedom, a new creation each and every day, because it is experience and life lived, which daily renews and transforms itself. Despite this, according to the Quran, humanity has rebelled against God throughout its history, and God has always patiently and mercifully continued to send new prophets to reveal his will. Every people and every age has been the recipient of a divine messenger, until the appearance of the Prophet Muhammad. In him, the history of prophecy reached its end. Muhammad is the ultimate prophet, who brought the revelation of the divine will to completion. The final revelation takes the form of the Quran, the Scripture sent by God, his own sacred word. Its advent was the dawn of a new epoch for humanity, defined by a community faithful to the revelation: the collectivity of Muslims who make up the *umma*.

Of course, human nature was not substantively altered by the final revelation of God's will in the Quran. Human beings continue to wander from the straight path and to challenge God, both personally and collectively. The *umma*, aware of its own history, freely admits its failure to always be faithful to God. Nevertheless, the *umma* has remained faithful in its central and essential task: to preserve the divine revelation contained in the Quran. Because of this humanity can never forget the will of God.

This is why *sharia* has a theological definition: the divine will for humanity, which humans are free to accept or reject. Acceptance brings the human being into harmonious relationship with the divine will, involving all of Creation, and leads to prosperity and well-being in both this world and the next. For this reason, Islam is called *din al-fitra*, the natural religion.

According to Islam, the nature and original state of the human being are goodness and truth, and the root of evil is an action taken with free will that deviates from the divine path. Accordingly, *fiqh* is governed by the principle that says "the origin of all things is lawful," meaning that nature and the human being are originally good, and therefore everything is lawful, save what has been explicitly prohibited by a clear and direct revelation. Therefore, law derives from the goodness that is rooted in humanity, and which is in harmony with nature. Perhaps this is why the jurists of the last century refused to codify *sharia*. Indeed, even if civil law does not derive from *sharia*, provided that the two do not conflict, it is still in line with the latter's goal: the achievement of justice.

The technical result of this in Islamic jurisprudence is that there are two distinct sources of law: public interest (*al-masalih al-mursala*) and custom or tradition (*al-'urf*). The first is a principle, embraced by the majority of scholars, which allows for many rules, typically accepted, to be put aside in the name of the public interest. Many traditional rules have been altered or modified in accordance with this principle. By contrast, the second source involves the adoption of customs and traditions that do not contradict Islamic principles and do not confuse what is lawful with what is unlawful. This, too, is a widely used principle, in particular by the Maliki and Hanafi schools of legal thought. The principle is captured by the maxim: "What custom has accepted is automatically incorporated."

Although these two sources are marginal compared to the Quran, the Sunna, the *qiyas*, and the *ijma'* (unanimous consensus) of the Companions of the prophet Muhammad, they nevertheless form the foundation of most of the laws, because *sharia*, in the words of Ibn al-Qayyim, "bases its foundation and its structure on what is good for humanity, in this life and on the Resurrection Day. It consists of justice, mercy, and benefit. Anything that moves away from justice towards oppression, from mercy towards its opposite, from benefit toward corruption, and from reason toward irrationality does not come from *sharia*, even if it has been presented to you as an interpretation thereof."[15]

It is clear that the true source of the law, according to *sharia*, is reality. The only principle that governs all laws is that of noncontradiction with *sharia*.

THE RELIGIOUS "OTHER" FROM AN ISLAMIC POINT OF VIEW

According to Abu Hurayra, the Messenger of God said: "My example, and that of the prophets who have gone before me, is that of a man who builds a house, making it beautiful and well done,

[15] Ibn Al-Qayyim al-Jawziyya, I'lam al-Muwaqqi'in (3/3)

except that he leaves out a single stone at one of the corners. The people walk around the house, admiring it, and ask: '[Why] did you leave out that stone?' [The Prophet] says: 'I am that stone and the Seal of the Prophets.'"[16]

In this *hadith*, the prophet reveals himself as a continuation and connection in the long, historical relationship between the heavens and the earth, the sacred and the human. He is a new connection, in which this relationship reaches its fulfillment, and through which the edifice of prophecy passes from imperfection to perfection. The perfection and completeness of this connection imply that its manifestations will cease. For this reason the prophet, in this *hadith*, also reveals himself as an "interruption": indeed, he is the seal, that is, the end, of all prophecy. Nevertheless, this end announces a new beginning, the start of a new phase in the relationship between the sacred and the human, which is no longer transitory and limited to a single prophet who hands down the message from Heaven. Now "the reason of the congregation of believers" has assumed the place of prophet, a transformation that would have been impossible without the fulfillment of prophetic revelation through the prophet-seal.

These dualisms of connection and interruption, imperfection and perfection, beginning and end do not, in this context, imply contradiction but rather difference or contrast, represented by the same principle that governs the relationship between Islam and the revealed religions that preceded it. It is even arguably true that the conflict between Islam and paganism was not, in essence, one of doctrine. Religion was not the epicenter around which turned the debate with the idolaters, who had not completely rejected Islamic monotheism. The Quran itself supports this view in many of its verses: "If you asked them: 'who created the heavens and the earth, and subjected the sun and the moon?' they would surely say, 'Allah!'" (Quran 29:61). Indeed, they worshiped idols only to grow nearer to God: "'We only worship them that they may bring us nearer to Allah in position'" (Quran 39:3). Nothing prevented them from embracing Islam, except for their attachment to the legacy of their ancestors: "And when it is

[16] Al-Bukhari, al-Sahih, Kitab al-Manaqib, n. 3535; Muslim, al-Sahih, Kitab al-Fada'il, n. 2286; Ahmad, al-Musnad, 2/312.

said to them: 'Follow what God has revealed,' they say: 'Rather, we will follow that upon which we found our fathers.'" (Quran 31:21). Islam's battle, therefore, was neither religious nor doctrinal. Instead, it was the struggle against the culture that had placed the tribal system outside of this world, although preserving its cohesiveness, turning its geographic isolation (in the desert) and its temporal isolation (in the past) into the defining element of its collective and individual identity.

Islam adopted many of the beliefs, religious practices, and ethical values that preceded it. Contrary to what is commonly written in the books of Islamic history, belonging both to the tradition and the contemporary age, the society in which Islam came into being was neither immoral nor lacking in virtue. Its people "were neither ignorant, nor stupid, nor vulgar, and neither were their lives cold and course; rather, they were possessed of knowledge, intelligence, fine emotions, and a life that was both sweet and comfortable."[17] In another *hadith*, the prophet says: "Truly, I came to bring virtue to its fulfillment."[18] But the act of fulfilling religion and moral virtue does not deny their existence. This was the state of Islamic society under the leadership of the prophet until the descent of some Quranic verses, during the Farewell Pilgrimage, which say: "This day I have perfected for you your religion and have completed My favor upon you, and I have approved for you Islam as religion" (Quran 5:3). Upon hearing this, 'Umar b. al-Khaṭṭāb burst into tears, and, when he was asked why, he replied: "After perfection there is nothing but incompleteness," meaning that the completion of the religion implied the absence of the prophet. Imperfection here does not suggest a moral judgment, because Islam wanted nothing more than to pass from a society consecrated to imperfection to a society that strives for perfection. Indeed, life itself is but a bridge between human imperfection and divine perfection, which is traversed by the human being.

Islam views all religions as members of the same body. If even one of them were missing, the prophetic edifice could not have been completed by the prophet Muhammad. This idea has existed in Islamic

[17] Taha Huseyn, Fi-l-Shi'r al-Jahili, 1st ed., Cairo: Dar al-Kutub al Misriya, 1926, p. 20.

[18] al-Bukhari, al-Adab al-Mufrad, n. 273.

tradition under different forms. In the fourth century of hijra, for example (the tenth century A.D.), the Brethren of Purity[19] used a different metaphor to express the same idea, describing humanity as a sick person beset by various illnesses. The doctor (God) prescribes different medications (religions) for different ailments, and the lack of a single medicine threatens the life of the patient (humanity). The *other*, in Islamic tradition, is the companion whose presence guarantees human fulfillment, and whose absence threatens human civilization.

It is therefore not surprising that Muhammad ʻAbid al-Jabri maintains that the concept of "other" (*al-akhar*) is unknown to the Arabic language, and that the closest word to this concept is *al-ghayr*, "the different," which means "whoever is not me." The term *ghayriyya*, which simply means "difference," derives from this word. As a result, according to al-Jabri, difference is not necessary for self-awareness, as it is in European thought. In Arabic, difference is an attribute, not a substance unto itself as in European languages. In the majority of cases, the term "other" is used to mean "to put in order," in the sense of listing or enumerating, rather than ranking things by preference or priority.

The Quran's position towards "non-Muslims" begins with their recognition not as "other" in the European sense of the word, but as "others" recognized as "people of religion." In any case, everyone, including "I/Islam" is equal before God. The Most High says: "Indeed, those who believed and those who were Jews or Christians or Sabeans [before Prophet Muhammad] – those [among them] who believed in Allah and in the Last Day and did righteousness – will have their reward with their Lord, and no fear will there be concerning them, nor will they grieve" (Quran 2:62).

DIFFERENCE AS A NATURAL RIGHT

The root *kh.l.f*, from which the word for difference, *ikhtilaf*, is derived, is among the most rich in the Arabic vocabulary, in terms of both the words that derive from it and its meaning. It can imply

[19] Muslim confraternity from Basra, in Iraq.

both positive and negative meanings, for example: *corruption, stupidity, resistance, contradiction, emirate, to give fruit, pray for rain*, and so on. But despite this wealth of meanings and forms, some dictionaries overlook that of *ikhtilaf* (difference), while others have related it back to the explanation of the term *khilfa*: "The peoples are *khilfa*, meaning that they come one after the other; and *khilfa* also refers to the succession of day and night." Ibn Manzour attributes multiple meanings to the verb *ikhtalafa*. It means a lack of conformity or correspondence and derives from "*ikhtalaftu-hu*, which means I have put it behind me."[20]

What can be understood from this examination of the meaning of *ikhtilaf* in Arabic dictionaries is that difference is neither a cause nor a consequence of conflict. Rather, a lack of conformity signals heterogeneity and distinctness, which form the basis of individual identity and pluralism. God did not make human beings to be identical to one another. Those who hide their differences in dialoguing with others, just like those who use differences as a pretext to make war against others, fail to understand the divine wisdom, which ordained that difference be a *sunna* of God (*sunnat allah*), that is, a law of nature that is continually present in his creatures. In this view, a careful observation of the universe, of which we occupy only a small part, reveals that God created it to be versatile and various. In the Quran, God himself says: "Do you not see that God sends down rain from the sky, and We produce thereby fruits of varying colors? And in the mountains are tracts, white and red of varying shades, and [some] extremely black. And among people and moving creatures and grazing livestock are various colors similarly" (Quran 35:27,28).

These two verses confirm for believers, leaving no room for doubt, that difference is a *sunna* of God, constantly present in his creation and his kingdom – so much so that it is impossible to find two creatures that are identical in every way. God even created each species in twofold form, making this a sign and point of reflection.

[20] Ibn Manzour, Lisan al-'Arab, section entitled kh.l.f., pp. 188–193; al-Zamakhshari, Asas al-Balagha, section entitled kh.l.f., p. 173; al-Jawhari, al-Sihah, section entitled kh.l.f., p. 313.

In the Quran, God says: "And of all things We created two mates: perhaps you will remember" (Quran 51:49).

The kind of difference pointed to in the Quran involves neither contradiction nor conflict, but rather multiplicity. For this reason, the word "multicolored" is used at least twice in more than one *sura*.

In fact, the Quran explicitly denies any hint of conflict or contradiction in the universe. God says: "You do not see in the creation of the Most Merciful any inconsistency" (Quran 67:3). And again, supporting the proposition that difference – whether among human beings, in the universe, or in life in general – implies only multiplicity and never conflict or contradiction, God says: "And of His signs is the creation of the heavens and the earth and the diversity of your languages and your colors. Indeed in that are signs for those of knowledge!" (Quran 30:22).

The Quranic commentator Ibn Kathir, in explaining this verse, writes:

> The Most High says that (among the signs) of His absolute power are (the creation of the heavens and the earth), that is the creation of the vast heavens above, the celestial bodies, the brilliance of the planets, the fixed and the wandering stars; and the creation of the solid earth below, with its mountains, its valleys, its seas, its deserts, its animals, and its trees. The Most High says, "the diversity of your languages," because there exist those who speak the language of the Arabs, those who speak the language of the Franks, those who speak the language of the Berbers, those who speak the language of the Abyssinians, those who speak the language of the Indians, and still others who speak other foreign languages; only God knows all the languages of human beings, as only He knows all their different colors. All the peoples of the world, from the creation of Adam until the Final Hour, have two eyes, two eyebrows, one nose, one forehead, one mouth, and two cheeks, and yet no two are identical; and even their bodies can always be distinguished by some obvious or hidden characteristic, or by their shape.
>
> Upon close observation, each person has a face endowed with a unique expression, and a body that is not identical to anyone else's. Even if people have common features such as beauty

or ugliness, within these they are different one from the other. (Indeed, in this are signs for those of knowledge!)[21]

Difference, therefore, is an innate characteristic with which God has stamped creation – a sign of his extreme power, one of his astonishing signs. The population of the universe, the flowering of existence, the flourishing of life: none of this could have come to fruition if human beings had been created identical, and each one is enabled to carry out that for which he or she has been created. In the Quran, God has said: "And if your Lord had willed, He could have made mankind one community; but they will not cease to differ ... and for that He created them" (Quran 11:118, 119).

Difference, in light of all of this, is a natural right, in the sense that it is present in every individual inasmuch as he or she is human. It is a feature of a person's humanity, and to vitiate it is to vitiate his or her humanity. Moreover, it is a permanent natural right, in the sense that it will exist for as long as humans continue to live on earth, that is, according to the Quran, until the Day of Judgment, on which God will judge the differences between people.

Pluralism is the sincere expression of difference in thought, opinion, and faith, and so it, too, is both general and permanent.

The Quran itself supports this truth when it says, in addition to the verses cited earlier (Quran 11:118, 119): "And mankind was not but one community [united in religion], but [then] they *differed.* And if not for a word that preceded from your Lord, *it would have been judged between them [immediately] concerning that over which they differ*" (Quran 10:19); "Had Allah willed, He would have made you one nation [united in religion], but [He intended] to test you in what He has given you; so race to [all that is] good. To Allah is your return all together, and He will [then] inform you *concerning that over which you used to differ*" (Quran 5:48); "Indeed, your Lord will judge between them on the Day of Resurrection concerning that *over which they used to differ*" (Quran 32:25); "And if they dispute with you, then say, 'Allah is most knowing of what

21 Ibn Kathir, *Tafsir al-Qur'an al-'Azhim*, vol. 3, Beirut: Dar al-Jil, p. 414.

you do. Allah will judge between you on the Day of Resurrection *concerning that over which you used to differ*'" (Quran 22:68, 69).[22]

It is clear that the right to difference, in the Islamic context, is a natural right, a general right applicable to all people, which is inalienable and will endure, according to the Islamic faith, until the Day of Resurrection, on which Almighty God will adjudicate the differences between people.

According to Islam, God does not prohibit difference. Muhammad Said al-Bouti writes:

> I searched the book of Almighty God for a verse that prohibits difference . . ., but I found nothing. However, He prohibits division and conflict, that is, the negative consequences of difference. He says, for example: "And hold firmly to the rope of Allah all together and do not become divided" (*The Quran* 3:103). He could instead have said "and let there be no differences among you." And in another place He says: "And obey Allah and His Messenger, and do not dispute and [thus] lose courage and [then] your strength would depart" (*The Quran* 8:46). And where He does prohibit difference, it is a particular type – that which characterizes certain defunct nations: "And do not be like the ones who became divided and *differed*[. . .]" (*The Quran* 3:105), that is "that your differences are not destabilizing, bringing you to conflict and disorder." Furthermore, we have all heard and read the words of Almight God "but they will continue *to be different*."[23]

The wisdom of the Islamic God is revealed in the *sunna* of difference, in the verse that says: "O mankind, indeed We have created you from male and female and made you peoples and tribes that you may know one another. Indeed, the most noble of you in the sight of Allah is the most righteous of you. Indeed, Allah is Knowing and Acquainted" (Quran 49:13). This verse is addressed to all people and was revealed,

[22] The italicized words in these Quranic verses have been, in accordance with the indications of the author, translated differently from the English version of the Quran used, to be more consistent with the meaning of the original Arabic. All involve the verb ikhtalafa or derivatives thereof, which has a wide spectrum of meanings in Arabic, including "to be different" and "to disagree."

[23] Muhammad Said Ramadan al-Bouti, al-Islam wa-Sunnat-al-Ikhtilaf, Beirut: Dar al-Fikr al-Mu'asir, 1995, p. 29.

according to Ibn Kathir, "after having prohibited mutual contempt between people and speaking ill of one another, with reference to the equality of people in their humanity."[24] So, difference is not the criterion for establishing who among the people is best, because people are as equal as the teeth of a comb. God says, "We have created you from male and female," because in this characteristic, all are equal. This confirms the conclusion that difference means distinction, and that the deeper meaning of this difference is knowledge. According to the Quran, God says: "know one another," or, according to Asim's reading: "know."

Thus, difference is the basis of knowledge, and dialogue is an instrument by which to pursue it. This makes clear that exclusion of difference in the name of dialogue is every bit as abhorrent as exclusion of the other because of his or her difference.

In difference itself there is no evil, which can instead be found in the rejection of difference, since, as Edgard Pisani writes, "intolerance is the rejection of difference; the search for identification carried out with bloody hands; the rejection of any form of independence and diversity. Intolerance rejects the exchange of ideas because it disperses hatred, and it refuses coexistence because that would mean accepting diversity."[25]

In conclusion, Pope Benedict's proposal – which maintains that the human being consists of will, spirit, and nature, and that this nature should occupy its natural place in legislation, in dialogue, and in the encounter with others – has solid support in Islamic tradition. Indeed, Islam pushes the proposal even a step further, asserting that each person had an inalienable right to difference, which is, in fact, the very thing that makes us individuals. Difference, therefore, can be neither reduced nor eliminated. On the contrary, the legislature must affirm and respect it, remaining bound by it as the ideal model. If it succeeds in doing so, the rule of the majority may inch closer to the rule of justice in contemporary society.

[24] Ibn Kathir, *Tafsir al-Qur'an al-'Azhim*, vol. 4, p. 218.

[25] E. Pisani, Fi Muwajaha 'Adam al-Tasamuh, trans. As'ad Halim, "Risala," UNESCO press, June 1992, p. 34.

5 THE SECULAR STATE, DEMOCRACY, AND NATURAL LAW

Benedict XVI's Address to the Bundestag from the Perspective of Legal Ethics and Democracy Theory

Martin Rhonheimer

A SPEECH THAT MADE HISTORY

Pope Benedict XVI's speech of September 22, 2011, before the Bundestag in Berlin was beyond question a speech of epochal significance. The unusual scene of the Pope standing before the German parliament reveals a relationship, intentionally or not, between spiritual and worldly power that corresponds to the contemporary self-image of the Church as established by the Second Vatican Council: a Church without any political power, but teaching with authority in the name of a higher truth, and doing so in the very power center of a secular, democratic state. What was the message of the speech? All worldly power, even democratically legitimate power, to avoid being misused, has to recognize that it is always subject to a higher truth beyond all human manipulation, because, in Benedict's words, "for the fundamental issues of law, in which the dignity of man and of humanity is at stake, the majority principle is not enough." And what was the underlying assumption? The Church teaches this truth and gives witness of it to a pluralistic society and to the decision makers of that society, but has no coercive means for erecting it into law. As the Pope said, "Everyone in a position of responsibility must personally seek out the criteria to be followed when framing laws." It is up to the people of every age to listen, and to be open in the freedom of their consciences to the guidance offered by the Church. In the public forum of democracy, nevertheless, the Church is only one voice among many, and the strength it possesses is only the strength of its arguments.

DEMOCRATIC ETHOS AND THE NATURAL LAW

Benedict also asked a question: "How do we recognize what is right?" In doing so, he recalled an essential historical fact: "Unlike other great religions, Christianity has never proposed a revealed law to the State and to society, that is to say a juridical order derived from revelation. Instead, it has pointed to nature and reason as the true sources of law – and to the harmony of objective and subjective reason, which naturally presupposes that both spheres are rooted in the creative reason of God." This refers to the separation of politics and religion that is typical of Christianity, which not only facilitated the reception of Roman law, but also, via natural law, the calling into question and abolition of the norms of Germanic customary law that opposed human dignity.[1]

In today's atmosphere the words of the Pope may well create the impression of a certain ambiguity. Does not this normative legal-theoretical recourse to nature and reason as the "true sources of law" serve to reduce and relativize the autonomy of politics and the decision-making processes of constitutional democracy that are so definitive for the free, secular state? Would the legitimacy of democratic and parliamentary legislation be held hostage to ecclesiastical criteria of morality and natural law? Nothing that the Pope said *necessitates* such an interpretation, but it is not expressly excluded, either – the Pope spoke too generally, and in too nonexplicit a way, for any such conclusion.

What might have caused the most irritation, perhaps, is that the speech, with its reference to the "true sources of law" founded on "nature and reason," reminded the audience of the earlier position of the Church that was so critical of democracy: by that view, the democratic principle of majority rule could be considered politically legitimate and viable only to the extent that it respected the fundamental requirements of the natural law – as interpreted by the

[1] See Harold J. Berman, *Law and Revolution: The Formation of the Western Legal Tradition* (Cambridge, Mass.: Harvard University Press, 1983), 144–151.

Church.[2] But to think in this way would be to misunderstand the autonomy, both institutional and procedural, of the democratic state vis-à-vis the religious institution of the Church, and thereby misunderstand as well the secularity and specific ethos of democracy. Is Benedict XVI really calling for a return to the traditional viewpoint – once criticized by himself, Joseph Ratzinger, as a "hypertrophied" conception of Catholic Natural Law doctrine, in which "the natural law idea was so heavily laden with Christian content, that the requisite ability to make compromises was lost, and the State could not be taken on its own terms as something essentially profane,"[3] an attitude that made it difficult to accept the peculiar ethos of democracy and its decision-making processes. Is this what Benedict was calling for? The strength of this ethos lies precisely in its being open to natural law normativity without, nevertheless, identifying a determinate, normative content to ground the legitimacy of democratic decision making and legislation. Such normative openness, in view of the pluralistic character of modern society, and in view of the need for human beings to live in peace and freedom, is really the virtue of the free, secular, and democratic state. But it is also its peril, since, precisely for this reason – to recall once again the "Böckenförde dictum" – this same state is founded on

[2] Ernst-Wölfgang Böckenförde, as is well-known, had already criticized this earlier position of the Church as early as 1957, when he was 27, in his now very famous article "Das Ethos der modernen Demokratie und die Kirche"; only recently he has again raised the issue as follows: "Of course there can be majority decisions in a democracy, but what belongs to the natural law is already valid and cannot be subject to any majority vote. To this extent democratic principles, and especially majority decisions, cannot have force. In this respect the compass of the natural law was determined by the Church itself as based on its understanding of the created order. The Church's Magisterium communicates that what follows from human nature in the realm of the natural law is what God has implanted in it": *Wissenschaft, Politik, Verfassungsrecht. Aufsätze von Ernst Wolfgang Böckenförde. Biographisches Interview von Dieter Gosewinkel* [*Science, Politics, Constitutional Law. Essays from Ernst-Wolfgang Böckenförde. Biographical Interview with Dieter Gosewinkel*], Frankfurt am Main: Suhrkamp, 2011, 394.

[3] Joseph Ratzinger, "Christliche Orientierung in der pluralistischen Demokratie?," in id., *Kirche, Ökumene, Politik. Neue Versuche zur Ekklesiologie* (Einsiedeln, 1987), 191.

presuppositions that it cannot itself guarantee: they flow, rather, from the moral substance of the society.[4]

BENEDICT'S PHILOSOPHY OF LAW

The ambiguity of Pope Benedict's remarks consists, as critics have noted, in his "not distinguishing adequately between lecturing on the philosophy and theology of law (on the one hand) and making an intervention in democratic theory (on the other)." This, one critic says, "is an obvious shortcoming of Benedict's speech."[5] In reality, however, the lack of distinction is characteristic of ecclesiastical and magisterial statements in general, whose main business is not, after all, the dimension of democratic theory or political science. Popes and bishops remind us of truths and ethical standards, they do not instruct us in politics – or at least they should not. Exactly for this reason, despite his not so much dogmatic as frankly academic and professorial manner, Benedict's speech is nevertheless subject to this logic of magisterial statement, and hence cannot but appear ambiguous when it refers to the natural law tradition without any further qualifications.

But if we interpret the address in the light of other statements made by this Pope, as well as statements made by him previously as Joseph Ratzinger the theologian, a significant portion of this ambiguity seems to disappear. First: with regard to the interpretation of the Second Vatican Council, Benedict is by no means, as has frequently been charged, simply an exponent of a "Hermeneutics of Continuity." Rather, he is in favor of what he himself called, in his Christmas Address to the Roman Curia of December 22, 2005, a "Hermeutics of Reform." "True reform", Benedict said, "consists . . . in this combination of continuity and discontinuity at different levels." In that

[4] Ernst-Wolfgang Böckenförde, "Die Entstehung des Staates als Vorgang der Säkularisation" (1967), reprinted in id., *Staat, Gesellschaft, Freiheit. Studien zur Staatstheorie und zum Verfassungsrecht* (Frankfurt am Main, 1976), 42–61, especially 60.

[5] Christian Geyer, "Die Sonne über Berlin: Der Papst bringt den Politikern Naturrecht bei," *Frankfurter Allgemeiner Zeitung*, September 23, 2011, 33.

speech, the Pope emphasized unmistakably that the Second Vatican Council "recognize[d] and [made] its own an essential principle of the modern state in the Decree on Religious Freedom." He thereby distanced himself from earlier papal positions that had judged the modern right to religious freedom as being in the same class as all the other so-called "modern freedoms." In his 2005 speech, Benedict XVI described the modern state in its gradual development since the American and French Revolutions as "a state that would make room impartially for citizens of various religions and ideologies, merely assuming responsibility for an orderly and tolerant coexistence among them and for the freedom to practice their own religion." The Second Vatican Council gave a "new definition to the relationship between the Church and the Modern State."[6]

Before the background of Papal statements such as these, open as they are to an explicit discontinuity in the Magisterium at the political level, and implicitly on the level of democratic theory, the address to the Bundestag can quite reasonably be understood as *not* calling into question the principle of majority rule – that, of course, being the strong point of a political system existing under the conditions of a religiously and morally pluralistic society – but rather as reminding those who practice politics that even democratic, procedurally correct majority decisions can legislate materially *unjust* decisions, and this precisely in those areas where human beings in one way or another exercise power over other human beings, that is, in the realm of "human ecology." This refers of course to certain fields of bioethics, but falls short of naming any specific normative contents; instead, there is simply a reminder of the fact that there do exist certain limits to the human power to make norms: limits, the Pope tells us, that

[6] Cf. also Martin Rhonheimer, *Christentum und Säkularer Staat. Geschichte – Gegenwart – Zukunft* (mit einem Vorwort von Ernst-Wolfgang Böckenförde); Freiburg i. Br., 2012), 46, note 10; a brief version of this book is: "Christianity and Secularity: Past and Present of a Complex Relationship," in Martin Rhonheimer, *The Common Good of Constitutional Democracy: Essays in Political Philosophy and on Catholic Social Teaching* (Washington, D.C.: The Catholic University of America Press, 2013), 342–428 (chapter 12). Cf. also Martin Rhonheimer., "Religionsfreiheit – Bruch mit der Tradition?" *Die Neue Ordnung*, 65, 4, August 2011, 244–261.

"reason and nature" can reveal to us. Nevertheless he acknowledges that "the question of what now corresponds to the law of truth, what is actually right and may be enacted as law, is not so obvious ... the question of how to recognize what is truly right and thus to serve justice when framing laws has never been simple, and today in view of the vast extent of our knowledge and our capacity, it has become harder still."

In saying this, the Pope did not reinterpret "a strength of the parliamentary system into a weakness,"[7] nor did he deny democracy its competence to pass laws and establish norms. Under a more accurate reading, Pope Benedict shows, rather, his understanding for democracy. Given the "vast extent of our knowledge and our capacity," democratic decision-making processes in the realm of "human ecology" – in anthropological questions, that is – requires a higher level of awareness on the part of democratic decision makers in order to avoid giving the force of law to what is unjust in reality. This is just the place where natural-law discourse comes into play: not in asserting that recourse to natural law can invalidate current laws or restrict democratic mechanisms such as popular elections, but instead in the knowledge that standards of justice do exist that can show even current law as being materially unjust and consequently illegitimate. Recourse to natural law is thereby a part of legal ethics: it "cannot be postulated as if it were already enacted law"; instead, it formulates an "ethical demand for law. As such, it plays an important role. It can legitimatize positive legislation, it can be an impetus for reform, and it can de-legitimatize, when positive law is in a fundamental internal contradiction with its own demands."[8] In this case, it is not the principle of democratic majority decision making

[7] According to Geyer, "Die Sonne über Berlin."

[8] Ernst-Wolfgang Böckenförde, *Wissenschaft, Politik, Verfassungsrecht (Biographisches Interview von Dieter Gosewinkel*, 376. Cf. also Martin Rhonheimer, "Unverzichtbarkeit und Ungenügen des Naturrechts. Über Politische Philosophie in der Tradition des Naturrechts," in Hans Thomas and Johannes Hattler (eds.), *Der Appell des Humanen: Zum Streit um Naturrecht* (Frankfurt am Main, 2010), 103–123; Robert Spaemann, "Die Aktualität des Naturrechts" (1973), in id., *Zur Kritik der politischen Utopie* (Stuttgart, 1977); and in id., *Philosophische Essays* (Stuttgart, 1983).

that is called into question; it is only, and exclusively, the material results of the process that are being subjected to critique. This is the democratic right of any citizen, of any political party or association of citizens, and also, of course, the Church.

POSITIVISM, NATURAL LAW, AND THE PROBLEM OF THE "BACKGROUND CULTURE"

To be sure, Benedict's reference to "reason and nature" seemed provocative to many. And yet right at this moment, the argument, when properly understood, takes a surprising turn – in a direction away from the feared push toward a criticism of democracy. For, as Benedict explained: "Where positivist reason dominates the field to the exclusion of all else – and that is broadly the case in our public mindset – then the classical sources of knowledge for ethics and law are excluded." This is no declaration about the legitimacy of democratic majority decisions, and thus does not lead to talk about the "natural-law limitations" of democratic legislative procedures. Rather, the question here concerns the identification of an epistemological problem with cultural impact: it is the restricted and "closed-off" nature of public consciousness with regard to sources of knowledge that are a part, as the Pope says, of our "cultural memory." This is "a dramatic situation which affects everyone." Indeed, an essential goal of his address, Benedict said, "is to issue an urgent invitation to launch . . . a public debate."

And this brings us to the very heart of the Pope's intention: in his view, the problem has really nothing to do with a critique of the democratic processes of the state under the rule of law, but rather with what John Rawls has called the *background culture*: that which provides the atmosphere we breathe in all our political actions, and on which we depend as living political beings. With his talk of a "cry for fresh air" and of a "concrete bunker with no windows," the Pope was not challenging our political institutions and decision-making techniques, but rather the public mindset, the culture that sustains those institutions and techniques and, indirectly, the legal–ethical consciousness of the persons who have political responsibility and play an active role in these institutions. He is also inviting us to let "reason and nature," as sources of justice, become a component of public democratic discourse, and to overcome our positivistic/functionalistic myopia about reason and nature in the public forum of democracy. This is something new for a Papal declaration in this form, and it is new in three respects. First, the ethos of democracy is not even in question, since in this instance no criteria are being formulated for the legitimacy of democratic decision-making procedures; second, because all concrete content is left undefined, the responsibility for developing it is left to public discourse, where the Church is only one voice among many; and third, because right on this very issue, more is left *unsaid* than *said*. Such a silence is irritating. And that, precisely, was part of the message of the speech.

But what really gave the message its wide intellectual scope was Benedict's way of calling to mind the foundations of European culture, not only as a Christian legacy, but as the fruitful synthesis of the pre-Christian inheritance as well: "The culture of Europe arose from the encounter between Jerusalem, Athens, and Rome – from the encounter between Israel's monotheism, the philosophical reason of the Greeks, and Roman law. This three-way encounter has shaped the inner identity of Europe. In the awareness of man's responsibility before God and in the acknowledgment of the inviolable dignity of every single human person, it has established criteria of law: it is these criteria that we are called to defend at this moment in our history."

Jerusalem, Athens, and Rome: they form together an overarching standard of human rationality. And it was Christianity, in fact, that made possible the creative interplay and mutual fructification of these three sources of reason: belief in God, philosophy and science, and law – and Europe grew out of this synthesis. This Europe was also the ancestral root of the secular state, and, although not immediately and directly, of the modern culture of human rights as well. In their specifically political dimension, these rights are actually a product of modernity – an aspect that Benedict left unmentioned in his address. Modern human and civil rights are not simply "natural law"; they have, rather, a specific political content, which presupposes the ideal and the reality of the secular, constitutional state. "Natural law" comprehends less than "human and civil rights" or constitutionally established rights; the latter do not derive immediately from the former, and still less are they identical with it – and the reason for this is that human and civil rights are written, positive, actionable laws. When defending the natural law, the Church did not always defend human rights in the modern sense; and for a very long time, it could not accept them.

But Pope Benedict is historically correct when he emphasizes that this culture of human rights is ultimately founded in the natural-law tradition of the Christian West, and thereby is founded on a broadened reason that is both conscious of its natural contingency and at the same time open to a higher reality, and which, without "positivistic" restrictions, is what really makes possible a view of the whole: "The conviction that there is a Creator God is what gave rise to the idea of human rights, the idea of the equality of all people before the law, the recognition of the inviolability of human dignity in every single person and the awareness of people's responsibility for their actions. Our cultural memory is shaped by these rational insights." Even if the secular state cannot be *derived* from this inheritance – that was brought about through the modern ethos of the primacy of the political, and thereby has a specifically modern legitimacy – nevertheless it still lives in the nutrient-rich soil of this culturallegacy, in that the inviolability of human dignity and the idea of the Creator God belong together. And that means that the public democratic discourse about the sources of law, even in a secular state, should keep its consciousness open to the transcendent origin of these sources – and that is just what the Preamble of the German Constitution declares.

Of course, something must be added here: secularity does not necessarily include religion or a belief in God; but it can never reasonably define itself in opposition to it. "Secular reason" is not by its nature godless or religion-free reason, but rather worldly human reason: while not controlled by supernatural revelation or religious institutions, it still remains open in an "upward" direction, and can thereby be understood to be rooted qua secular reason in a higher, transcendent reason. This is precisely why loyalty to the secular state can be reconciled with the Pope's appeal: for, as sources of law and of the recognition of inviolable human dignity, "nature and reason" are rooted in the belief in a Creator God.

"NATURE" AND "NATURAL LAW": RECOURSE TO THE CREATOR GOD AND SECULAR POLITICAL REASON

Even so, the concept of "nature" in Benedict's address remains unclear and underdetermined with respect to its relevance for moral reason.[9] "Human nature," to which he several times refers, is not simply "nature," certainly not the nature of the environmental movement. And the natural law, according to the tradition, is not simply a law that "nature" reveals to us in some unambiguous way. Instead, it is always and only an "ordering of *reason*" (*rationis ordinatio*), as Thomas Aquinas formulated it in agreement with canonical and early scholastic tradition. In order for natural law to lead to a concrete normativity, it cannot simply be read from the Book of Nature; "nature" as such is not yet a moral or legal norm. What is needed is rather recourse to nature *through the argumentative reason.*[10] Whatever is valid as natural law must be transparent to the reason: the "ought" of nature, or natural right, is always an "ought" of the reason, and only this can be the *regula moris* and thereby the standard of what is right, and can formulate an "ought" as a norm – and yet as soon as human reasoning concerns itself with a more specific concretizing of norms, it cannot be so certain, and needs the confidence that comes from the restraints of the living *ethos* of

[9] For more detail on what follows, see Martin Rhonheimer, "Benedict XVI über Rechtsstaat, Demokratie und Naturrecht: Die Reden in Berlin und London," [Benedict XVI on the Just State, Democracy and Natural Law: The speeches in Berlin and London], in Jan-Heiner Tück (ed.), *Der Theologenpapst: Eine kritische Würdigung Benedikts XVI* (Freiburg im Breisgau: Herder, 2013) 135–157.

[10] Cf. also Martin Rhonheimer, *The Perspective of Morality: Philosophical Foundations of Thomistic Virtue Ethics*, trans. G. Malsbary (Washington, D.C.: Catholic University of America Press, 2011); Martin Rhonheimer, *Natural Law and Practical Reason: A Thomist View of Moral Autonomy*, trans. G. Malsbary (New York: Fordham University Press, 2000); Martin Rhonheimer, "Natural Law as a 'Work of Reason': Understanding the Metaphysics of Participated Theonomy," *American Journal of Jurisprudence*, 55 (2010), 41–77.

society and its culture.[11] Recourse to God the creator does not give any assistance for knowing specific content, since, of course – and this is another teaching of Thomas Aquinas – the eternal law of God and his will can be recognized just by the natural reason, apart from supernatural revelation.[12] Pope Benedict knew this too, of course, and his message was quite reasonably limited to declaring that the openness of the reason to a creator God as the foundation of reason as well as nature permits us to see the natural in a new light, thereby helping us in turn to understand that "nature" also formulates the boundaries of what is morally permissible, and that the human and political reason are always required to locate these limits and respect them. Beyond that, the Pope did not go in the Bundestag Address. To be sure, as the Bishop of Rome, he has a clear conception of these limits. But he is also conscious that the Church, in its magisterial actions, has the task to remind us of these limits and exercise an influence on citizens and political leaders. But this will not endanger democracy or bring the principle of majority election into question, so long as it is remembered that a democracy too must always remain a state under the rule of law, and that current legislation even having been determined by majority choice can also be materially unjust.

It is an open question, whether a secular democratic culture of human rights can survive unimpaired without the support of knowledge about the Creator God who is the ground of all that is "right by nature," and the accompanying awareness that there are such things as ethical limits to what human beings can do to other human beings. Here is where Pope Benedict raises a finger of warning. If secular political reason were to define itself consciously as areligious or even as anti-Christian, it would, says Benedict, lose its "cultural memory."

[11] In Wolfgang Waldstein's book, *Ins Herz geschrieben: Das Naturrecht als Fundament einer menschlichen Gesellschaft* (Augsburg, 2010), to which Benedict refers a few times as a source of quotations in the footnotes to his Bundestag Address, there is, unfortunately, a notorious equating of "nature" and "norm" and of "nature" and "law," or at least an inadequate differentiation, giving rise to much methodological unclarity. This makes Waldstein's (fundamentally correct) critique of Kelsen and other representatives of legal positivism appear ultimately rather implausible.

[12] Thomas Aquinas, *Summa Theologiae*, I–II, q. 19, a. 4, ad 3.

"To ignore or dismiss" this "as a thing of the past would be to dismember our culture totally and to rob it of its completeness." One can only agree, since such a failure of memory would be bound up with the risk of new kinds of totalization of the political order that are not in keeping with a free and democratic state under the rule of law.[13] And in this respect the legal–philosophical and theological discourse of Benedict XVI does indeed indirectly attain relevance for democracy theory.

BENEDICT'S FUNDAMENTAL RECOGNITION OF THE SECULAR STATE AND THE LOGIC OF DEMOCRACY

But despite all the unanswered questions, one thing, it seems to me, became clear on September 22, 2011: what the Church is challenging the secular state and all its citizens to do is not to submit to the truth-claims of the Christian religion nor even to the Church's interpretation of the natural law. Instead, the challenge is to widen the horizon of the natural, "meta-religious" – and in this sense, also secular – reason, in order to include a glimpse of that higher, creative reason. That is the source for the standards (and they are not specifically Christian) that ground all rights, and thereby form the common ethical bond that unites from within the legitimate plurality of concrete political configurations. And yet it is not for the Church or for any other religious authority to define this political and juridical bond: Benedict was silent about this, and such silence is relevant from the viewpoint of democracy theory.

But that is not all: in the address given to the representatives of the Muslim community delivered the day after the Bundestag speech, Benedict made another explosive remark that was also relevant from the viewpoint of democracy theory, and something that no Pope had said before. Speaking of the German Basic Law (*Grundgesetz*), that is, the constitution of a secular, democratic state, he said, "In this law we find above all the common ethos that lies at the heart of human

[13] For more detail on this cf. Martin Rhonheimer, *Christentum und Säkularer Staat*, especially 209–245.

co-existence and that also in a certain way pervades the apparently formal rules of operation of the institutions of democratic life." This constitution, based as it is on natural–ethical values, laid "the foundations that we may consider valid for a markedly pluralistic era, foundations that actually point out the evident limits of pluralism: it is inconceivable, in fact, that a society could survive in the long term without consensus on fundamental ethical values." So this is an exhortation to a kind of "constitutional patriotism" founded on the secular democratic ethos built upon on the reality of pluralism, with its "apparently formal" rules such as the principle of majority rule – a Pope had never gone this far before. For what he is saying is that the very rules and regulations of democratic processes can express a fundamental ethical consensus: the basis, in fact, of human social cooperation, in the service of which law and the administration of law exist.

In his saying this, the Church recognizes that the political institutions of the secular state determine – ultimately, on the basis of the majority principle – the laws that are binding for society. And to recall that such positive law can also be materially unjust and thus a perversion of the law – that a democracy, that is, must always remain a state under the rule of law, and that there are limits to pluralism – does not work against democracy, but rather can help its members – both the politicians and all voting citizens – to behave with responsibility and expertise when using the power entrusted to them. This is to respect the rightful autonomy of the political realm, which means independence from religious institutions such as the Church but not independence with respect to the objective criteria of justice and fundamental moral standards. The essential secularity of politics, as here recognized by the Church, corresponds, again, to Pope Benedict's request for an "un-worldly" Church, as he put it in the final speech of his trip to Germany in the Freiburg Concert Hall: consciousness by the Church of its proper spiritual and pastoral task does not mean retreat from the world, but true missionary openness to it.

This is how the Church today can affirm the secular state, while speaking from the heart of its theology. In his Freiburg speech, Benedict XVI did not shrink from saying that "in a certain sense, history comes to the aid of the Church through the various periods of secularization, which have contributed significantly to her purification and inner reform." This sentence, which repays long and deep consideration, testifies once again to the intellectual breadth and sagacity of this Pope. In his – at first sight – rather abstract discourse on the philosophy of law, he is in reality able to think with great realism, and knows well how to let this ability bear fruit in his Magisterium.

Translation from the German original by Gerald Malsbary.

6 FROM REGENSBURG TO BERLIN – HOLINESS AND REASON

A Reflection on Pope Benedict XVI's Public Lectures

J.H.H. Weiler

I

A Pope speaks *Urbi et Orbi*, as Bishop of Rome and as a moral leader to the world. I expect that Pope Benedict XVI's intellectual legacy to the world will not reside in his encyclicals or apostolic letters, but in a remarkable set of speeches – at the UN, at the Colleges des Bernardins in Paris, at Westminster, and above all at Regensburg and Berlin in his address to the German Bundestag.

It would be redundant, perhaps even otiose, once again to parse through Regensburg and the Bundestag speeches. I will try first succinctly to recapture their most essential messages – and the nexus between the two. But the burden of this reflection will in going beyond the two speeches and exploring some of their implications and consequences – intended and unintended. Most important I will emphasize what lessons should not be taken from the Pope's remarkable discourse.

II

Benedict was shaped by and helped shape Vatican Council II. Ever since that seismic tremor, the Holy See in Rome has insisted on the importance of freedom of religion. John Paul II and Benedict were of the habit of claiming that it was the most fundamental of all freedoms. In our general secular culture this was and is typically received with a forgiving smile: "Which freedom would you expect a Pope to privilege?" construing this statement in a corporatist sense, as if the Pope was some trade union leader concerned about his members' benefits. There is of course this aspect to religious freedom and there is nothing ignoble in the shepherd watching out for his flock.

What had not received enough attention in all the brouhaha created by the comments of the Pope referencing Islam is the fact that in the context of the Regensburg Lectures the religious freedom the Pope was alluding to, was, it would appear, the opposite: The freedom to adhere to a religion of one's choice or not to be religious at all. The Pope, and the Church, embraced boldly the notion that freedom *of* religion includes freedom *from* religion. This is not simply or primarily an expression of liberal tolerance and liberty. It is an expression of a profound religious proposition with significant ramifications.

"We impose our faith on no one. Such proselytism is contrary to Christianity. Faith can develop only in freedom," the Pope lectured his own faithful at Regensburg. As I understand this teaching, a much deeper meaning of religious freedom than the freedom to practice religion emerges here. At the core of religious freedom is the freedom to say "No" to God. That is a religious proposition. Jews say: "All is in the hand of God except the fear of God"; that is how God wanted it. True religiosity, a true "Yes" to God, can only come from a being that has the internal spiritual ability, capacity, and external material condition to say "No." Benedict makes religious freedom a theological proposition, which, in turn, has a profound anthropological significance. Religious freedom goes to the deepest notion of the human as an autonomous agent with the faculty of moral choice even in the face of his creator. When Judaism and Christianity couch the relationship between God and man in covenantal terms "old" and "new" they celebrate that double sovereignty.

Choice over one's fate and destiny is all too often considered an artifact, a defining artifact, of modernity that distinguishes us from earlier epochs in which men and woman understood their condition as set by fate. I have always doubted that proposition, since it surely does not and cannot include this most fundamental of choices, which has been with man from the Garden of Eden onwards. From the onset of our civilization the freedom to say "No" to God was hard wired into our very essence as humans. That freedom is an expression of the deepest understanding of humans as autonomous, sovereign moral agents. For religious persons, we are autonomous, sovereign moral agents because we were thus created by, and in the image of, God with a specific Telos which gives meaning to one's existence that could not be achieved if we were not so created.

Even a secular atheist can understand that if one were to accept the existence of an omnipotent creator (which the atheist denies), to insist as an intrinsic religious proposition on the liberty to say "No" to such a creator is fundamental to the very understanding of the human condition within such a world view and is to stipulate a primordial notion of liberty. When the Pope stipulates freedom of religion as being the most fundamental, it is precisely because it stands as proxy to the very ontology of the human condition: What it is to be human.

Equally, one does not have to be religious in order to understand why an assault of religious freedom thus understood constitutes such a profound attack not only on the religious and not simply on a particular individual liberty of conscience but on the core of humanity.

One can go yet one step further, and in my understanding the Pope goes one step further. Citing James he explains, in the Regensburg homily rather than the discourse on science, that the "the royal law" the law of God's kingship is also "the law of freedom." If at the core of religious freedom is the ability to say "No" to God, how, then, does exercising that liberty by actually accepting the law of God's kingdom constitute an actual enhancement of one's freedom? It is not simply, although it is also that, a religious expression of the notion of rational liberty – the realization that it is only a legal framework which will allow us to exercise our liberty. No, it is deeper still: By acting outside the constraints of God's law I merely become a slave to my human condition including my human desires. A human sovereignty unbound is no sovereignty at all.

Likewise, to accept God's law, and no other, as "royal law," the law of he who transcends this world, is to assert my inner liberty vis-à-vis anyone who is of this world. There is no better antidote to totalitarianism in this world. It is sad that so many religious persons betrayed that royal law when fidelity to that law was most needed.

III

I will now try to spell out the connection between the "religious-freedom" theme of Regensburg and the "place-of-Christianity-in-general-public-discourse" theme of Berlin. At the core of the Bundestag discourse was an answer to the regnant Rawlsian orthodoxy that would exclude religious argument as legitimate input to public discourse and public normativity. Religion, after all, is predicated on a self-referential and immutable "article of faith" and thus unsuitable as a premise and a mode of discourse for defining the general public good. Rawlsian orthodoxy predicates a vocabulary of rationality, transcending closed and self-referential systems of belief, as the common language of public discourse and a condition for public normativity.

Benedict challenges that orthodoxy in more than one way. First, it is wrong to bundle all faiths under the generic "religion" as if they were all of the same cloth when it comes to the issue of public normativity. Even within the Abrahamic family there are marked differences on this issue – separating Christianity from Islam and Judaism.

Second, the Rawlsian reading of Christianity is misguided and mistaken. When the Christians step into the public space to make demands on public normativity, they do not make such demands based on revelation and predicated on faith or religion. It is, as we have seen, part of Christian anthropology that humans are endowed (so endowed by their creator – but this is neither here nor there) with the faculty of reason, common to humanity, which, indeed, constitutes the legitimate language of general public normativity. The content of the Christian demand will typically be in the realm of practical reason – morality and ethics as often expressed through natural law.

This is not a concession to secularism. It is an inevitable result of the religious propositions that informed the Regensburg discourse. To adopt a publicly binding norm predicated exclusively on religious faith and revelation would violate precisely that profound, religiously based commitment to religious freedom, whereby coerced faith is a contradiction and contrary to divine will.

It is courageous proposition because it is not only an entry visa into the normative public square, but imposes, too, a serious and severe discipline on the Christian community of faith. The stricture of reason might force one to revisit articles of faith. To reverse previous judgments, one no longer has that joker in the pack: "This is what God commanded." That is not reason. One might lose, reasonably, an argument rooted in reason. If one adopts a language, one has to speak it correctly to be understood, to be convincing. And that is true also for the language of reason.

Regensburg and Berlin belong, thus, to the same route, are predicated on the same logic. They are two sides of the same coin.

I can now also explain the sense in which not all religions are made from the same cloth. I should emphasize because of the sensitivity of the issue that though I think these notions are implicit in the Regensburg lectures, these are my constructs and should not be attributed to anyone but myself.

It is possible to arrange Christianity, Islam, and Judaism in accordance with two parameters: The reach of their normative claim and the nature of their normative claims in the general public space. As regards the first parameter, Christianity and Islam find themselves in the same bracket, both understanding themselves as universal with a strong missionary vocation – a missionary vocation that can, if not severely controlled, breed religious intolerance tendencies. Judaism is inward-looking with extremely weak proselytizing tendencies; its religious intolerance tendencies will be directed at fellow Jews but not at gentiles. As regards the second parameter, Islam and Judaism find themselves in the same bracket; both of them have a normativity that is partly consistent with a universal moral ethic (thou shalt not kill) but a very substantial part of which is revelational and not cannot have any suasive power vis-à-vis nonbelievers or believers of other faiths. Christianity, by contrast, not necessarily historically, but certainly in its contemporary understanding at least since Vatican II (and probably long before it), stands with a general public normativity rooted in the universal ethical idiom and, in its official position, abjures any form of religious coercion. Revelation, as we saw, is excluded as a legitimate consideration for any form of public coercion. That, of course, neutralizes the possible intolerance tendency that might flow from its universalism. The reader of this chapter can work out the various permutations these parameters produce, but it is clear that when discussing the issues of religious normativity in the public space it serves no purpose to lump all these religions together the way the Rawlsian orthodoxy does.

IV

I now begin to explore some of the implications and consequences and dangers – dangers that might result from a careless reading of the papal message. The nexus between general normativity and reason is seductive and in some ways constitutive of Christian identity – it is part of the Pauline message, part of the Christian jettisoning of much of the rituals of the "old covenant" and a core element in the "new covenant." (Let us set aside the delicate question whether the so called "old" covenant still endures for the Jews, as I naturally believe it does. This issue is not germane to the issues I discuss nor to the profound message of the Pope in his lectures.) Keeping the moral and ethical wine – jettisoning the irrational ritualistic vessel. Part of the Christian message and mission highlighted by the Pontiff in the oft-neglected Regensburg homilies was the concern for the weak and the meek, for the less fortunate in our society and in the world, for those on the margins, for the much discussed "other." It is an appealing message. It transcends Christianity: It is central to Judaism, finding expression in the Pentateuch, in the Prophets, and in the Oral Law and the mitzvot of loving kindness. It is equally integral to Islam. It is, too, part of many worldviews rooted in secular ethics. Religion, as such, has no monopoly over the ethical – though religious ethics may be differently grounded.

In the Regensburg Homilies the Pope does not shy away from the discomfiting and the difficult. The way he puts it to his flock is uncompromising: "Social Issues and the Gospel are inseparable." It is a striking phrase and for me the most interesting question is: Why does the Pope feel that it is necessary to remind his flock that social concerns and the gospel are inseparable?

In my reconstruction answering this question is of utmost urgency and importance in reflecting on the relationship of the religious and unreligious in today's largely secular societies and mostly secular states in the West.

In my view, the Pope is alerting us, religious people in general, and more specifically his Catholic flock of the danger of taking the view that the Christian demand on public normativity expressed through the language of general reason applicable to all humans exhausts the meaning of a religious life or even of Christian normativity.

I will now begin to answer this question, with the obvious humility and diffidence that derives from the fact that I, an outsider, am engaging with the words of the Pontiff. As the reader will see, there is more than one layer to my answer to this question.

The "social issues," as an expression of morality and ethics, is central to the Abrahamic religions, but alone it does not define the religious sensibility, the religious impetus, and the religious sense. On the one hand, religion does not have a monopoly over morality and ethics. On the other hand, to reduce religion to social issues is precisely that – an impoverishing reductionism. The quintessential religious categories, the ones that have no equivalence, no correspondence in a secular world view, are holiness and sanctity. To reduce religion to social concern is to diminish fatefully the meaning of holiness and sanctity. To be sure, holiness and sanctity are not disconnected from ethics and morality. The immoral and unethical are antithetical to holiness and sanctity. One cannot aspire to holiness and sanctity if one is unethical and immoral. But holiness and sanctity are not exhausted in the ethical and moral. They denote something more.

First, in the Judaeo-Christian tradition the *collective* imperative is clear: "And the LORD spake unto Moses, saying, Speak unto all the *congregation* of the children of Israel, and say unto them, Ye shall be holy: for I the LORD your God am holy" (Lev. 19:1,2).

Verses 18 and 19 are emblematic of the mission of holiness and sanctity. They contain, *side by side*, the ethical and the sacramental:

> Thou shalt not avenge, nor bear any grudge against the children of thy people, but thou shalt love thy neighbour as thyself: I am the LORD.
>
> Ye shall keep my statutes. Thou shalt not let thy cattle gender with a diverse kind: thou shalt not sow thy field with mingled seed: neither shall a garment mingled of linen and woollen come upon thee.

When the Pope inveighs in his homily, "Social Issues and the Gospel are inseparable," derives directly from the Leviticus phraseology. The famous imperative is not: "Love thy neighbour as thyself" *simpliciter*, but "Love thy neighbour as thyself, *I am the Lord*" – social and issues and the Gospel are inseparable.

The insistence on this nexus in the words of the Pontiff encapsulates a remarkable historical irony. In the period of the prophets such as Amos and Isaiah, and when Jesus preached his message, the faithful needed to be exhorted and reminded that faith and holiness could not be achieved and did not exhaust themselves in the ritual and the sacramental, important as these are. Today, the scales are turned and even the religious have to be reminded that the richness of the religious sense is not exhausted in simply leading an ethical and caring life. It is part of the modern condition that makes the modern faithful almost embarrassed by the gospel, by the sacramental, and by the claims, vocabulary, and practices that express the sanctity aspects of their religion and faith. These appear, irony of ironies, as "unreasonable." And this phenomenon is widespread among all the children of Abraham, Sarah, and Hagar.

It is thus of more than symbolic significance that part of the Regensburg Trilogy is, in the Catholic context, a Eucharistic celebration and that at the very moment of underscoring the importance of social concern and human solidarity the Pope insists on the gospel and sacramental context in which that social concern must be situated.

V

Faithful to the papal notion of religious liberty in Regensburg and the insistence on a general public reason, the Christian would clearly not step into the public square and demand that the sacraments and a great deal more of Christian normativity bound up with the discipline of holiness become binding law on all. But from this affirmation one should not fall into a second mistake, which is to conclude from this that if there is something in one's religion that cannot be made binding on all it does not belong to the universe of reason.

The reason it is not to be binding on all is not because it is not predicated on reason. It is not to be made binding on all, because it depends and is predicated on entering into the covenant of faith, in accepting the specificity of a particular religion. It is certainly not unreasonable in the eyes of the Christian to respond to the "Good News" and respond to the call of "the Redeemer." But, in line with the deepest meaning of religious freedom as explicated by the Pope, that choice has to be freely made, not coerced. To accept that part of Christian normativity that is not unreasonable but is predicated on the entering the faith and to make it binding on all would violate the religious imperative of religious freedom. But it is erroneous to think that within the covenant of faith somehow reason departs – consider the writings of Maimonides or Aquinas. The state-of-art philosophical and metaphysical reflection – for some time now – is and has been that it is no more unreasonable to embrace a religious world view that accepts the transcendent than it is to reject such, an epistemic status which should teach humility both to the believer and the atheist. Put differently, the fact that the believer will not seek to impose on the public square a normativity that is not rooted in general reason does not mean that the choice of faith is unreasonable.

Be that as it may, there can be rightly reasoned and wrongly reasoned propositions within the covenantal universe – which is one way that allows for renewal and self-correction – and reason becomes, in this case, the medium and idiom of interpreting and understanding the specificities of *imitatio dei*.

It is also entirely wrong to think that the normativity of holiness is confined to the ritualistic (such as the interdiction of intermingling of wool and linen that is presented in Leviticus). There is a large zone of charity, of care, of love that derives from the specific Christian narrative and is part of Christian normativity – what it is to be a Christian –but would not be appropriate to make part of general coercive normativity. These are things that a good Christian must do, but that he or she would not presume that others must do, at least not in the same sense of the word "must."

I want to express the idea in a different more accessible way. The Christian in this world is meant to live a normative life of *imitatio dei*. Some of that normativity is universal – ought to be followed whether one is a Christian or not, though the Christian understands his or her humanity, including human reason, as part of God's creation as explicated in Scripture. But that normativity has a universal validity independent of that particular conceptual genealogy. But there will be plenty of things that a Christian will feel obliged to do, such as go to Mass, to confess, and to get married in a certain way, that are not part of that universal normativity and oblige him or her because he or she answered the "Good News."

Though the universal moral normativity is an integral part of the Christian, it is the particularist normativity of holiness which underscores the specific Christian identity. "We do this or refrain from doing this," says the Christian to his or her son or daughter, "because we are part of the human family and this is something every one should be doing. We expect such from everyone." But no less important are the instances where the Christian message will be, "We do this or that or refrain from doing this or that, because we are Christian. We might hope that all would join our covenantal community, but until such time, we will not seek to coerce them to these aspects of our way of life."

And the same is true for the way secular society views the Christian. Helping the poor? General morality? Conceptually at least, the Christian does not stand out. (Though statistically Christian communities give more to charity than secular communities.) But prayer, mass, and other things are a clear distinct badge. I hazard to think that both are indispensable dimensions of the Christian identity.

It is wrong to think that this part of Christian testimony, because its normativity is internal, should not be part of Christian discourse in the public square. On the contrary, it should most emphatically be part of that discourse, albeit in a noncoercive, normative manner. To abstain from such would not only be an internal betrayal – a Peter-like public denial – but would be a loss to the general political culture. A vegetarian may not necessarily seek to impose vegetarianism on all, but is there not much one can learn and take inspiration from a life determined by a care for all living creatures, which recoils from cruelty and exploitation of living creatures? In other words, the fact that Christian public normativity is rooted in the universal idiom of reason does not mean that it is only that part of the Christian narrative which is suitable for manifestation in the public square and in public discourse.

VI

To conclude, I come to what will no doubt be the most controversial part of this reflection. We are looking at two religious normativities. One – general practical reason and morality – which is derived from universal reason, and does not require a specific religious commitment, and another – holiness and sanctity – which instead depends on such a commitment which essentially means a human telos of a conscious *imitatio dei* rooted in a specific historical narrative, institutional arrangements, and sacramental practices.

The most delicate question is into which box one fits which norm. Does, for example, a Catholic say that the prohibition on divorce derives from universal reason and is, as such, something that one should or at least may legitimately seek to impose on all, or should it be something about which one says that it is an internal norm, deriving – in reason (and thus open to internal discussion on what reason demands) – from the text of Scripture and the logic of the Catholic sacrament of marriage and the Christian narrative, but not opposable to the whole human community and alternative understandings of marriage? If the latter is chosen it becomes an explicit identity marker, one of many, of what it means to be a Catholic. As I explained earlier, the fact that it is a norm that derives from and is explicated within the Christian covenant does not mean that it cannot and should not be part of a societal discourse on the meaning of marriage, conjugal love, and commitment. It simply should not be presented as something that general reason would demand of everyone to follow.

Let us spell it out in the personal way I used earlier to highlight the internal and external dimensions. When he or she educates his or her children does a Catholic say: "Once married, there should be no divorce because that is what marriage must mean to all men and women?" Or does he or she say: "Once married, there should be no divorce, because this is how we Catholics, following the teaching of our Lord and Church understand marriage?" Does he or she say to his or her Muslim or Jewish neighbors (the religions of whom allow divorce): "If you followed universal reason you would not allow divorce." Or does he or she say: "I understand you and respect you, but I suppose that is one of the things that differentiate us from you and secular society, that we do not have divorce."

There can be many *social* consequences to choosing to throw the norm into the box of either general reason or particular reason. Let us think of the internal ramifications. I already suggested that characterizing a norm as belonging to general reason involves a great deal of courage. It is a debate one can lose in the social sense – by which I mean that the general public square finds the reasoning unconvincing and irrational. Even if one sticks to one's rational convictions, the persuasive power even over the community of believers is weakened. A majority does not make a thing right, of course. But it surely makes persuasion more difficult. Disconcerting as it may appear, it is even part of the story of the shift in scientific paradigms. Likewise, in a secular society where the religious community seeks the freedom to live with the freedom to practice their faith, if the norms of faith are couched in terms of general reason, it makes it more difficult to persuade society to make allowance for difference – reason, after all, is universal. Again, I will give an example. Think of the Muslim and Jewish community who insist on halal and kosher slaughtering. If the members of these communities were to make the argument for this slaughter based on the proposition that in reason it is the most humane way of slaughtering, and then society found (rightly or wrongly) that it was not, it would be much more difficult to sanction the practice than if they justified it as part of their ritualistic and particularlistic practice. The religious identity is more visible, both internally and externally in relation to the second normativity.

This question becomes much more delicate if posed in relation to the debate *du jour* regarding same-sex marriage. I certainly do not want to express an opinion on the substance of this debate save to say that as a matter of public reason, I believe there are nonhomophobic strong arguments as to why there might be a societal interest to seek to preserve the traditional understanding of marriage. There are, too, powerful arguments to extend "marriage for all."

The sacramental logic of marriage, a holy union in the eyes of God, within religion generally and within the Judeo-Christian tradition more specifically, which restricts marriage in a whole variety of ways, among which is the exclusion of same sex marriage, can be seen to follow a different logic altogether deriving from that very fact of being a holy sacrament and from a different view of human sexuality.

I am not sure, certainly as regards Christianity, how one makes the choice into which normative box this type of issue is to fall. Traditionally, in relation to, say, opposing same-sex marriage, the tendency of religious leaders has been to opt for universal reason and natural law – the only option if one wants legitimately to be part of the general public discourse and normativity. But it comes with a double price: If the argument is so couched and, as an empirical matter, one is seen to lose the public debate couched in universal reason, the internal authority of the norm within the community of faith is correspondingly weakened, since it thus becomes a question of simple public good in which the religious and the secular are indistinguishable and in which one's identity as, say, a Catholic is not at issue. Holiness norms and identitarian norms are more impervious to such challenge.

Additionally, it becomes more difficult subsequently to claim a consciousness exception based on religion to a general norm. If the norm is presented as a matter of public reason and one loses that debate deliberatively and democratically, why should one be given an opt-out from the general norm? If it is presented as part of a religious logic and thus an expression of freedom of religion, the case is much stronger. These prudential considerations are not given as a reason to opt for one characterization or the other, but as clarifying some of the stakes in contemporary society.

7 "TO SERVE RIGHT AND TO FIGHT WRONG"*

Why Religion, Human Rights, and Human Dignity Need Each Other

John Witte, Jr.

THE MODERN CONTEXT

"A sense of the dignity of the human person has been impressing itself more and more deeply on the consciousness of contemporary man," Pope Paul VI declared in his preface to *Dignitatis Humanae* (1965). "And the demand is increasingly made that men should act on their own judgment, enjoying and making use of a responsible freedom, not driven by coercion but motivated by a sense of duty."[1]

This was a historic statement about human dignity, signaling a momentous swing in the pendulum of world opinion. Only two decades before, the world had stared in horror into Hitler's death camps and Stalin's gulags where all sense of humanity and dignity had been brutally sacrificed. In response, the world had seized anew on the ancient concept of human dignity, claiming this as the "ur-principle"[2] of a new world order. The Universal Declaration of Human Rights of 1948 opened its preamble with classic words: "recognition in the inherent dignity and of the equal and inalienable

* The quote in the title is from Pope Benedict XVI, Visit to the Bundestag, Reichstag Building, Berlin, September 22, 2011, ¶2.

[1] Walter M. Abbott and J. Gallagher, eds., The Documents of Vatican II (New York: Herder & Herder, 1966), 675.

[2] Louis Henkin, et al., Human Rights (New York: Foundation Press, 1999), 80.

rights of all members of the human family is the foundation of freedom, justice, and peace in the world."[3]

By the mid-1960s, church and state alike had translated this general principle of human dignity into specific human rights precepts. In *Dignitatis Humanae* and several other documents produced during and after the Second Vatican Council (1962–1965), the Roman Catholic Church took some of the first decisive steps. Every person, the Church now taught, is created by God with "dignity, intelligence and free will ... and has rights flowing directly and simultaneously from his very nature."[4] Such rights include the right to life and adequate standards of living, to moral and cultural values, to religious activities, to assembly and association, to marriage and family life, and to various social, political, and economic benefits and opportunities. The Church emphasized the religious rights of conscience, worship, assembly, and education, calling them the "first rights" of any civic order. The Church also stressed the need to balance individual and associational rights, particularly those involving the church, family, and school. It urged the abolition of discrimination on grounds of sex, race, color, social distinction, language, or religion.[5] Within a decade, various Ecumenical groups, some Protestants, and a few Orthodox Christian groups crafted comparable comprehensive declarations on human rights and human dignity.[6]

Not only the world's churches, but also the United Nations and several nation-states issued a number of landmark documents on human dignity and human rights in the 1960s. Foremost among these were the two international covenants promulgated by the United Nations in 1966, each of which confirmed the belief in the "inherent dignity" and "the equal and inalienable rights of all members of the human family," and the belief that all such "rights derive from the

3 Ian Brownlie, ed., Basic Documents on Human Rights, 3rd ed. (New York: Oxford University Press, 1992), 21.

4 "Pacem in Terris" (1963), paragraph 9, in Joseph Gremillion, ed., The Gospel of Peace and Justice: Catholic Social Teachings Since Pope John (Maryknoll, N.Y.: Orbis Books, 1976), 203.

5 Ibid.; Abbott and Gallagher, *Documents of Vatican II*, 675.

6 See sources in John Witte, Jr. and Frank S. Alexander, eds., Christianity and Human Rights: An Introduction (Cambridge: Cambridge University Press, 2011).

inherent dignity of the human person."[7] The International Covenant on Economic, Social, and Cultural Rights (1966) posed as essential to human dignity the rights to self-determination, subsistence, work, welfare, security, education, and cultural participation. The International Covenant on Civil and Political Rights (1966) set out a long catalogue of rights to life and to security of person and property; freedom from slavery and cruelty; basic civil and criminal procedural protections; rights to travel and pilgrimage; freedoms of religion, expression, and assembly; rights to marriage and family life; and freedom from discrimination on grounds of race, color, sex, language, and national origin. Other international and domestic instruments issued in the later 1960s took close aim at racial, religious, and gender discrimination in education, employment, social welfare programs, and other forms and forums of public life – viewing such discrimination as a fundamental betrayal of the "dignity and equality inherent in all human beings."[8]

So matters stood a half century ago. Today, the concept of human dignity has become ubiquitous to the point of cliché – a moral trump frayed by overuse, a general principle twisted by repeated manipulation. We now read regularly of the dignity of luxury, pleasure, and leisure; the dignity of identity, belonging, and difference; the dignity of ethnic, cultural, and linguistic purity; the dignity of sex, gender, and sexual preference; the dignity of aging, dying, and death. At the same time, the corpus of human rights has become swollen to the point of eruption – with many recent rights claims no longer anchored in universal norms of human dignity, natural justice, or the common good, but aired as special aspirations of an individual or a group.

Even more worrisome is that the place of religion in human rights, and the protection of religious freedom as an essential first principle of any just legal order, has become increasingly contested today. Religion, many critics now argue, is too expansionistic and monopolistic, too patriarchal and hierarchical, too antithetical to the very ideals of pluralism, toleration, and equality to be useful for a modern human rights regime. Religion should be treated as just another category of private liberty, expression, and association and given no more preference than

[7] Basic Documents on Human Rights, 114, 125.
[8] See documents in id., 148, 162, 169.

its secular counterparts. Indeed, to accord religion special human rights treatment is to discriminate against nonreligious claimants in the same position. Purge religious freedom entirely, this argument concludes, and the human rights paradigm will thrive better.[9]

POPE BENEDICT'S CHALLENGE

Pope Benedict XVI challenged this alarming new trend and called church, state, and the world back to the founding human rights principles of the mid-twentieth century. Standing in Westminster Hall in 2010 – on the very spot where Thomas More had stood a half millennium before in sacrificial defense of freedom – the Pope praised the British common law tradition of democracy, human rights, and the rule of law, with its guarantees of liberty, equality, and due process of law. But he then warned Parliament that religion "is not a problem for legislators to solve, but a vital contributor" to the cultivation of a "better understanding" and more "effective implementation" of a just legal and political system. The Pope challenged "the increasing marginalization of religion, particularly of Christianity" in England and the West more generally. He challenged "those who advocate that the voice of religion be silenced" or privatized. He challenged the growing campaign to rid the public square of its religious symbols, ceremonies, and speech. All this deprecation of religion, the Pope declared, comes from a massive "failure to appreciate not only the rights of believers to freedom of conscience and freedom of religion, but also the legitimate role of religion" in public life and public law.[10]

This new deprecation of religion also fails to appreciate the essential role of religion in building and maintaining the modern legal regime of human rights, the Pope continued in his address to the Parliament of Germany in 2011. "In history, systems of law have almost always been based on religion." And in the West, this has

[9] See Mary Ann Glendon, "Religious Freedom: A Second Class Right?" Emory Law Journal 61, 2012, 971–990.

[10] Pope Benedict XVI, Meeting with the representatives of British society, Westminster Hall, Westminster, September 17, 2010, ¶¶ 3, 6, 7.

been especially true in the development of the law of human rights. Already early Church Fathers such as Origen claimed the freedom of association, speech, and conscience. Later fathers, such as Ambrose and Augustine, claimed the freedom of the clergy and laity alike "to serve right and to fight against wrong," whether perpetrated by a tyrannical monarch or a tyrannical majority. Medieval and early modern writers such as Thomas Aquinas and Francisco de Vitoria combined reason and nature, Greek philosophy and Roman law, to build much of the basic architecture of public, private, penal, and procedural laws and rights. These early intellectual achievements, the Pope declared, opened up "the path that led via the Christian Middle Ages and the juridical developments of the Age of Enlightenment all the way to the [Universal] Declaration of Human Rights [of 1948] and to our German Basic Law of 1949, with which our nation committed itself to 'inviolable and inalienable human rights as the foundation of every human community, and of peace and justice in the world.'"[11] (This Protestant historian must add that early modern Lutherans, Calvinists, Anglicans, and Anabaptists played vital roles in this development of human rights and rule of law as well.[12])

But Christianity and other religious traditions are not just a historical source of our modern norms of human rights, the Pope argued in his 2008 address to the United Nations General Assembly. Religion was not just the scaffolding that was used to build the edifice of human rights, and should now be taken down lest the full view of this new legal structure be obstructed. To the contrary, the Pope argued, religion remains an essential part of the foundation and infrastructure of the modern human rights regime. For religious communities teach and insist on the most fundamental "idea of the person as image of the

[11] Visit to the Bundestag, ¶¶2–5. See also his Address for the Collège des Bernardins, Paris (September 12, 2008) and his Address at the University of Regensburg (September 12, 2006) on the Christian foundations of Western culture.

[12] See John Witte, Jr., The Reformation of Rights: Law, Religion and Human Rights in Early Modern Calvinism (Cambridge: Cambridge University Press, 2007); John Witte, Jr., Law and Protestantism: The Legal Teachings of the Lutheran Reformation (Cambridge: Cambridge University Press, 2002).

Creator," which is "the absolute and the essence of freedom." It on the foundation of the inherent dignity of "the human creature" that the world could agree to issue a "universal declaration of human rights," despite the vast differences among modern cultures and faiths. "The rights recognized and expounded in the *Declaration* apply to everyone by virtue of the common origin of the person, who remains the high-point of God's creative design for the world and for history."[13]

To ignore that essential foundation of human dignity – and the religious communities that uniquely support this anthropology – is to destroy the "inner unity" of the Universal Declaration and to move human rights inevitably "towards the satisfaction of simple interests, often particular interests." It is to destroy the "commonly held sense of justice built primarily upon solidarity among the members of society" and to replace it with a "narrowly utilitarian" concern for private happiness and the attainment of personal desire. It is to destroy its common commitment to the Golden Rule – "Do unto others as you would have done unto you" – to a narrowly legalistic notion of "applying correct procedures." And it is to separate the essential connection between human rights and human responsibilities.[14]

Human rights, the Pope argued, are ultimately too important to be left to only for individuals to pursue or for individual states to protect, even with the backing of the United Nations. Human rights also require the continued nurture and challenge of the world's faith communities. The Pope put it thus to the UN General Assembly:

> [A] vision of life anchored in the religious dimension can help to achieve this, since recognition of the transcendent value of every man and woman favours conversion of the heart, which then leads to a commitment to resist violence, terrorism and war, and to promote justice and peace. This also provides the proper context for the inter-religious dialogue that the United Nations is called to support.... It pertains to the nature of religions, freely practiced that they can autonomously conduct a dialogue of thought and life.... Their task is to propose a vision of faith not in terms of

[13] Pope Benedict XVI, United Nations General Assembly, New York, April 18, 2008, ¶5–6.

[14] Id., ¶¶6–8.

> intolerance, discrimination, and conflict, but in terms of complete respect for truth, coexistence, rights, and reconciliation.[15]

It is for this reason, among others, that religious freedom is so vital to the entire apparatus of human rights today, the Pope concluded. Not only is religious freedom the bedrock of other rights, but the free exercise of religion is essential for the maintenance of other rights. "It is inconceivable that believers should have to suppress a part of themselves – their faith – in order to be active citizens. It should never be necessary to deny God in order to enjoy one's rights. The rights associated with religion are all the more in need of protection if they are considered to clash with a prevailing secular ideology or with majority religious positions of an exclusive nature."[16]

As a Protestant, interested in the religious foundations and dimensions of human rights and the robust protection of religious freedom, I agree wholeheartedly with the Holy Father that religion and human rights need each other. On the one hand, human rights norms need religion. There is, of course, some value in simply declaring human rights norms of "liberty, equality, and fraternity" or "life, liberty, and property" – if for no other reason than to pose an ideal against which a person or community might measure itself, to preserve a normative totem for later generations to make real. But, ultimately, these abstract human rights ideals of the good life and the good society depend on the visions and values of human communities and institutions to give them content and coherence – to provide what Catholic philosopher Jacques Maritain once called "the scale of values governing [their] exercise and concrete manifestation."[17] It is here that religion must play a vital role. Religion is an ineradicable condition of human lives and human communities. Religions invariably provide many of the sources and "scales of values" by which many persons and communities govern themselves. Religions inevitably help to define the meanings and measures of shame and regret, restraint and respect, responsibility

[15] Id., ¶10. [16] Id., ¶11.

[17] Jacques Maritain, "Introduction," in UNESCO, Human Rights: Comments and Interpretations (New York: Columbia University Press, 1949).

and restitution that a human rights regime presupposes. Religions must thus be seen as indispensable allies in the modern struggle for human rights. To exclude them from the struggle is impossible, indeed catastrophic. To include them, by enlisting their unique resources and protecting their unique rights, is vital to enhancing the regime of human rights and to easing some of the worst paradoxes that currently exist.

Conversely, religion needs human rights norms both to protect them and to challenge them. There is, of course, some merit in religious believers and groups quietly accepting the current protections of a modern human rights regime – the guarantees of liberty of conscience, freedom of exercise, rights to religious self-determination, and the like. But passive acquiescence in a secular scheme of human rights ultimately will not prove effective. And failure to press the unique rights claims of religious believers and communities will eventually leave many religious beliefs, practices, and communities too vulnerable. Religious communities must reclaim their own voices within the secular human rights dialogue, and reclaim the human rights voices within their own internal religious dialogues. Religious communities must be open to a new human rights hermeneutic–fresh methods of interpreting their sacred texts and traditions that will allow them to reclaim their essential roots and roles in the cultivation of human rights. Religious traditions cannot allow secular human rights norms to be imposed on them from without; they must (re)discover them from within.

Both theses – that human rights need religion, and that religion needs human rights – are controversial. The next two sections seek to defend both theses.

RELIGION IN HUMAN RIGHTS

A number of distinguished commentators have argued that religion should have no place in a modern regime of human rights. Religious ideas may well have been the sources of human rights in earlier eras, they allow. Some religious groups might even have helped to inspire the modern human rights revolution that began with the promulgation of the Universal Declaration of Human Rights (1948). But religion, these religious skeptics argue, has now outlived its utility. Even Judaism, Christianity, and Islam do not speak unequivocally about human rights, and none has amassed an exemplary human rights record over the centuries. Their sacred texts and canons say much more about commandments and obligations than about liberties and rights. Their theologians and jurists have resisted the importation of human rights as much as they have helped in their cultivation. Their internal policies and external advocacy have helped to perpetuate bigotry, chauvinism, and violence as much as they have served to propagate equality, liberty, and fraternity. The blood of thousands is at the doors of our churches, temples, and mosques. The bludgeons of pogroms, crusades, jihads, inquisitions, and ostracisms have been used to devastating effect within and among these faiths. They must now move aside.

This argument proves too much to be practicable. In the course of the twentieth century, religion defied the wistful assumptions of the Western academy that the spread of Enlightenment reason and science would slowly eclipse the sense of the sacred and the sensibility of the superstitious. Religion also defied the evil assumptions of Nazis, Fascists, and Communists alike that gulags and death camps, iconoclasm and book burnings, propaganda and mind controls would inevitably drive religion into extinction. Yet another great awakening of religion is upon us – now global in its sweep and frightening in its power.

It is undeniable that religion has been, and still is, a formidable force for both political good and political evil, that it has fostered both benevolence and belligerence, peace and pathos of untold dimensions. But the proper response to religious belligerence and pathos cannot be to deny that religion exists or to dismiss it to the private sphere and sanctuary. The proper response is to castigate the vices and to cultivate the virtues of religion, to confirm those religious teachings and practices that are most conducive to human rights, democracy, and rule of law.

Human rights norms ultimately need religious ideas, institutions, and rights claims to survive and thrive. First, without religion, many rights are cut from their roots. The right to religion, Georg Jellinek once wrote, is "the mother of many other rights."[18] For the religious individual, the right to believe leads ineluctably to the rights to assemble, speak, worship, proselytize, educate, parent, travel, or to abstain from the same on the basis of one's beliefs. For the religious association, the right to exist invariably involves rights to corporate property, collective worship, organized charity, parochial education, freedom of press, and autonomy of governance. To ignore religious rights is to overlook the conceptual, and often the historical, source of many other individual and associational rights.

Second, without religion, the regime of human rights becomes infinitely expandable. Many religious communities adopt and advocate human rights in order to protect religious duties. A religious individual or association has rights to exist and act not in the abstract but in order to discharge discrete religious duties. For many religions, freedoms and commandments, rights and duties belong together. To speak of one without the other is ultimately destructive. Rights without duties to guide them quickly become claims of self-indulgence. Duties without rights to exercise them quickly become sources of deep guilt.

Third, without religion, human rights become too captive to Western libertarian ideals. Many religious traditions cannot conceive of, nor accept, a system of rights that excludes, deprecates, or privatizes religion. Religion is for these traditions inextricably integrated into every facet of life. The rights of religion are, for them, an inherent part of rights of speech, press, assembly, and other individual rights as well as ethnic, cultural, linguistic, and similar associational rights. No system of rights that ignores or deprecates this cardinal place of religion can be respected or adopted.

Fourth, without religion, the state is often given an exaggerated role to play as the guarantor of human rights. The simple state-versus-individual dialectic of many modern human rights theories leaves it to the state to protect and provide rights of all sorts. In reality, the state is not, and cannot be, so omnicompetent, as the fantastic failures

[18] Georg Jellinek, Die Erklärung der Menschen- und Bürgerrechte: ein Beitrag zur modernen Verfassungsgeschichte (Liepzig: Duncker and Humblot, 1895), 42.

of the twentieth-century Communist states made all too clear. Numerous "mediating structures" stand between the state and the individual, religious institutions prominently among them. Religious institutions, among others, play a vital role in the cultivation and realization of rights. They can create the conditions (sometimes the prototypes) for the realization of first-generation civil and political rights. They can provide a critical (sometimes the principal) means to meet second-generation rights of education, health care, child care, labor organizations, employment, and artistic opportunities, among others. They can offer some of the deepest insights into norms of creation, stewardship, and servanthood that lie at the heart of third-generation rights.

HUMAN RIGHTS IN RELIGION

My converse thesis is that human rights must have a more prominent place in the theological discourse and institutional practice of modern religions. Many would consider this second thesis to be as misguided as the first. It is one thing, such human rights skeptics argue, for religious believers and bodies to accept the freedom and autonomy that a human rights regime allows. This at least gives them unencumbered space to pursue their divine callings. It is quite another thing for religious communities to import human rights within their own polities and theologies. This exposes them to all manner of unseemly challenges.

Human rights norms, these skeptics argue, challenge the structure of religious bodies. While human rights norms teach liberty and equality, most religious bodies teach authority and hierarchy. While human rights norms encourage pluralism and diversity, many religious bodies require orthodoxy and uniformity. While human rights norms teach freedoms of speech and petition, several religions teach duties of silence and submission. To draw human rights norms into the structures of religion would only seem to embolden members to demand greater access to religious governance, greater freedom from religious discipline, greater latitude in the definition of religious doctrine and liturgy. So why import them?

Moreover, human rights norms challenge the spirit of religious bodies. Human rights norms, these skeptics argue, are the creed of a secular faith born of Enlightenment liberalism, humanism, and rationalism. Human rights advocates regularly describe these norms as our new "civic faith," "our new world religion," "our new global moral language." The influential French jurist Karel Vasak pressed these sentiments into a full confession of the secular spirit of the modern human rights movement:

> The Universal Declaration of Human Rights [of 1948], like the French Declaration of the Rights of Man and Citizen in 1789, has had an immense impact throughout the world. It has been called a modern edition of the New Testament, and the Magna Carta of humanity, and has become a constant source of inspiration for governments, for judges, and for national and international legislators.... [B]y recognizing the Universal Declaration as a living document ... one can proclaim one's faith in the future of mankind.[19]

In demonstration of this new faith, Vasak converted the "old trinity" of "liberté, equalité, et fraternité" taught by the French Revolution into a "new trinity" of "three generations of rights" for all humanity. The first generation of civil and political rights elaborates the meaning of liberty. The second generation of social, cultural, and economic rights elaborates the meaning of equality. The third generation of solidarity rights to peace, orderly development, and environmental protection elaborates the meaning of fraternity. Such language has become not only the *lingua franca* but also something of the *lingua sacra* of the modern human rights movement. In the face of such an overt confession of secular liberalism, religious skeptics conclude, a religious body would do well to resist the ideas and institutions of human rights.

[19] Karel Vasak, "A 30-Year Struggle," *UNESCO Courier*, November 1977, 29; Karel Vasak, "Pour une troisième génération des droits de l'homme," in Christophe Swinarski, (ed.), Études et Essais sur le Droit International Humanitaire et sur les Principes de la Croix-Rouge en l'Honneur de Jean Pictet (The Hague: Martinus Nijhoff, 1984), 837–845.

Both these skeptical arguments, however, presuppose that human rights norms constitute a static belief system born of Enlightenment liberalism. But the human rights regime is not static. It is fluid, elastic, and open to challenge and change. The human rights regime is not a fundamental belief system. It is a relative system of ideas and ideals that presupposes the existence of fundamental beliefs and values that will constantly shape and reshape it. The human rights regime is not the child of Enlightenment liberalism, nor a ward under its exclusive guardianship. It is the *ius gentium* of our times, the common law of nations, which a variety of Hebrew, Greek, Roman, Christian, and Enlightenment movements have historically nurtured in the West and which today needs the constant nurture of multiple communities around the world. It is beyond doubt that many current formulations of human rights are suffused with fundamental liberal beliefs and values, some of which run counter to the cardinal beliefs of various religious traditions. But liberalism does not and should not have a monopoly on the nurture of human rights; indeed, a human rights regime cannot long survive under its exclusive patronage.

I use the antique term *ius gentium* advisedly – to signal the place of human rights as "middle axioms" in our moral and political discourse. Historically, Western writers spoke of a hierarchy of laws – from natural law (*ius naturale*), to common law (*ius gentium*), to civil law (*ius civile*). The natural law was the set of immutable principles of reason and conscience, which are supreme in authority and divinity and must always prevail in instances of dispute. The civil law was the set of enacted laws and procedures of local political communities, reflecting their immediate policies and procedures. Between these two sets of norms was the *ius gentium*, the set of principles and customs common to several communities and often the basis for treaties and other diplomatic conventions. The contents of the *ius gentium* did gradually change over time and across cultures as new interpretations of the natural law were offered, and as new formulations of the positive law became increasingly conventional. But the *ius gentium* was a relatively consistent body of principles by which a person and a people could govern themselves.

This antique typology helps us to understand the intermediate place of human rights in our hierarchy of legal and cultural norms today. Human rights are the *ius gentium* of our time, the middle axioms of our discourse. They are derived from and dependent upon the transcendent principles that religious traditions (more than any other group) continue to cultivate. They also inform, and are informed by, shifts in the customs and conventions of sundry state law systems. These human rights norms do gradually change over time: just compare the international human rights instruments of 1948 with those of today. But human rights norms are a relatively stable set of ideals by which a person and community might be guided and judged.

This antique typology also helps us to understand the place of human rights within religion. My argument that human rights must have a more prominent place within religions today is not an attempt to import libertarian ideals into their theologies and polities. It is not an attempt to herd Trojan horses into churches, synagogues, mosques, and temples to assail secretly their spirit and structure. My argument is, rather, that religious bodies must again assume their traditional patronage and protection of human rights, bringing to this regime their full doctrinal vigor, liturgical healing, and moral suasion. Using our antique typology, religious bodies must again nurture and challenge the middle axioms of the *ius gentium* using the transcendent principles of the *ius naturale*. This must not be an effort to monopolize the discourse, nor to establish by positive law a particular religious construction of human rights. Such an effort must be part of a collective discourse of competing understandings of the *ius naturale* – of competing theological views of the divine and the human, of good and evil, of individuality and community – that will serve constantly to inform and reform, to develop and deepen, the human rights ideals now in place.

A number of religious traditions of late have begun the process of reengaging the regime of human rights, of returning to their traditional roots and routes of nurturing and challenging the human rights regime. This process has been incremental, clumsy, controversial, and at times even fatal for its proponents. But the process of religious engagement of human rights is now under way in Christian, Islamic,

Judaic, Buddhist, Confucian, Hindu, and indigenous communities alike. Something of a new "human rights hermeneutic" is slowly beginning to emerge among modern religions.[20]

This is, in part, a "hermeneutic of confession." Given their checkered human rights records over the centuries, religious bodies have begun to acknowledge their departures from the cardinal teachings of peace and love that are the heart of their sacred texts and traditions. Christian churches have taken the lead in this process – from the Second Vatican Council's confession of prior complicity in authoritarianism, to the contemporary Church's repeated confessions of prior support for apartheid, communism, racism, sexism, fascism, and anti-Semitism.

This is, in part, a "hermeneutic of suspicion," in Paul Ricoeur's famous phrase. Given the pronounced libertarian tone of many recent human rights formulations, it is imperative that we not idolize or idealize these formulations. We need not be bound by current taxonomies of "three generations of rights" rooted in liberty, equality, and fraternity. Nor do we need to accept the seemingly infinite expansion of human rights discourse and demands. Rights bound by moral duties, by natural capacities, or by covenantal relationships might well provide better boundaries to the legitimate expression and extension of rights.

This is, in part, a "hermeneutic of history." While acknowledging the fundamental contributions of Enlightenment liberalism to the modern rights regime, we must also see the deeper genesis and genius of many modern rights norms in religious texts and traditions that antedate the Enlightenment by centuries, even by millennia. We must return to our religious sources. In part, this is a return to ancient sacred texts freed from the casuistic accretions of generations of jurists and freed from the cultural trappings of the communities in which these traditions were born. In part, this is a return to slender streams of theological jurisprudence that have not been part of the mainstream of the religious traditions, or have become diluted by too great a commingling with it. In part, this is a return to prophetic

[20] See examples in John Witte, Jr. and M. Christian Green, Religion and Human Rights: An Introduction (Oxford: Oxford University Press, 2012).

voices of dissent, long purged from traditional religious canons, but, in retrospect, prescient of some of the rights roles that the tradition might play today.

And this is, in part, a "hermeneutic of law and religion." A century of legal positivism in the Western academy has trained us to think that law is an autonomous discipline, free from the influence of religion and belief. A century of firm laicization and strict separation of church and state has accustomed us to think that our law and politics must be hermetically and hermeneutically sealed from the corrosive influences of religious believers and bodies. The reality is that law and religion need each other, especially in the vital regime of human rights.

All four of these hermeneutics are brilliantly exemplified in Pope Benedict XVI's five lectures analyzed in this volume. One can find comparable such statements from Chief Rabbi Lord Jonathan Sacks and His Holiness the XIVth Dalai Lama, among others.[21] If other religious leaders around the world would also take seriously the challenge of religion and human rights, the world might slowly develop a new "concordance of discordant canons" and actions about the most fundamental value of human persons and peoples – their inherent and inviolable human dignity.

[21] See their articles in the symposium issue, "The Pursuit of Happiness in Interreligious Perspective," *Journal of Law and Religion* 29, 2014, 5–123.

PART II Fundamental Rights and Freedom of Religion

8 FAITH AND REASON IN THE REGENSBURG ADDRESS

Giuliano Amato

There is a clear thread running through the address Pope Benedict XVI delivered at the University of Regensburg. While its course is evident, its many implications have yet to be brought to light and explored.

The thread is present from the beginning of the speech, where the Pope Emeritus dedicated a recollection to the ancient university where he himself taught, to the meetings with colleagues and to the *universitas scientiarum* in which everyone participated and felt to be a part. This introduction may be perceived as a mere protocol or embellishment, since it is certainly an elegant, perhaps even a charming way for a former professor who became Pope to begin a university lecture. But in reality there is much more to that recollection of the *universitas scientiarum*. In it we find the germ of the theme that will be unpacked in the lecture: the theme of theology belonging to the sciences, according to his vision of these, which challenges the limitation of science only to those disciplines that can empirically prove their claims. We also find in it the implicit consequences of this view: the constitutive link between faith and reason.

Benedict's speech grounds the link between faith and reason historically and conceptually on the encounter between the Greek spirit and the Christian one, and therefore on "the God who has revealed himself as *logos* and, as *logos*, has acted and continues to act."[1] This, according to Benedict, is a fundamental point in understanding the Christian faith and it leads him to critically evaluate the various forms, Christian

[1] This quote, and the following quotes without citations, are found in Pope Benedict XVI, Meeting with the Representatives of Science, Aula Magna of the University of Regensburg, Regensburg, September 12, 2006.

and non-Christian, of voluntarism and transcendentalism (including the image of the arbitrary God). This also leads him to distance himself from Kant, who grounded faith in practical reason, believing that in order to make room for faith, it was necessary "to set thought aside."

Since Kant himself said it, how can we avoid crediting him with the identification of only the natural sciences as sciences – those in which true and false can only be established by experimental proofs? The consequence of this approach is the elimination not only of theology, but of all the sciences whose object is not the *composition* of matter, but rather its *meaning* – including Kant's own field, philosophy. In other words, the elimination of all those disciplines that respond not only to the question, "Where are we?" but also to, "Where did we come from? And where are we going?"

Posing these questions and, at the same time, reacting against the de-Hellenization of Christianity in the name of *logos*, the Pope Emeritus affirms a kind of reason that goes beyond the reason of rational argumentation in public debate (important though it is), as in Rawls.[2] It is also the form of reason that gives a foundation of rational truth to *ethos* (ethics) and, therefore, to the recognition of the other, with everything that implies. For Christians, certainly, the recognition of the other has yet another framework: that love which "as Saint Paul says, 'transcends' knowledge and is thereby capable of perceiving more than thought alone." This powerful force toward what is right is and always remains the love for the God-*logos*. And it is the *logos* which, pointing us in a common direction and toward a common goal, also keeps us away from *hybris*, which Benedict calls one of the most dangerous poisons that pollutes human relationships.

THE CRITIQUE OF THE POSITIVIST CLOSING OF THE SCIENCES

Within the framework described earlier, the Pope Emeritus crosses paths with philosophy, and not coincidentally it forms the basis of one of the fundamental points of agreement between himself and Jürgen

[2] J. Rawls, Political Liberalism, New York: Columbia University Press, 1993.

Habermas in their dialogue of January 2004.[3] Habermas kept secular philosophical discourse distinct from religious discourse, expecting the former to be characterized by an awareness of its own fallibility and fragility (qualities that certainly do not characterize the latter, which is founded on nonnegotiable truths). But he shared his interlocutor's critique of the positivistic closing of the sciences within the confines of the experimental disciplines and his belief in everyone's need, secular or religious, for rational discourse as the only means of reciprocal communication. He and Benedict also agree on another crucial point: the risk involved when a society entrusts *ethos* only to individual conscience and the discretionary valuation of the individual.

Here the Hellenism of the Christan faith serves Ratzinger – as we have noted – to anchor *ethos* to an objective value, which is the sum of faith and reason together. Habermas reaches a similar conclusion, but predictably not in the name of faith, nor recognizing in religion, in his words, the "cognitive guarantee" of the collective *ethos*, which religion would preestablish *ab externo*, from without.[4] Rather he reaches it in the name of shared values, which are at the basis of the constituent agreement of every democratic society, and which, moreover, largely coincide with the religiously-derived *ethos*. Both points of view reject ethical subjectivism, since for both such subjectivism is the harbinger of social disintegration.

This (almost) shared premise has its own historically and culturally important value, as we will see. But we must first ask ourselves if the premise is sufficient to avoid, or to carry toward a positive solution, the possible conflicts concerning the *ethos* that inspires the social and common life. Is the Hellenism of the *logos* enough to make everyone, in all circumstances, share in a single form of reason? Certainly not; not all people share in a single form of reason.

[3] J. Habermas and J. Ratzinger, Ragione e fede in dialogo, Venice: Marsilio, 2005, reproduced in English in Hent de Vries and Lawrence E. Sullivan, (eds.), Political Theologies: Public Religions in a Post-Secular World, New York: Fordham University Press, 2006.

[4] Id.

If it is indeed true that moving beyond the positivist perspective can provide a common framework, the fact remains that Ratzinger's reasoning contains an essential teleological component, which necessarily points to the ultimate, objective ends of humankind. These do not belong to the realm of secular reason, which is satisfied with finding an objective foundation for *ethos* in the values and principles that have emerged as human civilization has progressed.

Therefore, the (almost) common premise remains, nurtured by the partial overlap between religious and civil values. On its own, this testifies to a not-insignificant cultural shift compared to the cultural context of some decades ago. At that time, French secularism, *laïcité*, was the dominant model for secular culture, and it was mainstream to equate religion with superstition. At the same time, religion resisted modernity, including the results of scientific developments, up until the Second Vatican Council. Today, in what Habermas calls "post-secular society" religion is accepted in the public sphere, and religion, in turn, not only accepts reason, but proclaims itself to be a participant in it, and even the offspring thereof.[5]

The Pope Emeritus is the first to point out the implications of this transition, and his speech particularly highlights those implications that concern believers. To do so he uses a quote from Manuel II Palaiologos: "Not to act reasonably, not to act with logos, is contrary to the nature of God." It is a clear-cut assertion, which nevertheless opens up a wide range of issues and related solutions, all to be explored. What is against reason? To kill in the name of God? To discriminate between believers in one's own religion and believers in other religions? To renounce one's own truths to avoid discrimination, or to impose a truth on others simply because one has the power to do so, even if they are not convinced? And what does it mean to "discriminate?" And is the fact that another disagrees enough to silence the claims of one's own faith in the public sphere?

The Regensburg speech does not address each of these questions in turn. But on the basis of what was said there, we can deduce that it would be easy for the Vicar of Christ to respond to the first of them,

[5] Id.

since for him it is certainly against reason to kill in the name of God. And it would be relatively easy to respond to the second as well, by stating that the law of the state cannot be asked to discriminate on the basis of religion (even if this has occurred many times in the past), while the Church, despite the salvific value that it attributes to its faith, blesses and looks with affection on anyone who, with a sincere heart, seeks the light that reveals his or her path. While it is true that the Church's teaching institutions do not treat teachers and doctrines from other faiths with the same pride of place that is reserved for Catholic teachers and teachings, it would be unreasonable to consider this as a form of discrimination.

The response to the third question is more complicated, since it concerns the defense of religious truths that are not shared but are nevertheless impacted by public decision making. Not by chance, the most commonly encountered problems are rolled into it, not only because of the dilemmas it poses for Christians, but also because of those it poses for others, since it is here that the paradigms dictating their interaction are determined. Let us also assume that in post-secular societies, while religious and secular discourse are in part asynchronous, religious truth is nevertheless considered by its interlocutors to be the expression not of superstition, but of a culture that, to borrow again from Habermas, nourishes the normative conscience and the solidarity of citizens in a positive way. Here, the doubts formulated earlier become more pressing. Is this mutual recognition, and the partial overlap between civil and religious values, enough to make for a shared judgment not so much about religious truth, but about its reflections on the civil question at issue? Is it enough to create a common solution as a result?

SHARED SPACES OF INQUIRY

We place our hope in these premises, and in the rational argumentation that everyone must use to maintain their ideas in the public arena, where *ipse dixit* is not tolerated. But this would not be enough if the encounter between religious and secular discourse in the public sphere did not rely on something more, something that comes from the depths of religion itself: tolerance – mutual tolerance, obviously (which Rawls places at the foundation of his view of "rational" encounter between diverse groups). This should be inherent in secular discourse (even if the secularists who snub religious convictions and all that they imply seem not to know it). John Locke wrote that: "The Toleration of those that differ from others in Matters of Religion, is so agreeable to the Gospel of Jesus Christ, and to the genuine Reason of Mankind, that it seems monstrous for Men to be so blind, as not to perceive the Necessity and Advantage of it, in so clear a Light."[6] It is true that Locke's tolerance stopped well before reaching nonbelievers, but in more recent times, on the basis of the Christian message, which proposes itself as a universal message, Benedict XVI has highlighted the necessity of shared spaces of inquiry for both believers and nonbelievers. These surely presuppose mutual tolerance, and hopefully do much to further the inquiry as well.[7]

Why is tolerance important? For two reasons: the first has to do with the declension of each person's own principles and values. These, as described earlier, can correspond to the general notions to which they refer – life, dignity, and personhood – but they can also be understood differently, and if they are interpreted too differently, no correspondence is possible. Consider, for example, the defense of life, which is shared by all, but becomes highly controversial when it comes to its implications for the embryo, the fetus, and for individuals in a vegetative state or the final stages of life.

In short, this is the classic terrain where religious discourse and secular discourse, even in dealing with absolutes that correspond to one another, run the risk of irreparable conflict. And tolerance helps them, for starters, to listen to one another, to hear one another's reasons, and to turn away from the prejudiced rejection of the other.

[6] J. Locke, A Letter Concerning Toleration, trans. W. Popple, 2nd. ed., London: Awnsham Churchill, 1690, reprinted in J. Locke, A Letter Concerning Toleration and Other Writings, Indianapolis: Liberty Fund, 2010, 11.

[7] It has given rise to the Cortile dei Gentili, which has already created a space for dialogue and publications (www.cortiledeigentili.com). On the crucial openness of religion, which gives universal value to its message, see A. Ferrara, Democrazia e apertura, Milan: B. Mondadori, 2011.

To the extent this occurs, they can establish the first grounds for understanding, thus preventing themselves, in the name of tolerance, from getting to the point of intolerable conflict. This brings us to the second reason in support of tolerance: the power it has to stop at the penultimate questions, hiding from the ultimate ones. Is it possible, in spite of this, to successfully come up with acceptable solutions?

Today, science accepts – as it tells us in a solemn way (in the 2006 Venice Charter of the Veronesi Foundation[8] shared by notable signatories) – that something that is technically feasible may yet not be worth doing, because there can be moral reasons, traceable to principles that are absolute for everyone, which oppose it. So, to foreshadow examples we will return to later, there is no possible concretization of human dignity that accepts the production of chimeras or the selection of embyos and interruption of pregnancy for eugenics purposes. In addition, science acknowledges mystery, on the noncontrovertible grounds that no one is able to conclusively prove that the universe and the complex forms of life therein are not the fruit of a superior intelligence. Science does not follow the same path as religion, which not only makes this conclusion, but derives from it the further conclusion that the creator God is also attentive to the life of his creatures, responsive to their prayers, and involved in modifying, if he wishes, the course of their affairs. On this point there is no mutual understanding, but there is also no reason to create and maintain conflict about it in the public sphere.

Nor is there a reason to do so whenever a solution exists that is capable of partially satisfying the demands of both camps. This is the crucial point, because, beyond tolerance, one could argue with good reason that this kind of solution reflects the principle of "reasonable accommodation," which, according to authors such as Jocelyn Maclure and Charles Taylor,[9] springs from the rights of equality and nondiscrimination in pluralistic societies. They conceive of the idea as a protection of minority groups, and, therefore, as an accommodation of their reason, adjusting norms and general applications

[8] www.fondazioneveronesi.it

[9] J. Maclure and C. Taylor, Secularism and Freedom of Conscience, Cambridge: Harvard University Press, 2013.

which would otherwise violate them. But the principle can easily have a more general scope, which anchors it to the very foundations of democracy, and which deals with different, clashing elements that are present in its social fabric. Carlo Lavagna wrote many years ago that democracy must lead to "proportional harmonization of all demands" in accordance with "a principle that is coessential to the very concept of law and of legal discipline."[10] Which, in his culture, meant coessential to reason.

Therefore when convictions of a religious origin are at stake, reason, democracy, and tolerance together demand that the believer not impose them on those who do not share in his or her belief. But, by the same token, who does not share the belief must know how to stop at solutions that do not directly target them, and which both believer and nonbeliever can then be responsible to accept. These are, as they are called earlier, the penultimate solutions.

THE GROUNDS FOR A PRACTICABLE ENCOUNTER

Experience is already rich with situations and events in which this encounter, however difficult, is practicable (even if it has not always been successfully carried out). Let us consider only a few examples, beginning with embyos, which are already human creatures for Catholic believers, and not for others. For believers it is unacceptable to create them solely for research purposes, and therefore no one should claim that the law allows it, and certainly not that it encourages it. But if there remain excess leftover embryos created for implantation, the decision between eliminating them and using them for research purposes should be shared by everyone, at least to determine the lesser evil.

Euthanasia, for a believer, is an expression of impermissible *hybris*, a violation of the commandment "thou shalt not kill," and for this reason is devastating if permitted by the law of the state. But no one can be prevented from making decisions concerning his or her own

[10] C. Lavagna, "Considerazioni sui caratteri degli ordinamenti democratici," in Riv. trim. dir. pubbl., 1956, 392.

life. For example, in discussing end-of-life issues for people in a vegetative state, it can be required that someone's will on these matters be unambiguous, or that it be formed in full consciousness. But then there must also be consensus on executing such will, so that it can occur not in an active way, but by refusing to allow life to continue by artificial means.

A more complicated issue is that of genetic modification, and yet it is precisely here that the kind of convergence I am proposing seems to take place most consistently. This is only the latest chapter in a long history of alteration of nature. Humans have made themselves the protagonists of this history by dint of their intelligence, which has allowed them to see in nature long-hidden potentialities. It was in this way that, through the use of seeds and all the various farming developments, they completely altered their way of sustaining themselves and the human way of life. The same has occurred with many other discoveries and innovations, which have taught people to capitalize upon elements that already existed in nature by breaking them down and recombining them in a new way.

Genetic modifications are, among all of these, the most significant, because they alter a living being by inserting the genes of a different living being, thereby offering the possibility of making organisms for a particular purpose. It is a power that humanity has never had before, which does not necessarily mean we should consider it to be beyond the boundaries marked by the Herculean pillars of ethics and religion, but which – we must admit – is not far from them.

It is not beyond them in and of itself, since many modifications fit in with those betterments of the environment, of food, and of health which in various forms have always characterized the history of *homo sapiens*, the stewards of the world we live in and bearers of the responsibility (for both religion and secular ethics) to both safeguard it and to better it. Consider the creation of enzymes that trap nitrogen in the atmosphere, or of bacteria that help plants fend off parasites. Here the only shared precaution is the adoption of prudential measures to protect health and the environment, in the presence of modified organisms that are placed in the outside environment before the potential effects are fully known.

But the boundary can be easily surpassed when the organisms involved are human organisms, which are genetically modified in order to enhance their strength or abilities. It is one thing to do this to avoid serious hereditary illness, and quite another to make a person fine-tuned for extreme sports, for war, or for work that will expose him or her to nuclear radiation. Not to mention the (still theoretical) hypotheses of prenatal genetic treatments that result in predetermining the life and identity of the neonate-to-be, or even of entire generations, as a consequence of eugenetic politics with pseudoracial purposes.

In all of these developments, principles have been affirmed through the elaboration and approval of conventions, charters, and directives in which any discrepencies between the secular and religious voices who collaborated in their production appear only minimally, if at all. Recall the Charter of Fundamental Rights of the European Union of 2000, in which Article 3 forbids both reproductive cloning and eugenics, or the Council of Europe's 1997 Oviedo Convention on Human Rights and Biomedicine, in which Article 13 rejects any intervention whose purpose is to introduce genetic modifications inhereitable by future generations, and Article 14 forbids sex selection as a valid procreative choice, unless to avoid the transmission of hereditary illnesses tied to gender.

Whether we speak about respect for creation on the part of the creature, or about respect for human dignity, integrity, and liberty, the final conclusion is nearly always the same, and the pillars of Hercules are for everyone, in almost all cases, in the same place. Once again it is embryos that create discord, accentuated by the fact that the genetic modifications they are subjected to can even be interspecies, culminating in the creation of the chimera embryo. In 2007 the British Human Fertilization and Embryology Authority authorized preliminary research in this direction, awakening passionate debate on the ethical validity of the combination of human organic material with that of animals, which entailed, even if in small quantities, the introduction of animal cytoplasmic DNA into human embyos. The purpose was the cure of particularly severe illnesses, but religious voices were not alone in seeing an impermissible *hybris* in this development.

The creation of chimeras that involve human beings is absolutely rejected by everyone, just as animal chimeras are considered problematic where the market potential and the scientific purpose is unknown, and are rejected where animal suffering is involved. But when this is done to the human embryo, the same question reemerges, and the only way to avoid it is the rejection of hybridization, at least whenever it cannot be determined that the object of the experiment is an animal embyo, modified with nonembryonic human genetic materials.

REASON, TOLERANCE, AND DEMOCRACY

This rapid overview does not provide a comprehensive account of the themes that implicate the intrinsic relationship between faith and reason, which is at the heart of Benedict XVI's idea. Nor is the treatment of these themes here exhaustive, but only serves to highlight possible points of encounter between religious and secular discourse within the realm of reason. The profitability of the proposed approach should be evident, and with it the clear possibility to have a coherent encounter between reason, tolerance, and democracy in order to find solutions that are useful for the common good, and which do not call into question the ultimate convictions that would make conflict unavoidable.

Even if this is already a satisfying result, we cannot conclude our analysis without taking stock of what Benedict XVI said four years after Regensburg, in his speech at Westminster Hall in September 2010. On that occasion, the Pope Emeritus said that "the objective norms governing right action are accessible to reason, prescinding from the content of revelation."[11] As a result, "the role of religion in political debate is not so much to supply these norms, as if they could not be known by non-believers – still less to propose concrete political solutions, which would lie altogether outside the competence of

[11] Pope Benedict XVI, Meeting with the Representatives of British Society, Westminster Hall, Westminster, September 17, 2010.

religion – but rather to help purify and shed light upon the application of reason to the discovery of objective moral principles."[12]

Based on these passages, we could reopen the debate between Ratzinger and Habermas, since – as mentioned earlier – Habermas attributed to religion the claim of providing *ab externo* the contents of civil ethics, and for this reason stressed that the nonsubjective foundation of that ethics should be found in the values enshrined in the constitutional covenant between citizens. In 2010 Benedict rejected that claim and attributed to religion – ever faithful to the Hellenic roots of Christianity, and therefore to the *logos* – the unique but fundamental task of casting light on the application of reason in the search for objective moral principles, preventing reason from falling prey to the tragic distortions it has undergone in history, from the slave trade to the totalitarian madness of the twentieith century.

Of course, this is not enough to erase the enduring differences between a reason that teleologically considers the ultimate ends (and derives "objective" moral principles from them) and a reason that stops short of considering them. It is nevertheless worthwhile to reflect on the meaning of the passages presented earlier, which are so clear and – let us be honest – so surprising for those who, one moment supporting them and the next opposing them, throw themselves for or against "concrete political solutions" attributed to religion.

In the context of the foregoing analysis, the speech at Westminster is the best affirmation of a possible encounter, in postsecular society, between all those who feel the need to strengthen the ethical fabric and who have the wisdom to understand that this is only possible if there are shared solutions, going beyond each person's position as a believer or nonbeliever. It is up to them to achieve this; it is enough that the impulse toward mutual intolerance is pushed to the margins. What Benedict XVI tells us is that we can help one another to do this. An extraordinary conclusion and a wonderful premise.

[12] Id.

9 RELIGIOUS FREEDOM IN THE POLITICAL SPEECHES OF POPE BENEDICT XVI

Mary Ann Glendon

Cardinal Joseph Ratzinger was widely regarded as rather apolitical, but as Pope Benedict XVI, he brought a forceful and distinctive approach to the duty of offering principles for reflection, criteria for judgment, and guidelines for action in public life. His mode of engaging the issues of the day is particularly well illustrated in his frequent treatment of religious freedom. The speeches dealing with that subject are deeply marked by his longstanding preoccupation with the synergy between faith and reason, as well as by the synergy between religion and freedom postulated in Vatican II's Declaration on Religious Freedom, *Dignitatis Humanae*.

"Religious freedom," as the Council Fathers pointed out, "has to do with immunity from coercion in civil society."[1] Thus it is not surprising that many of Pope Benedict's most penetrating observations on religion and politics have been delivered directly to political actors in such bastions of worldly power as the White House, the United Nations, the Elysée Palace in Paris, Britain's Westminster Hall, and the Reichstag Building in Berlin. The basic elements of his thinking on those topics, however, were already present in the words he addressed to an academic audience in Regensburg in September 2006.

Although the content of the Regensburg speech precisely reflected its title, "Faith, Reason, and the University," the Pope's extended meditation on that subject was ignored by most commentators amidst the controversy that broke out over his quotation from a fourteenth

[1] Dignitatis Humanae, 1.

century Byzantine Emperor who had said that the prophet Mohammed had brought "things only evil and inhuman, such as his command to spread by the sword the faith he preached."[2]

It must have been disappointing to the relatively new Pope that so little attention was paid to his central messages born of a lifetime's study: his call for a "profound encounter of faith and reason . . ., an encounter between genuine enlightenment and religion"; his appreciation of the positive aspects of modernity combined with his critique of an impoverished concept of reason limited to the empirically verifiable; his warning that "disturbing pathologies of religion and reason" erupt when faith and reason are separated, and his expression of hope for a "genuine dialogue among religions and cultures."

He took up those themes again just three months later, this time with more specificity. In his pre-Christmas message to the Roman Curia, he observed with sympathy that "the Muslim world today finds itself facing an extremely urgent task that is very similar to the one that was imposed upon Christians beginning in the age of the Enlightenment, and that Vatican Council II, through long and painstaking effort, resolved concretely for the Catholic Church."[3] That process of self-renewal, he explained, necessarily entails a commitment to freedom of religion.

> [I]t is necessary to welcome the real achievements of Enlightenment thinking – human rights, and especially the freedom of faith and its exercise, recognizing these as elements that are also essential for the authenticity of religion. Just as in the Christian community there has been lengthy inquiry into the right attitude of the faith toward these convictions – an inquiry that will certainly never be concluded definitively – so also the Islamic world, with its own tradition, stands before the great task of finding the appropriate solutions in this regard.

He concluded his address to the curia with an expression of solidarity with "all those who, precisely on the basis of their religious

[2] Pope Benedict XVI, "Faith, Reason, and the University: Memories and Reflections," Meeting with the representatives of science, Aula Magna of the University of Regensburg, Regensburg, September 12, 2006.

[3] Address to the Roman Curia, December 22, 2006.

convictions as Muslims, struggle against violence and in favor of synergy between faith and reason, between religion and freedom."

Two years later, Pope Benedict took the occasion of his visits to the United States and France to advance the concept that he calls "positive secularism" – an approach to the relation between church and state that is marked by respect for religion and its public role, rather than by hostility to religion. In April 2008, en route to Washington, D.C., he told journalists on the plane that he was "fascinated" by the fact that the United States "began with a positive concept of secularism."[4] The American founders, he observed, had "intentionally created a secular state" – not out of antagonism toward religion, but quite the contrary – out of respect for it. He drew a sharp contrast with the "negative" European form of secularism, noting that the branch of the Enlightenment that was essentially anticlerical and irreligious had so little influence in early America, that the American system was devised to protect religion and churches from government, not to protect government from religion and churches.

Upon his arrival in Washington, the Pope was met by President George W. Bush, the first and only time President Bush so greeted a visiting head of state. To the assembled welcoming party, the president explained why he had come out to Andrews Air Force Base to welcome the Pope. "It's very simple," he said, "he is the greatest spiritual leader in the world."

In a ceremony on the south lawn of the White House, the Pope expressed his respect for America's "vast pluralistic society" and his appreciation for "a nation that welcomes the role of religion in the public square." Later in his trip, he referred to the United States as a model of a secular state where many religions not only coexist in relative harmony, but have actually flourished. He noted approvingly that, historically, Americans "do not hesitate to bring moral arguments rooted in Biblical faith into their public discourse."[5] And upon his return to Italy, the Pope spoke of American society as characterized by a "healthy secularism" through which "the religious dimension, with the diversity of its expressions, is not

[4] Benedict XVI, Interview with journalists, April 15, 2008.
[5] Pope Benedict XVI, Address to U.S. Bishops, April 16, 2008.

only tolerated but appreciated as the nation's 'soul' and as a fundamental guarantee of human rights and duties."[6]

Those words of praise, however, were accompanied by notes of caution. The Pope was well aware that the positive form of secularism that he admires is under increasing assault in the United States. Accordingly, he took the occasion of his speech at the White House to warn that religious freedom cannot not be taken for granted, and that its erosion could have deleterious effects on the American democratic experiment. "The preservation of freedom," he said, "calls for the cultivation of virtue, self-discipline, sacrifice for the common good and a sense of responsibility toward the less fortunate. It also demands the courage to engage in civic life and to bring one's deepest beliefs and values to reasoned public debate. In a word, freedom is ever new. It is a challenge held out to each generation, and must constantly be won over for the cause of good."[7]

Moving on to New York and the United Nations headquarters, Pope Benedict devoted part of his April 18 address to the General Assembly to the need to protect a capacious concept of religious freedom.

> It is inconceivable ... that believers should have to suppress a part of themselves – their faith – in order to be active citizens. It should never be necessary to deny God in order to enjoy one's rights. The rights associated with religion are the more in need of protection if they are considered to clash with a prevailing secular ideology or with majority religious positions of an exclusive nature. The full guarantee of religious liberty cannot be limited to the free exercise of worship, but has to give due consideration to the public dimension of religion and hence to the possibility of believers playing their part in building the social order.[8]

As it happens, I had the good fortune to be present at the UN when the Holy Father delivered that speech, and to witness the enthusiastic standing ovation that it received. At the time, however, I could not

[6] Pope Benedict XVI, General Audience, April 30, 2008.

[7] Pope Benedict XVI, White House Address, April 16, 2008; cf. Benedict XVI, Encyclical Letter *Spe Salvi*, Rome, 30 November 2007, 24.

[8] Address to the General Assembly of the United Nations, April 18, 2008.

help wondering whether those who applauded the Pope with such gusto had really grasped the full implications of his words, especially where religious freedom was concerned.

Later that year, in September 2008, the Pope took his message about religious freedom to the cradle of antireligious secularism. When reporters asked him what his message in France would be, he replied that it seemed evident to him that "secularism in itself is not in contradiction with faith" and that "religion and politics should be open to each other."[9] Speaking to French politicians at the Elysée Palace, he said:

> At this moment in history when cultures continue to cross paths more frequently, I am firmly convinced that a new reflection on the meaning and importance of "*laïcité*" is now necessary. In fact, it is fundamental, on the one hand, to insist on the distinction between the political realm and that of religion in order to preserve both the religious freedom of citizens and the responsibility of the state towards them; and, on the other hand, to become more aware of the irreplaceable role of religion for the formation of consciences and the contribution which it can bring to, among other things, the creation of a basic ethical consensus within society.[10]

Although France has explicitly enshrined the principle of *laïcité* in its constitution,[11] then-President Nicolas Sarkozy showed his receptiveness to the idea that *laïcité* should be open to religion. He referred in his welcoming speech to religion – "especially the Christian religion" – as France's "living patrimony."[12] He went on to remark that "It would be crazy to deprive ourselves of religion; quite simply, a failing against culture and against thought.... A positive secularity offers our

[9] Rachel Donadio, "Pope Addresses Secularism in France," New York Times, September 13, 2008.

[10] Pope Benedict XVI, Address to French Politicians, September 12, 2008.

[11] French Constitution of 1958, Article 1: "La France est une République, indivisible, laïque, démocratique et sociale."

[12] Sarkozy, "Declaration on the place of religion in France and on his concept of positive secularity," September 12, 2008, http://discours.vie-publique.fr/notices/087002825.html.

consciences the possibility of dialogue, above and beyond our beliefs and rites, concerning the meaning we want to give to our lives."[13]

Exactly two years to the day after Regensburg, the Pope used his speech at the Collège des Bernardins to expand his warning against the separation of faith and reason – and to renew his critique of an excessively narrow conception of reason. Whereas his Regensburg address had focused on the pathologies of fundamentalist religion divorced from reason, he now turned the tables on militant secularists. To "drive the question concerning God into the subjective realm, as being unscientific," he said, is just as irrational as religious fundamentalism; in fact, it represents "the capitulation of reason, the renunciation of its highest possibilities."[14]

Concerns about how the Pope's visit would be regarded by France's Muslim community were allayed when the President of the French Muslim Council referred to the Regensburg controversy as a thing of the past, and the Rector of the Paris Mosque stated that, "Through his speeches we know that he is a man of peace and dialogue."[15]

Given the negative connotations of the word "secularism" in several religious circles, many people must have been surprised to see the head of the Roman Catholic Church emerge as an advocate for a form of secularism. Pope Benedict's bold bid to reinterpret and redirect the concept of secularism, however, has been long in the

[13] Two years later, on a visit to the Vatican, Sarkozy reaffirmed his support for a fresh concept of secularism: "I believe in secularity as a principle of respect. But the Church cannot be indifferent in the face of the problems of the society to which she belongs as an institution, and politics cannot be indifferent in the face of the religious event and spiritual and moral values. There is no religion without social responsibility; there is no politics without morality." Jesus Colina, "Sarkozy Seeks to Confirm Collaboration with Church," *ZENIT*, October 8, 2010.

[14] Meeting with Representatives from the World of Culture, Paris, September 12, 2008. See also "World Day of Peace Message," 2011 (8).

[15] Associated Press, *Pope Speaks of Secularism in first France visit*, September 15, 2008, http://usatoday30.usatoday.com/news/religion/2008–09–12-pope-france_N.htm; www.nytimes.com/2008/09/13/world/europe/13pope.html.

making. As Cardinal Ratzinger, he had already developed a contrast between secularism as a posture of neutrality and secularism as a posture of opposition to religion, pointing out that while the former opens up areas of freedom for persons of all faiths, the latter "imposes itself through politics and leaves no public space for the Catholic and Christian vision, which thus risks becoming something purely private and essentially mutilated."[16]

When it was announced that the Pope would visit Britain in 2010, many predicted that he would receive a chilly reception. In some ways, Britain with its officially established religion was a more challenging destination than secular France. This, after all, is the country where former Prime Minister Tony Blair had refrained from making religious references in his speeches out of fear that voters would think him a "nutter."[17] Queen Elizabeth, however, set a welcoming tone, telling Pope Benedict that his visit was an important reminder that all Britons shared a common Christian heritage, and affirming that "freedom to worship is at the core of our tolerant and democratic society."[18]

The Pope took up those themes in his own speech, remarking on Britons' shared Christian heritage and offering a "hand of friendship" to the British people.[19] Later, in Westminter Hall, he evoked the proud British tradition of parliamentary government. He urged his listeners to consider religion as "a vital contributor to

[16] Joseph Cardinal Ratzinger, interview reported in S. Magister, *The Church Is Under Siege. But Habermas, the Atheist, Is Coming to its Defense*, November 22, 2004, http://chiesa.espresso.repubblica.it/articolo/20037?eng=y.

[17] Recently, Blair acknowledged that he had once removed the words "God bless Britain" from a speech after being told by his public relations advisor that "We don't do God." Tim Ross, "Tony Blair Wanted to End Speech with "God Bless Britain," *Telegraph*, www.telegraph.co.uk/news/politics/tony-blair/9265571/Tony-Blair-wanted-to-end-speech-with-God-bless-Britain.html

[18] Martin Beckford, "Pope visit: Queen says freedom to worship is at 'core' of British society," *Telegraph*, www.telegraph.co.uk/news/religion/the-pope/8007100/Pope-visit-Queen-says-freedom-to-worship-is-at-core-of-British-society.html

[19] David Willey, "Papal visit: Pope offers 'hand of friendship' to UK," *BBC*, www.bbc.co.uk/news/uk-11313328

the national conversation," and to be wary of the risks to a regime of ordered liberty when religious freedom is eroded.[20]

> I cannot but voice my concern at the increasing marginalization of religion, particularly of Christianity, that is taking place in some quarters, even in nations which place a great emphasis on tolerance. There are those who would advocate that the voice of religion be silenced, or at least relegated to the purely private sphere. There are those who argue that the public celebration of festivals such as Christmas should be discouraged in the questionable belief that it might somehow offend those of other religions or none. And there are those who argue – paradoxically with the intention of eliminating discrimination – that Christians in public roles should be required at times to act against their conscience. These are worrying signs of a failure to appreciate not only the rights of believers to freedom of conscience and freedom of religion, but also the legitimate role of religion in the public square.

Prime Minister David Cameron noted after the Pope's departure that the speech had made the UK "sit up and think."[21]

Despite scattered protests, the public reaction to the Pope's person and message was unexpectedly positive, prompting historian Paul Johnson to refer to the pontiff as "the world's best salesman."[22] The speech on the vital contribution that religion can make to public life, according to Johnson, held the audience of former prime ministers, Members of Parliament, Lords, and other officials "transfixed." In fact, Johnson observed, "the secret of the Pope's success is that he was not selling. He was giving. He was introducing a great many people to a world with which they are unfamiliar, and reassuring others that their world is still there, brighter and more welcoming than ever."

[20] Pope Benedict XVI, Meeting with the representatives of British society, Westminster Hall, Westminster, September 17, 2010.

[21] Mark Greaves, "Cameron tells Pope: 'you have made Britain sit up and think," *Catholic Herald*, www.catholicherald.co.uk/news/2010/09/19/cameron-tells-pope-you-have-made-britain-sit-up-and-think/

[22] Paul Johnson, "The Pope in a British Comeback," *Forbes Magazine*, November 8, 2010.

The following year, with religious liberty under growing threat from statist regimes, cultural relativists, aggressive secularists, and sexual liberationists, the Pope launched a frontal attack against the slogan – almost a mantra in secular circles – that religion is a major source of strife. He gave his 2011 World Day of Peace message the contrarian title, "Religious Freedom: The Path to Peace," and proceeded to defend a broad conception of religious liberty as essential not only for individuals, but for the well-being of society and for peace on earth.

"Without openness to the transcendent," he said, "the human person withdraws within himself, fails to find answers to the heart's deepest questions about life's meaning, fails to appropriate lasting ethical values and principles, and fails even to experience authentic freedom and to build a just society."[23] But when religious freedom is protected, "the dignity of the human person is respected at its root, and the ethos and institutions of peoples are strengthened."[24]

To diminish the public role of religion, he said, "is to create a society which is unjust, inasmuch as it fails to take account of the true nature of the human person; *it is to stifle the growth of the authentic and lasting peace of the whole human family*."[25]

Recent scholarship provides support for the Pope's challenge to the claim that religion fosters violence. According to one study, violence actually tends to be greater in societies where religious practice is suppressed,[26] and according to another, promotion of religious freedom actually reduces inter-religious conflict.[27] A Swedish analysis of conflicts occurring between 1989 and 2003 found that religion was rarely a primary or exclusive factor in conflicts

[23] "Religious Freedom, the Path to Peace," World Day of Peace Message, 2011, 2.

[24] Id., 5. [25] Id., 1 (emphasis in original).

[26] Brian Grim and Roger Finke, The Price of Freedom Denied: Religious Persecution and Conflict in the 21st Century (Cambridge: Cambridge University Press, 2011).

[27] Thomas Farr, World of Faith and Freedom (New York: Oxford University Press, 2008).

where it was implicated.[28] Rather, such conflicts often have more to do with issues of individual and group identity than with theological differences.[29] As Jacques Maritain once observed, "nothing is easier for human weakness than to merge religion with prejudices of race, family, or class, collective hatreds, passions of a clan and political phantoms."[30]

In his 2011 World Day of Peace Message, Pope Benedict postulated that religious freedom has a "special status" among fundamental rights and freedoms: "It is an essential element of a constitutional state; it cannot be denied without at the same time encroaching on all fundamental rights and freedoms, since it is their synthesis and keystone."[31] Then, touching on current events, he deplored the fact that there are "some areas of the world where it is impossible to profess one's religion freely except at the risk of life and personal liberty, while in other areas "we see more subtle and sophisticated forms of prejudice and hostility towards believers and religious symbols."[32]

It seems likely that the Pope was aware of the alarming finding of the Pew Forum in 2009 that nearly 70 percent of the world's

[28] The study is reported in Isak Svenson, "Fighting with Faith: Religion and Conflict Resolution in Civil Wars," Journal of Conflict Resolution 51, 932, 2007.

[29] Malise Ruthven, Fundamentalist and other Obstacles to Religious Toleration in Universal Human Rights in a World of Diversity: The Case of Religious Freedom, ed. Mary Ann Glendon (Vatican City: Pontifical Academy of Social Sciences, 2011), 456.

[30] Jacques Maritain, Christianity and Democracy (San Francisco: Ignatius Press, 2012), 39.

[31] Pope Benedict XVI, World Day of Peace Message, 2011, 5. Here, he was following the view of Pope John Paul II who maintained that religious freedom "is so closely linked to the other fundamental rights, that it can rightly be argued that respect for religious freedom is, as it were, a touchstone for the observance of the other fundamental rights.... The State's respect for the right to freedom of religion is a sign of respect for the other fundamental human rights, in that it is an implicit recognition of the existence of an order which transcends the political dimension of existence." John Paul II, Address to the Diplomatic Corps, 1989.

[32] World Day of Peace Message 2011, 1.

population lives in countries where there are "high restrictions" on religious freedom due to governmental policies, social hostilities, or both.[33] The same survey also brought sobering news regarding countries that impose only "low" to "moderate" restrictions on religious freedom. Although the threats are less dramatic in the liberal democracies of the West, religious freedom there is at heightened risk due to erosions of conscience protection for religious individuals and institutions, restrictions on the autonomy of religious institutions, and constraints on the rights of parents regarding the education of their children.

A few days after his World Day of Peace Message, Pope Benedict outlined several ways in which religious freedom was being violated in his annual address to the diplomats accredited to the Holy See:[34]

> Religious freedom is infringed when it is reduced to freedom of worship; when a majority religion uses blasphemy laws to justify discrimination and violence against minorities; and when the regime is inspired by "political or philosophical systems which call for strict control, if not a monopoly, of the state over society."
>
> Religious freedom is infringed when it is marginalized, as even happens in countries which pay great lip service to pluralism and tolerance, but treat religion as "something insignificant, alien or even destabilizing to modern society." Christians in such countries, he noted, are "required at times to act in the exercise of their profession with no reference to their religious and moral convictions, and even in opposition to them, as for example where laws are enforced limiting the right to conscientious objection on the part of health care or legal professionals."
>
> Religious freedom is infringed when religious feasts and symbols are banned from civic life under the guise of respect for other religions or non-believers. "By acting in this way, not only is the right of believers to the public expression of their faith restricted, but an attack is made on the cultural roots which nourish the profound identity and social cohesion of many nations."

33 Pew Forum on Religion and Public Life, Global Restrictions on Religion, December 2009, 1. The study covered 198 countries and territories, representing more than 99.5% of the world's population.

34 Address to the Diplomatic Corps, 2011.

> Religious freedom is infringed "when religious communities cannot operate freely in society through initiatives in the social, charitable, or educational sectors," as when a state monopoly of education, or mandatory participation in certain types of sex education, violates "the primordial right of families to make decisions about the education of their children."
>
> Religious freedom is threatened by "the dangerous notion of a conflict between religious freedom and other human rights, or with alleged new rights which lack a foundation in authentic human nature," a trend which risks downgrading religious freedom to a second-class right, one that is easily trumped by other rights, claims or interests.

Not surprisingly, one discerns in the speeches discussed here a practical application of ideas that had long been gestating in the theology of Joseph Ratzinger. Running through them like an electric current are the twin synergies of faith and reason, religion and freedom. Particularly striking are the author's efforts to reclaim Enlightenment rationality and to promote a revised conception of secularism.[35]

His method of reappropriation in each of these cases involves a careful winnowing of the wheat from the chaff, discerning and building on what is sound, while naming and discarding the elements that have not proved conducive to human flourishing. Never before has a Pope spoken so fulsomely in praise of the Enlightenment inheritance as Benedict did at Regensburg and in his 2006 Address to the Curia. Yet that praise must be understood against the background of Cardinal Ratzinger's discourse at Subiaco in 2005 where he pointed out that Enlightenment philosophy was "incomplete" because it had consciously severed its own historical roots in Christianity, thus "depriving itself of the regenerating forces from which it sprang."[36]

[35] The Pope renewed his advocacy for an understanding of the role of religion in public life free of historical prejudices in 2011 while greeting the new ambassador from Brazil, the country with the world's largest Catholic population. In that speech, he called again for a "healthy secularism" that does not treat religion as a mere private sentiment but accords it appropriate public recognition. Address to Brazilian Ambassador to the Holy See, November 2, 2011.

[36] Cardinal Joseph Ratzinger, "On Europe's Crisis of Culture," April 1, 2005.

Just as the Enlightenment needs to be reconnected to its roots, so religion needs to embrace reason in its fullness. That was the Pope's message at Regensburg. A cramped conception of "reason," he pointed out at the Collège des Bernardins, will not do. Reason cannot fulfill its own potential if it is limited to what is empirically verifiable.

It was but a step from reconnecting the best of Enlightenment thought with Christianity to arguing that the secular state must be freed from antireligious fundamentalism. And it was but a step from contesting the secularist myth that religion is a source of strife to proclaiming that religious freedom is, in fact, a "path to peace."

Benedict's discourses on religion and public life can be likened to the pleas that Alexis de Tocqueville addressed to different sectors of French society nearly two centuries ago. In his preface to *Democracy in America*, Tocqueville made two novel claims. To allay the fears of devout Catholics such as his mother, he claimed that the American example proved that religion could flourish in freedom. And to enlightened skeptics, such as most of his friends, he argued that religion (by which he meant Biblical religion) would be beneficial for emerging free societies. He was emphatic in advising his fellow sons of the Enlightenment to get over their prejudices against religion. Lovers of liberty, he said, "should hasten to call religion to their aid, for they must know that one cannot establish the reign of liberty without that of mores, and mores cannot be firmly founded without beliefs."[37]

Two centuries later, with Tocqueville's propositions still contested by religious and secular fundamentalists alike, Pope Benedict took up the challenge of trying to persuade the former to welcome the good gifts of modernity and the latter to abandon their hostility to religion. Whether and to what extent these efforts will be successful no one knows, but it is not too soon to say that the scholarly Pope became an eloquent public intellectual, bringing a bold, distinctive, and theologically informed voice to the discussion of religion in public life.

[37] Alexis de Tocqueville, Democracy in America, ed. J. P. Mayer (New York: Doubleday Anchor, 1969), 17.

10 FREEDOM OF RELIGION
The Contribution of Benedict XVI to a Universal Guarantee from a European Perspective

Christoph Grabenwarter

INTRODUCTION

In his address to members of the General Assembly of the United Nations on April 18, 2008, Benedict XVI made a clear statement of commitment to the protection of human rights, in particular to the freedom of religion. While it is clear that within the framework of such a meeting, the role of the United Nations is being discussed in this speech, some of the key issues addressed by Benedict XVI have to be seen in a broader context of the international protection of human rights. It is remarkable that the pope finds such clear words in favor of international human rights when he stresses the importance of the Universal Declaration of Human Rights:

> Indeed, the victims of hardship and despair, whose human dignity is violated with impunity, become easy prey to the call to violence, and they can then become violators of peace. The common good that human rights help to accomplish cannot, however, be attained merely by applying correct procedures, nor even less by achieving a balance between competing rights. The merit of the *Universal Declaration* is that it has enabled different cultures, juridical expressions and institutional models to converge around a fundamental nucleus of values, and hence of rights. Today, though, efforts need to be redoubled in the face of pressure to reinterpret the foundations of the *Declaration* and to compromise its inner unity so as to facilitate a move away from the protection of human dignity towards the satisfaction of simple interests, often particular interests. The *Declaration* was adopted as a

> "common standard of achievement" (*Preamble*) and cannot be applied piecemeal, according to trends or selective choices that merely run the risk of contradicting the unity of the human person and thus the indivisibility of human rights.

Based on the assumption of the unity of the human person and the universality of human rights, Benedict XVI, among others, touches upon three issues in his widely remarked speech: the role of the State in the protection of the citizens against violations of human rights, the role of freedom of religion in a democratic state, and the dimensions of freedom of religion. All three issues are related to each other and have common roots in the Universal Declaration of Human Rights of 1948. This declaration is based on values that are the values of Christianity and of the Catholic Church as well. It served as an important basis, as well, for regional human rights as for the Covenant on Civil and Political Rights (CCPR).

The three aspects shall be discussed in this paper, and they will be reflected against the background of the scientific work of the author in the field of the European context of human rights protection, that is, the European Convention on Human Rights (ECHR). In particular, it will be shown how the European heritage is expressed in the current case law of the European Court of Human Rights (ECtHR).

FREEDOM OF RELIGION AS AN INTERNATIONAL GUARANTEE IN HUMAN RIGHTS CATALOGUES

The Universal Declaration of Human Rights, as adopted by the General Assembly of the United Nations on December 10, 1948,[1] forms not only the "basis for a peaceful world"[2] but also the basis and starting point for virtually all international human rights texts that have been proposed and ratified in the second half of the twentieth

[1] Res. 63/116.

[2] E. Roosevelt, "Writing the Universal Declaration of Human Rights: Some Recollections," in B. Fassbender, Menschenrechteerklärung. Universal Declaration of Human Rights – Allgemeine Erklärung der Menschenrechte. Neuübersetzung, Synopsen, Erläuterungen, Materialien, Munich: 2009, 31 seq. at 44.

century. In particular, Article 18 of the declaration is the first text in a row of international instruments that guarantee freedom of religion. Its wording is still up to date, and it has become the model for later guarantees of this freedom: "Everyone has the right to freedom of thought, conscience and religion; this right includes freedom to change his religion or belief, and freedom, either alone or in community with others and in public or private, to manifest his religion or belief in teaching, practice, worship and observance." It is short – much shorter than the equivalent guarantee in Article 18 CCPR – and still it covers all relevant aspects of the freedom.

Therefore, little change was necessary when the final draft of the Article on freedom of religion in the ECHR was agreed in the following year. Article 9 of the Convention guarantees to everyone the right to freedom of thought, conscience, and religion, including freedom to change his or her religion or belief and freedom, either alone or in community with others and in public or private; and to manifest this religion or belief, in worship, teaching, practice, and observance. These freedoms are subject to limitations, that is, those that are prescribed by law and which are necessary in a democratic society for a number of so called "legitimate aims."

As a whole, freedom of thought, conscience, and religion as enshrined in Article 9 is also to be seen as an independent international guarantee. It has to be distinguished from any form of religious freedom guaranteed by national constitutional orders as its interpretation is in no way bound by national ideas and values. National constitutional orders regularly stipulate explicit regulations with regard to the relationship between the state and the churches or between the state and religion in addition to a fundamental right of freedom of religion; however, they do not call for a particular "model." International guarantees, such as Article 9 ECHR, can have an effect on these institutional regulations of the state-church relations. Some of the guarantees shaping the law regulating the relationship between state and church – such as the right to self-determination of religious communities – correspond to parts of Article 9 (1). In the area of education and teaching there is another important guarantee, Article 2 of Protocol No. 1, which in this field is the *lex specialis* to Article 9 of the Convention, at least where the dispute concerns the obligation imposed on member states by the second sentence of Article 2 of Protocol No. 1 to respect the right of parents to ensure such education and teaching in conformity with their own religious and philosophical convictions in the exercise of any functions which they assume in that area.[3]

THE ROLE OF THE STATE IN HUMAN RIGHTS PROTECTION

Although the universal dimension of human rights protection is common ground among lawyers today it remains clear that it is the state that is responsible for the respect of human rights. Benedict XVI finds clear words in his UN speech when he says: "Every State has the primary duty to protect its own populations from grave and sustained violation of human rights."

Admittedly, this statement is directed above all against gross violations of human rights touching upon questions not only of the most fundamental human rights (such as right to life, prohibition of torture, and prohibition of slavery) but also of humanitarian law. But there is also another general message behind this sentence that reflects the state of the art of modern human rights law – the responsibility or the obligation to protect the individuals living in a country. European human rights law has become an "avant garde" in the development and formulation of "positive obligation" on the side of the state.[4]

The Strasbourg Court proceeds from a general "obligation to secure"[5] in the field of human rights, and it has developed manifold positive obligations in its case law. There is of course an efficient legal basis for such an assumption already in the text of some Articles of the

[3] ECtHR, 29/6/2007 (Grand Chamber), *Folgerø et al. v Norway*, No. 15472/02, §§ 54, 84; ECtHR, 18/3/2011 (Grand Chamber), *Lautsi v Italy*, No. 30814/06, § 59.

[4] Cf. G. Ress, "The Duty to Protect and to Ensure Human Rights under European Convention on Human Rights," in E. Klein (ed.), The Duty to Protect and to Ensure Human Rights, Berlin: Berlin Verlag Arno Spitz GmbH 2000, 165 et seq.

[5] ECtHR, 19/2/1989 (Grand Chamber), *Guerra a.o. v Italy*, No. 14967/89, § 60.

ECHR. At the very beginning of the Convention, an Article obliges member states to "secure to everyone within their jurisdiction the rights and freedoms" defined in the Convention. It is an important step in human rights history that there is no idea of limiting the scope to the nationals of a particular state and that the legal basis for the obligation is not a national one or a constitutional one but of an international treaty.

Other concrete rights have been extended by the case law to positive obligations, some with a quite solid basis already in the text. Article 2 of the Convention is the most prominent example, not only because of its fundamental significance but also because of its wording. Its first sentence reads: "Everyone's right to life shall be protected by law." In the way the right to life is formulated in the first sentence of Article 2 (1), it imposes upon the national authorities an obligation to protect every human life provided by law. Thus, the state is obliged to protect the lives of individuals against the acts of third parties (so-called positive obligations) as well as against interferences by the state itself. The state may also, to a certain extent, be obliged to safeguard the lives of those within its jurisdiction from natural hazards, negative environmental conditions, or other external circumstances. Although in fulfilling these obligations the States are granted a margin of appreciation, an effective protection of life is requested. The principle of effectiveness determines the nature and degree of the obligation.

Some examples show the quality of the effectiveness of the European approach. The first essential part of the protection of life is the state's obligation to implement a general ban of killing.[6] The Convention does not as such enjoin whether a provision of a criminal-law remedy or a remedy in the civil courts is necessary for compliance with the positive obligation to ban killing. A list of acts of killings that must be prosecuted by the state cannot be established from Article 2.[7] The margin of appreciation of a state is limited by the principle of effectiveness and the principle of

[6] C. Grabenwarter, K. Pabel, Europäische Menschenrechtskonvention, 5th ed., Munich: Verlag C. H. Beck, 2012, § 20, 17 with further references.
[7] ECtHR, 17/1/2002 (GC), *Calvelli a. Ciglio v Italy*, No. 32967/96, § 51.

proportionality.[8] In cases of medical negligence causing the death of the patient, the obligation may, for instance, also be satisfied if the legal system affords victims a remedy in the civil courts, enabling any liability of the doctors concerned and any appropriate civil redress to be established. The court found that Article 2 does not necessarily require a criminal-law remedy.[9]

However, there are limits to the obligation, especially with a view to unborn life and to the end of life. In the case of the death of a fetus against the will of the mother due to the negligence of a doctor, the court held that Article 2 did not require that the state provides for a criminal-law remedy; therefore no violation of the right to life was found in the case law.[10] An obligation to prohibit euthanasia or assisted suicide by law does not follow from Article 2.[11] Given the lack of uniform regulation in the laws of the contracting states and the existing public controversy, the court found no European consensus, and therefore the permissibility of national pro-euthanasia laws cannot be presumed. This was also established in the *Pretty* case, which attracted international public attention. The applicant – a woman who was suffering from a certain type of neuropathy which causes physical incapacity – was unable to commit suicide herself and therefore applied for permission for lawful euthanasia. Without the possibility of ending her life she faced the prospect of a distressed death. The court had to examine a possible infringement of Articles 2, 3, 8, 9, and 14 of the Convention. It concluded that no positive obligation arises under the Convention to require the respondent state either to give an undertaking not to prosecute the husband if he assisted the applicant to commit suicide or to provide a lawful opportunity for any other form of assisted suicide. Accordingly, the court did not find a violation of any provision.[12]

8 ECtHR, 4/5/2001, *Jordan v United Kingdom*, No. 24746/94, § 104.

9 ECtHR, 17/1/2002 (GC), *Calvelli a. Ciglio v Italy*, No. 32967/96, § 51.

10 ECtHR, 8/7/2004 (GC), *Vo v France*, No. 53924/00, §§ 93 et seq.

11 The Court expressly left the question open: ECtHR, 29/4/2002, *Pretty v United Kingdom*, No. 2346/02, § 41.

12 ECtHR, 29/4/2002, *Pretty v United Kingdom*, No. 2346/02, §§ 42, 56, 78, 83, 90; Morris, "Assisted Suicide under the European Convention on Human Rights: a Critique," *Eur. Human Rights Law Rev.*, 2003, 65 et seq. at 68.

These examples show that international protection has its limits. State constitutions may go further in their level of protection and they often do, especially in the context of protection of life – at both ends of life. The Basic Law of Germany, drafted and enacted against the background of the Nazi regime, is perhaps the most important example for this observation. And it leads as back to the general issue of this chapter, that is, the relation between international human rights law and the state with its national (constitutional) law. International human rights law and national fundamental rights must complement each other; the international level is the ultimate guarantor, especially in cases when national mechanisms fail. However, international human rights protection does not substitute the national system of protection. In particular, international guarantees are not deemed to limit the state sovereignty, or as Benedict puts it: "The action of the international community and its institutions, provided that it respects the principles undergirding the international order, should never be interpreted as an unwarranted imposition or a limitation of sovereignty. On the contrary, it is indifference or failure to intervene that do the real damage."

FREEDOM OF RELIGION IN A DEMOCRATIC STATE

Freedom of religion in a European context is constructed on the basis of and necessarily linked with the concept of a democratic constitution. A democratic constitution of European style contains the preconditions for true and effective exercise of the human right of freedom of religion.

While the ECHR does not preclude the existence of a state church,[13] it is common ground today that even if a legal order provides for a state church, the freedom to change one's religion or faith and the rights of those of different faith have to be assured. The idea behind this position is the separation of state and church. This separation is the precondition, not an impediment or obstacle

[13] Grabenwarter, Pabel, op.cit. n. 5, § 22 para. 96 with further references.

for effective freedom in the field of human rights. Benedict XVI was aware of this relation and expressed it on the occasion of his meeting with the members of the General Assembly of the United Nations. While he proceeds from the vision of unity of the person he argues in favor of clearly distinguishing "between the dimension of the citizen and that of the believer". He expressly acknowledges the activity of the United Nations that has ensured that public debate gives space to viewpoints inspired by a religious vision in all its dimensions, including ritual, worship, education, dissemination of information, and the freedom to profess and choose religion.

In the near future, freedom of religion will need more and more protection also in Europe in dimensions that might have been undisputed in the past. Believers should not have to suppress their faith in order to be active citizens – again a wording Benedict used in his UN speech. And: "It should never be necessary to deny God in order to enjoy one's rights. The rights associated with religion are all the more in need of protection if they are considered to clash with a prevailing secular ideology or with majority religious positions of an exclusive nature. The full guarantee of religious liberty cannot be limited to the free exercise of worship, but has to give due consideration to the public dimension of religion, and hence to the possibility of believers playing their part in building the social order."

This is an important reminder and a program at the same time. It leads us to think that the task of human rights lawyers is to consider that freedom of religion is not a "single issue" guarantee. It rather unifies various dimensions that are important all together in order to provide for an effective protection of this fundamental right.

DIMENSIONS OF THE FREEDOM OF RELIGION

In his speech to the UN Benedict XVI does not only recall the necessity of distinction between the citizen and the believer. He also refers to the activity of the United Nations that has ensured a public debate that "gives space to viewpoints inspired by a religious vision in all its dimensions, including ritual, worship, education, dissemination of information and the freedom to profess and choose religion."

In fact, as a consequence of various activities of international organizations in the field of human rights at different levels, we have a much more precise understanding of the concept of religion and its manifold dimensions, including freedom of religion, than we had twenty years ago. Again the Strasbourg Court in its case law on Article 9 of the Convention has contributed considerably to this positive development. While it refrained from defining the concept of "religion" (1 as follows), it gave clear indications on the scope of the fundamental right in the fields of manifestation (2 through 5), that is, the "negative freedom," the right to change a religion and finally the right of religious communities "collective dimension".

1. *No definition of "religion."* Article 9 protects the freedom of religion and belief. A generally accepted definition of religion can be found neither in the national legal orders of the Member States nor in the ECHR itself.[14] However, it is safe to assume that a religion includes a denomination, guidelines on how to live, and a cult.[15] At the same time the court made it clear that the propaganda for Islamic *political* organizations does not constitute an expression of a religious belief.[16]

Article 9 is not restricted to common religions. It protects all religions that are "identifiable," not only "common" or "traditional" religions. However, an exact definition of religion in the meaning of Article 9 is not required, since beliefs are protected to the same extent. Irreligious and nonreligious acts are also protected by Article 9, as long as they are an expression of a certain belief.

In its constant case law the court does not find itself responsible to decide *in abstracto* whether or not a body of beliefs and related practices may be considered to be a "religion" within the meaning of Article 9 of the Convention. In the absence of a European

[14] Evans, "Freedom of Religion under the European Convention on Human Rights," 2001, 51 et seq.

[15] M.N. Shaw, "Freedom of Thought, Conscience and Religion," in R.St.J. Macdonald, F.Matscher, and H. Petzold (eds.), The European System for the Protection of Human Rights Dordrecht: M. Nijhoff, 1993, 445 seq. at 448.

[16] ECtHR, 18/01/2001, *Zaoui v Switzerland*, No. 41615/98.

consensus on the religious nature of Scientology teachings, and being sensitive to the subsidiary nature of its role, the court considered that it must rely on the position of the domestic authorities in the matter and determine the applicability of Article 9 of the Convention accordingly.[17] On the other hand there is no doubt that religions that are not formally registered as such in all member states form a religion within the meaning of Article 9.

2. *Freedom to manifest.* Article 9 not only conveys the freedom to have a religion or belief as a matter of individual conscience (*forum internum*),[18] but it also implies, *inter alia*, the freedom to "manifest [one's] religion." Bearing witness in words and deeds is bound up with the existence of religious convictions (*forum externum*).[19] According to Article 9, freedom to manifest one's religion is not only exercisable in community with others, "in public" and within the circle of those whose faith one shares, but can also be asserted "alone" and "in private."[20] Those who choose to exercise the freedom to manifest their religion cannot reasonably expect to be exempt from all criticism. However, the manner in which religious beliefs and doctrines are opposed or denied is a matter which may engage the responsibility of the state, notably its responsibility to ensure the peaceful enjoyment of the right guaranteed under Article 9 to the holders of those beliefs and doctrines.[21]

The right to manifest one's religion or belief can be exercised in worship, teaching, practice and observance. This list is not exhaustive. It is left to the individual to decide the form in which his or her belief should be exercised. The two alternatives mentioned in Article 9 to manifest one's religion, that is, either alone or in community with others, can not be considered as being mutually exclusive, or as leaving a choice to the authorities, but only as recognizing that

[17] ECtHR, 1/10/2009, *Kimlya v Russia*, No. 76836/01, §§ 79 et seq.

[18] ECtHR, 25/5/1993, *Kokkinakis v Greece*, No. 14307/88, § 31; ECtHR, 1/7/1997, *Kalaç v Turkey*, No. 20704/92, § 27.

[19] ECtHR, 25/5/1993, *Kokkinakis v Greece*, No. 14307/88, § 31.

[20] ECtHR, 25/5/1993, *Kokkinakis v Greece*, No. 14307/88, § 31; ECtHR, 1/7/1997, *Kalaç v Turkey*, No. 20704/92, § 27.

[21] ECtHR, 20/9/1994, *Otto Preminger Institut v Austria*, No. 13470/87, § 47.

religion may be practiced in either form.[22] In the context of Article 9 "teaching" is not to be understood as academic education, which is protected by Article 2 of Protocol No. 1. It is to be understood as the general communication of religious knowledge. Proselytizing of adults as well as children is therefore also protected by Article 9. To manifest one's religion or belief in "observance", on the one hand, refers to ritual customs. Processions or pilgrimages are examples of this being traditional forms of manifesting one's religion, just like the bell-ringing or the muezzin's call. On the other hand, certain acts of a daily routine, such as a particular dress code, a special way to wear one's hair or beard,[23] or observing certain dietary rules, are protected.[24] The court also considers ritual slaughtering, during which the animals are not stunned, to be a religious ritual falling in the scope of Article 9.[25]

The term "practice" as employed in Article 9 (1) does not cover each act that is motivated or influenced by a religion or belief. In fact, the act is required to express the belief concerned.[26] An act that is not customary in the religious community at question cannot be considered as a manifestation of one's beliefs in observance or practice.[27] A general right to refuse to comply with certain legal obligations

[22] Shaw, "Freedom of Thought," 450; EComHR, 12/3/1981, *X. v United Kingdom*, No. 8160/78.

[23] ECtHR, 10/11/2005 (GC), *Leyla Şahin v Turkey*, No. 44774/98, § 78; Burgorgue-Larsen/Dubout, "Le port du voile à l'université. Libres propos sur l'arrêt de la grande chambre Leyla Şahin c. Turquie de 10 Novembre 2005," RTDH 66/2006, 183 et seq.; see already ECtHR, 15/2/2001, *Dahlab v Switzerland*, No. 42393/98; ECtHR, 23/2/2010, *Ahmet Arslan et al. v Turkey*, No. 41135/98, § 35.

[24] ECtHR, 7/12/2010, *Jakóbsky v Poland*, No. 18429/06, § 45.

[25] ECtHR, 27/6/2000, *Cha'are Shalom Ve Tsedek v France*, No. 27417/95, §§ 77 et seq.; thereto Flauss, "Observations, Abattage rituel et liberté de religion: le défini de la protection des minorités au sein des communautés religieuses," RTDH 2001, 195 et seq.

[26] EComHR, 12/10/1978, *Arrowsmith v United Kingdom*, No. 7050/75, § 71; p. 5; EComHR, 15/12/1983, *C. v GBR*, No. 10358/83; EComHR, *V. v Netherlands*, No. 10678/83.

[27] EComHR, 6/12/1983, *D. v France*, No. 10180/82: refusal of a Jewish believer to hand a letter of repudiation to his ex-wife, which would enable her to remarry while making it impossible for him to remarry his divorced wife.

relying on religious or ideological commandments cannot be derived from Article 9.[28] Therefore, neither the noncompliance with working hours,[29] nor the refusal to pay taxes, falls within the scope of Article 9.

3. *"Negative" freedom.* The freedom to practice a religion entails the freedom not to practice a religion ("negative freedom").[30] The state must not enforce the practice of religious rituals or the integration in a religious community.[31] The freedom not to hold religious beliefs and not to practice a religion includes the right not to be compelled to swear allegiance to a particular religion.[32] Furthermore, there is no obligation to attend religious events and education. In consequence, an exemption from religious education in school must be possible.[33] According to the court's case law, the negative freedom of religion also includes the right not to be obliged to reveal one's confession or conviction or to give information from which the confession or conviction can be deduced.[34] The freedom of religion does not guarantee a right not to be confronted with religious symbols or contents. This is true even for state schools.[35]
4. *Right to change one's religion or belief.* From a universal perspective, perhaps the most interesting issue in the text is the freedom to change a religion. The right to change one's religion or belief

[28] ECtHR, 2/10/2001, *Pichon and Sajous v France*, No. 49853/99: a pharmacist cannot rely on Article 9 to refuse to sell the birth control pill.

[29] ECtHR, 13/4/2006, *Kosteski v Macedonia*, No. 55170/00, §§ 38 et seq.; EComHR, 3/12/1996, *Konttinen v Finland*, No. 24949/94.

[30] ECtHR, 18/2/1999, *Buscarini v San Marino*, No. 24645/94, § 34.

[31] The court considered the liability to pay church taxes of a person who was not a member of the religious community to be a violation of Article 1 Protocol No. 1: ECtHR, 3/10/1990, *Darby v Sweden*, No. 11581/85, § 33.

[32] ECtHR, 18/2/1999, *Buscarini v San Marino*, No. 24645/94, § 34.

[33] From the perspective of the parental rights: ECtHR, 9/10/2007, *Zengin v Turkey*, No. 1448/04, § 76.

[34] ECtHR, 21/2/2008, *Alexandridis v Greece*, No. 19516/06, § 38; ECtHR, 15/6/2010, *Grzelak v Poland*, 7710/02, § 87; ECtHR, 3/6/2010, *Dimitras v Greece*, No. 42837/06 et al, § 78; ECtHR, 3/11/2011, *Dimitras (No. 2) v Greece*, No. 34207/08 et al, § 28.

[35] Under the head of right to education ECtHR, 18/3/2011 (GC), *Lautsi v Italy*, No. 30814/06, §§ 63 et seq.

is also explicitly enshrined in Article 9 (1). It entails the right to leave a religious denomination[36] without having to join another one. Where the religious community does not know a possibility to leave, the state is obliged to introduce sufficient safeguards to ensure the individual's freedom of religion.[37] It is worth mentioning that this dimension was one of the most disputed in the process of drafting the Universal Declaration. At first, in the committee, Muslim representatives were against such a right with reference to their religion. However, in the assembly the head of delegation made a clear statement in favor of this dimension – and it was voted for in the end.[38]

5. *Collective dimension.* Article 9 protects the religious communities' right to found themselves and the ability to establish a legal entity,[39] as well as their right to an autonomous existence, which ensures that they can function free from arbitrary State intervention in their organization ("collective dimension").[40] In the case law this is referred to as the "autonomous existence of religious communities," which is at the very heart of the protection afforded by Article 9.[41] As a general rule, the member states have to refrain from interfering with internal affairs of the churches and religious communities. The determination of the content of certain

36 EComHR, 4/12/1984, *Gottesmann v Switzerland*, No. 10616/83: a church tax does not violate Article 9 if a possibility to leave the church is given, regarding the compatibility of the German system of church taxes with the convention in general, see ECtHR, 17/2/2011, *Wasmuth v Germany*, No. 12884/03, §§ 50 et seq.

37 EComHR, 14/5/1984, *E. and G.R. v Austria*, No. 9781/82, 45; EComHR, 4/12/1984, *Gottesmann v Switzerland*, No. 10616/83.

38 Roosevelt, "Writing the Universal Declaration of Human Rights," 43.

39 ECtHR, 13/12/2001, *Metropolitan Church of Bessarabia et al. v Moldova*, No. 45701/99, §§ 105 et seq.; ECtHR, 5/10/2006, *The Moscow Branch of the Salvation Army v Russia*, No. 72881/01, § 71.

40 ECtHR, 26/10/2006, *Hasan and Chaush v Bulgaria*, No. 30985/96, § 62; ECtHR, 13/12/2001, *Metropolitan Church of Bessarabia et al. v Moldova*, No. 45701/99, § 115; ECtHR, 22/1/2009, *Holy Synod of the Bulgarian Orthodox Church et al. v Bulgaria*, No. 412/03 et al, § 103.

41 For example: ECtHR, 10/6/2010, *Jehova's Witnesses of Moscow v Russia*, No. 302/02, § 99.

religious beliefs and the means used to practice those beliefs are examples of such internal affairs, just like the internal organization of the community or the appointment of the religious leader.[42] Furthermore, under certain circumstances specific requirements for ecclesiastic employees can be part of this autonomy.[43] Also, the exemption from certain provisions governing the employment of aliens granted to specific representatives of religious societies comes within the scope of Article 9, where such privileges are intended to ensure the proper functioning of religious groups.[44]

CONCLUSION

Human rights protection and, in particular, the protection of freedom of religion are not an end in themselves. As the preambles of the Declaration of Human Rights and of later conventions in the field, among them most prominently the ECHR, make clear, all these catalogues constitute a "common standard" that is precondition and basis for further reaching goals, such as peace and justice. Today, a democratic state without the freedom of religion is unthinkable. Defending democracies against attempts to destroy them means to defend human rights and free speech and to propagate respect for private law, right to life, human dignity – and the freedom of religion. The responsibility lies above all in the hands of the state and its institutions. If they fail, international instruments such as the ECHR

[42] ECtHR, 26/10/2006, *Hasan and Chaush v Bulgaria*, No. 30985/96, § 78; ECtHR, 18/10/2002, *Agga v Greece*, No. 50776/99 et al, §§ 56 et seq; ECtHR, 16/12/2004, *Supreme Holy Council of the Muslim Community v Bulgaria*, No. 39023/97, §§ 81 et seq; ECtHR, 22/1/2009, *Holy Synod of the Bulgarian Orthodox Church et al. v Bulgaria*, No. 412/03 et al, § 103; ECtHR, 15/9/2009, *Mirojubovs et al. v Latvia*, No. 798/05, § 77.

[43] ECtHR, 23/9/2010, *Obst v Germany*, No. 425/03, § 49; ECtHR, 23/9/2010, *Schüth v Germany*, No. 1620/03, §69; ECtHR, 3/2/2001, *Siebenhaar v Germany*, No. 18136/02, § 41.

[44] ECtHR, 25/9/2012, *Jehovas Zeugen in Österreich v. Austria*, No. 27540/05, § 31.

are called to work as "emergency" tools until the state has regained its ability to ensure the rights at national level.

The "safety net" is provided by the international community, more precisely by the member states of the United Nations, in Europe by those being members of the Council of Europe. In the field of freedom of religion another safety net exists, which has been established by the various religions, at the universal level, at the regional level, and at the national level – by dialogue. I shall conclude by quoting Benedict XVI once more:

"Dialogue should be recognized as the means by which the various components of society can articulate their point of view and build consensus around the truth concerning particular values or goals. It pertains to the nature of religions, freely practised, that they can autonomously conduct a dialogue of thought and life. If at this level, too, the religious sphere is kept separate from political action, then great benefits ensue for individuals and communities. On the other hand, the United Nations can count on the results of dialogue between religions, and can draw fruit from the willingness of believers to place their experiences at the service of the common good. Their task is to propose a vision of faith not in terms of intolerance, discrimination and conflict, but in terms of complete respect for truth, coexistence, rights, and reconciliation."

11 BENEDICT'S LEGACY

Human Rights, Human Dignity, and the Possibility of Dialogue

Christopher McCrudden

The contributors to this volume have been asked, in what surely was an inspired moment, to reflect on several of the major speeches that Pope Benedict XVI delivered over the course of his pontificate, including those delivered in Westminster Hall, at Regensburg, to the United Nations, at the Collège des Bernardins, and to the Bundestag. We were asked to contribute a personal reaction to the Pope's ideas about law and justice. Little did we know that our reflections would take place in the transition from Pope Benedict to Pope Francis! My reflections therefore, unsurprisingly, look partly to the future, and to the legacy of Benedict,[1] as much as to the past. I shall focus on the understanding of human rights and human dignity on which Benedict's speeches appear to me to be based.[2]

* * *

It is evident that there are major tensions between some aspects of secular human rights discourse and the Catholic Church.[3] The period

[1] I shall use this way of describing the former Pope rather than the more formal Pope Emeritus Benedict XVI, I hope without offense. I am most grateful to James Hanvey SJ and Timothy Radcliffe OP for comments on my earlier version.

[2] I have drawn extensively on papers delivered to an interdisciplinary conference on human dignity, subsequently published in Christopher McCrudden, ed., *Understanding Human Dignity* (British Academy/Oxford University Press, 2013), without further attribution. My introduction to the collection is available at http://ssrn.com/abstract=2218788.

[3] I have explored these tensions elsewhere; see Christopher McCrudden, "Legal and Roman Catholic Conceptions of Human Rights: Convergence, Divergence, and Dialogue?," Oxford Journal of Law and Religion, 1, 1, 2012,

of rapprochement between the two, evident during the papacy of John XXIII (reflected by *Pacem in Terris)*, and the papacy of John Paul II (regarding the need for freedom and democracy in central and eastern Europe), now seems under severe challenge. The Church's approach to the role of women, issues of sexual orientation, contraception, abortion, genetic manipulation, and physician-assisted suicide, to name but a few current issues, increasingly appear to conflict with emerging human rights norms. Given that, as Benedict said at the United Nations, "[h]uman rights are increasingly being presented as the common language and the ethical substratum of international relations,"[4] to be seen to be out of sympathy with secular human rights discourse is not a comfortable position to be in. The scandals that have beset the Church, from the failure to address the abuse of children, to financial irregularities in the conduct of the affairs of the Holy See, have also risked calling the Church's credibility into question, even in those areas where there is a close working relationship between the Church and human rights activists, such as in the elaboration and protection of socio-economic rights, and the rights of children.

One of the strengths of the Church has been the extent to which it engages with the world on the basis of reason, and one of the defining characteristics of the speeches that we have been invited to discuss is Benedict's evident desire to reason with the secular world, including the human rights community. A recurring theme of the speeches was the desire to have a genuine "dialogue," as he put it, "between faith and reason." The issue I consider in these brief reflections is whether such a dialogue is indeed possible. I want to consider the possibility that the preconditions that Pope Benedict appeared to set for such a dialogue may mean that the desired engagement is not feasible.

* * *

We can begin with the basics. What did Benedict consider human rights to be? We shall see that this is a vexed question, but some things

185–201; Christopher McCrudden, "Catholicism, Human Rights and the Public Sphere," International Journal of Public Theology, 5, 2011, 331–351.

4 Pope Benedict XVI, Meeting with the Members of the General Assembly of the United Nations Organization, New York, April 18, 2008.

are clear. Benedict, for example, did not adopt a purely descriptive approach to identifying human rights. A descriptive approach attempts to answer the question by setting out, for example, how the term has come to be used historically, and how it may have changed over time. Another type of descriptive approach is that which lawyers often adopt. We are prone to say that human rights are those rights designated as such by law, whether domestic law or international law.

Benedict challenged such descriptive approaches, and adopted a more explicitly normative approach to the idea of human rights. By this, I mean that he reasoned through to the position that a particular claim is appropriately considered to be a human rights claim from a moral or ethical position. In the United Nations speech, he made this explicit. "Human rights," he said, "must be respected as an expression of justice, and not merely because they are enforceable through the will of the legislators."[5] Rights are not "exclusively" or "purely" the creation of law.

Nor should rights be subject to the whim of shifting majorities. Whatever the benefits of democracy, Benedict made clear, majoritarian preferences should not be seen alone as the basis for human rights standards. Perhaps not surprisingly, it was in the Bundestag address that we hear this most clearly articulated. "For most of the matters that need to be regulated by law, the support of the majority can serve as a sufficient criterion."[6] But democracy has important limits, and one of those limits is in the area of human rights. It is "evident that for the fundamental issues of law, in which the dignity of man and of humanity is at stake, the majority principle is not enough."[7]

So, if human rights are not based "exclusively" in law, and they are not determined by the principle of majority rule, on what exactly are

[5] Pope Benedict XVI, Meeting with the Members of the General Assembly of the United Nations Organization, New York, April 18, 2008.

[6] Pope Benedict XVI, Visit to the Bundestag, Reichstag Building, Berlin, September 22, 2011.

[7] Pope Benedict XVI, Visit to the Bundestag, Reichstag Building, Berlin, September 22, 2011.

they based? Recently political philosophers have taken to distinguishing between three broad, normatively based, theories of human rights: naturalistic theories, agreement-based theories, and political theories. The normative position Benedict adopted was, essentially, naturalistic. We have seen already that political agreement or societal consensus did not impress him as the basis of human rights, but at the United Nations he was even clearer: "it is a mistake," he said, speaking of human rights, "to fall back on a pragmatic approach, limited to determining 'common ground,' minimal in content and weak in its effect."[8] Nor did he base his human rights theory on the political role that human rights play; he does not appear, in Charles Beitz's words, to consider human rights to be simply "political doctrine constructed to play a certain role in global political life."[9]

The adoption of his favored naturalistic approach involved identifying a particular, preexisting norm or value from which human rights are derived, and which therefore delimits their scope and application. For Benedict, it is clear that human rights are derived from the idea of "human dignity."[10] The protection of human dignity is, he said on another occasion, "the first and last of the fundamental rights" and should be "the criterion that inspires and directs all ... efforts."[11] At the United Nations, this stance was made crystal clear. When speaking to the United Nations, he referred to human dignity as an "objective foundation of the values inspiring and governing the international order," including human rights.[12] The centrality of human dignity was emphasized by the wide range of terms he used to

[8] Pope Benedict XVI, Meeting with the Members of the General Assembly of the United Nations Organization, New York, April 18, 2008.

[9] Charles Beitz, The Idea of Human Rights (Oxford: Oxford University Press, 2009), 49.

[10] See, in general, David G Kirchhoffer, "Benedict XVI, Human Dignity, and Absolute Moral Norms," New Blackfriars, 91, 1035, 2009, 586–608.

[11] Message to Mr. Jacques Diouf, Director General of FAO on the occasion of World Food Day 2005 (October 12, 2005), quoted in Kirchhoffer, "Benedict XVI, Human Dignity, and Absolute Moral Norms," 589.

[12] Pope Benedict XVI, Meeting with the Members of the General Assembly of the United Nations Organization, New York, April 18, 2008.

describe its moral status. He described it on several occasions as fundamental, inalienable, inherent, innate, and essential.[13]

Adopting a naturalistic approach did not take Benedict outside the mainstream of political philosophers who have engaged with human rights theory. Indeed, on one reading, a naturalistic theory is the traditional or orthodox approach within secular political philosophy. There is, therefore, at least on this basis, significant ground for engagement with secular human rights philosophy. The debates between those adopting naturalistic approaches and others are not conflicts between the Church on the one hand, and political philosophers on the other, but rather debates within political philosophy, to which the Church can, and should, contribute.

Naturalistic approaches may be either metaphysical or nonmetaphysical. Taking the example of human dignity, some argue that the concept of dignity depends on a metaphysical understanding of the human in relation to a deity. But there are also nonmetaphysical understandings of "human dignity" that are nevertheless naturalistic, where the dignity of the person is seen to derive from an understanding of what it means to be human, based on our observations of human experience. Proponents of natural law theories of human rights argue that such theories are of this type.

Benedict's theory of human rights was both metaphysical and nonmetaphysical. It was metaphysical in emphasizing that human persons are made in the image of God. This is a constant theme: at Westminster, he referred to the "overriding concern to safeguard the unique dignity of every human person, created in the image and likeness of God."[14] His human rights theory, based on human dignity, was also nonmetaphysical, emphasizing that human dignity is based on an anthropological understanding of what it is to be human and that this is derived from human reasoning, reflecting on experience. At the Bundestag, he stressed the importance of reason and nature. "Christian theologians," he said, "aligned themselves . . . on the

[13] See Kirchhoffer, "Benedict XVI, Human Dignity, and Absolute Moral Norms," 591, where supporting references are given.

[14] Pope Benedict XVI, Meeting with the representatives of British society, Westminster Hall, Westminster, September 17, 2010.

side of philosophy, and ... acknowledged reason and nature in their interrelation as the universally valid source of law."[15] He returned to this theme even more explicitly at Westminster: "The Catholic tradition maintains that the objective norms governing right action are accessible to reason, prescinding from [i.e., leaving out of consideration] the content of revelation."[16] There is no conflict between the metaphysical and nonmetaphysical approaches because "not to act in accordance with reason is contrary to God's nature"[17] and so being created in the image of God requires the exercise of reason.

Human dignity, then, is an intrinsically valuable status possessed by all human beings simply in virtue of their humanity, and discoverable by ordinary moral reasoning or through natural reason. Human rights concern those rights derived from human dignity. This approach has several significant implications, which we shall come to in due course. One implication is that it emphasizes, and supports, the universality of human rights, because such rights are grounded in the dignity of the human person, which is itself a universal idea. The rights recognized and expounded in the Universal Declaration of Human Rights, he insisted, "apply to everyone by virtue of the common origin of the person.... They are based on the natural law inscribed on human hearts and present in different cultures and civilizations.... This great variety of viewpoints must not be allowed to obscure the fact that not only rights are universal, but so too is the human person, the subject of those rights."[18] Not to base human rights on the secure foundations of the human person was to risk relativism and the destruction of the universality of human rights: "Removing human rights from this context would mean restricting their range and yielding to a relativistic conception, according

[15] Pope Benedict XVI, Visit to the Bundestag, Reichstag Building, Berlin, September 22, 2011.

[16] Pope Benedict XVI, Meeting with the representatives of British society, Westminster Hall, Westminster, September 17, 2010.

[17] Pope Benedict XVI, Meeting with the representatives of science, Aula Magna of the University of Regensburg, Regensburg, September 12, 2006.

[18] Pope Benedict XVI, Meeting with the Members of the General Assembly of the United Nations Organization, New York, April 18, 2008.

to which the meaning and interpretation of rights could vary and their universality would be denied in the name of different cultural, political, social and even religious outlooks."[19]

⋆ ⋆ ⋆

Benedict's understanding of human rights as set out in his speeches demonstrates several key areas of agreement with a significant proportion of secular human rights discourse: the centrality of human dignity, the universality of human rights, the need for a normative foundation for human rights, and the possibility of a nonmetaphysical justification for this normative foundation. Profoundly important though these areas of agreement are, the puzzle is why, given the areas of overlapping consensus, there appears now to be greater distance than at any time since 1948 between the Church and secular human rights discourse in the application and understanding of each of these areas of apparent agreement. Given this disagreement, the need for a dialogue is all the more important. From what I have said so far, it seems possible to conduct such a dialogue both on the basis of the importance of reason in addressing problems, and (perhaps particularly) on the basis of the centrality of human dignity to both the social teaching of the Church, and (increasingly) the normative foundations of secular human rights.[20]

It was a constant theme in the Pope's speeches that dialogue was seen as positive. The Pope referred, approvingly, at the Collège des Bernardins, to "dialogue between Christian Wisdom and the cultural, intellectual, and artistic currents of contemporary society."[21] At the United Nations, he acknowledged that "[d]ialogue should be recognized as the means by which the various components of society can articulate their point of view and build consensus around the truth

[19] Pope Benedict XVI, Meeting with the Members of the General Assembly of the United Nations Organization, New York, April 18, 2008.

[20] Christopher McCrudden, "Human Dignity and Judicial Interpretation of Human Rights," European Journal of International Law, 19, 4, 2008, 655–724.

[21] Pope Benedict XVI, Meeting with Representatives from the World of Culture, Collège des Bernardins, Paris, September 12, 2008.

concerning particular values or goals."[22] At Regensburg he encouraged the "wide-ranging dialogue of sciences,"[23] a dialogue which he wanted theology to join. Above all, at Westminster Hall, he emphasised the need for dialogue as his central message. "[T]he world of reason and the world of faith – the world of secular rationality and the world of religious belief – need one another and should not be afraid to enter into a profound and ongoing dialogue, for the good of our civilization."[24] His closing lines, indeed, return to this theme: "I would invite all of you, therefore, within your respective spheres of influence, to seek ways of promoting and encouraging dialogue between faith and reason at every level of national life."[25]

It is clear that Benedict considers that there is a fundamental contribution that religion can bring to public reason. The relationship between faith and reason that he called for is not without considerable subtlety. He clearly does not envisage the Church as simply representing "faith," and secular society representing "reason." Dialogue is essential for Benedict partly because of the sheer complexity of many of the issues faced by humanity. In an important statement to the Bundestag, Benedict appears to acknowledge the difficulty of moving from an understanding of human rights based on the fundamental dignity of the human person to the identification of the precise practical implications of this insight. He asks, straightforwardly, "how do we recognize what is right?,"[26] and answers thoughtfully and modestly that "in terms of the underlying anthropological issues, what is right and may be given the force of law is in no way simply self-evident today. The question of how to recognize what is truly right and thus to serve justice when framing laws has never been

[22] Pope Benedict XVI, Meeting with the Members of the General Assembly of the United Nations Organization, New York, April 18, 2008.

[23] Pope Benedict XVI, Meeting with the representatives of science, Aula Magna of the University of Regensburg, Regensburg, September 12, 2006.

[24] Pope Benedict XVI, Meeting with the representatives of British society, Westminster Hall, Westminster, September 17, 2010.

[25] Id.

[26] Pope Benedict XVI, Visit to the Bundestag, Reichstag Building, Berlin, September 22, 2011.

simple, and today in view of the vast extent of our knowledge and our capacity, it has become still harder."[27] When we read this together with his Westminster speech, the role of the Church he envisaged does not appear to be one of prescribing detailed solutions to fiendishly difficult practical problems, but one of helping people to orient their decisions correctly. "[T]he role of religion in political debate," he says, "is not so much to supply ... norms, as if they could not be known by non-believers – still less to propose concrete political solutions, which would lie altogether outside the competence of religion – but rather to help purify and shed light upon the application of reason to the discovery of objective moral principles."[28]

* * *

However, is a "profound and ongoing dialogue" possible with the Church on human rights? Despite the evident desire for such a dialogue, and the significant degree of overlapping consensus, Benedict's speeches may be seen as offering a dialogue with secular human rights only on terms that may mean that no genuine dialogue is possible, except with others of faith, excluding secular nonbelievers. Why might this be the case?

We saw the importance that Benedict attached to the difficulty of deciding what is right, and how the Church should not rush to "concrete political solutions." Having apparently freed us to exercise our reason, however, we are then confronted with a set of very specific norms that Benedict found to be inherent in natural law, objectively valid, and, as David Kirchhoffer observes, "more importantly, non-negotiable."[29] Part of the problem the Church faces in engaging in a dialogue with secular human rights is that these specific dogmatic norms appear to be statements of objective truth which are not open to the type of dialogue that appears to be offered elsewhere. Experience teaches us that it is when the Church moves from

27 Id.

28 Pope Benedict XVI, Meeting with the representatives of British society, Westminster Hall, Westminster, September 17, 2010.

29 Kirchhoffer, "Benedict XVI, Human Dignity, and Absolute Moral Norms," 597

"purifying and shedding light on the application of reason to the discovery of objective moral principles" to "proposing concrete political solutions," that it is most likely to run up against competing secular human rights approaches.

One example must suffice to illustrate the general point, involving the profoundly tragic position that women contemplating abortions face. In a speech in January 2013, he noted "with dismay" how in various countries, "even those of Christian tradition," "efforts are made to introduce or expand legislation which decriminalizes abortion."[30] The reason for this dismay, he said, is because direct abortion is "gravely contrary to the moral law." He appeared to link this directly with a concern "lest the law unjustly alter the balance between the right to life of the mother and that of the unborn child, a right belonging equally to both."

The issue I raise here is not whether abortion is morally wrong. Assuming it is, what is the role of the state? What is troubling in Benedict's remarks was the specificity of the political function that law was expected to play in regulating abortion. There are two particularly problematic assumptions. First, the implication that state law should generally prohibit that which is "gravely contrary to the moral law" gives little or no attention to the problems such an approach generates in a pluralistic democracy where what is the morally right course of action is essentially contested. Second, the implication that the best way of balancing the right to life of the mother and that of the unborn child is by *criminalizing* abortion assumes a particular role for the criminal law. Several problems arise. If abortion is criminalized, how does this "balance" the two rights? Does it not simply prioritize the right of the unborn child over that of the mother in all circumstances? And even if the primary concern is with the right to life of the unborn child, why is criminalization necessarily the best way to achieve this aim? What if there is empirical information that shows that the destruction of unborn life is *less* likely if abortion is decriminalized? Or is the law in this area to be seen as primarily expressive

[30] Address of His Holiness Pope Benedict XVI to the Members of the Diplomatic Corps Accredited to the Holy See, January 7, 2013, emphasis added.

rather than instrumental? In short, the strong preference for criminalization of abortion, apparently in all circumstances, generates exactly the sort of "concrete political solutions," which Pope Benedict said "would lie altogether outside the competence of religion."[31]

It seems doubtful that a black and white rule that abortion should be criminalized in all circumstances encourages "the application of reason"[32] either by the legislature, or, more importantly, by the woman herself. Criminalization, rather, involves the application of state coercion on the basis of a simple rule of thumb: it precisely *prevents* the application of reason in highly complex, individual moral contexts; it substitutes brute force, applied by the state. How is the absoluteness of the norm reconcilable with the highly nuanced, complex understanding of the human that human dignity requires?

Another dimension of the possible limits on the dialogue offered lies in the somewhat limited conception of human dignity that Benedict adopted not just in the abortion context but more broadly. While it is clear that human freedom was an essential element in his understanding of human dignity, what he meant by human freedom appeared rather constrained. Benedict rejected a conception of dignity based primarily in an individualistic understanding of autonomy; he emphasized instead the web of relationships that individuals inhabit. It was essentially a conception of freedom as positive freedom, while a significant dimension of the practice of human rights emphasizes the importance of negative freedoms against the state.

At the United Nations, he adopted an understanding of freedom that incorporated the need for restrictions that recognized responsibilities as well as rights: "rules and structures that are intrinsically ordered to promote the common good," he said, "do not limit freedom."[33] Rather, "[i]n the name of freedom, there has to be a correlation between rights and duties, by which every person is called to assume responsibility for his or her choices, made as a consequence

[31] Pope Benedict XVI, Meeting with the representatives of British society, Westminster Hall, Westminster, September 17, 2010.

[32] Id.

[33] Pope Benedict XVI, Meeting with the Members of the General Assembly of the United Nations Organization, New York, April 18, 2008.

of entering into relations with others."[34] He returned to this theme at the Collège des Bernardins: "It would be a disaster," he said, "if today's European culture could only conceive freedom as absence of obligation."[35]

What is the appropriate balance to be struck between positive and negative freedom, between the individual and community, and between subjectivity and objectivity, in arriving at a rich analysis of the concept of human dignity? Too often it can appear that Benedict was only willing to see human dignity from an objective-communitarian standpoint, in part because he perceived the secular world as only conceiving it from a subjective-individualistic standpoint. In correctly identifying the overidentification of human dignity with autonomy, he risked sliding too far toward the other extreme, where interiority, negative freedom, subjectivity, and individuality were substantially driven away from an understanding of what dignity involves.

One of Benedict's specific targets also related to the threat of excessive individualism. Although not identified as such, this concerned the antiessentialist, constructivist turn that secular human rights (and, particularly, equality) discourse began to take from the 1960s. With the increasing emphasis on racial and gender equality, developing into a more general concern to enable individual identities to be valued and protected, equality discourse took on an antiessentialist and constructivist quality. By "essentialist" I mean the idea that "definitions are descriptions of the essential properties of things, and that one can evaluate attempts at definitions in terms of the falsity or truth of the descriptions given by them."[36] As Simon Blackburn explains, "[e]ssentialism is used in feminist writing of the view that females (or males) have an essential nature (e.g. nurturing and caring versus being aggressive and selfish), as opposed to differing by a

34 Id.

35 Pope Benedict XVI, Meeting with Representatives from the World of Culture, Collège des Bernardins, Paris, September 12, 2008.

36 Entry on "essentialism," in John Scott and Gordon Marshall, A Dictionary of Sociology (Oxford: Oxford University Press, 2009), www.oxfordreference.com/views/ENTRY.html?subview=Main&entry=t88.e745, accessed April 10, 2012.

variety of accidental or contingent features brought about by social forces."[37] It is this understanding that *anti*essentialism seeks to challenge, preferring to view institutions and roles as socially constructed and provisional. In particular, social identities are seen as changeable. Secular human rights discourse and, to a notable extent, human rights *law*, has significantly (but by no means uniformly) adopted an antiessentialist understanding of dignity.[38]

While this antiessentialist turn is problematic in several ways, not least in its apparent hunger to see *everything* as socially constructed, leaving no role for genetics, for example, Benedict was in danger of sliding again to the other extreme. His understanding of anthropology appears to be strikingly essentialist and anticonstructivist in its understanding of social roles. Benedict's understanding of dignity was that it refers to a particular kind of excellence that each thing has. For example, "matter is not just raw material for us to shape at will . . ., the earth has a dignity of its own and that we must follow its directives."[39] Human dignity, then, involves recognition of the particular excellence that persons have; their inherent worth as persons. In the Bundestag, following a reference to "the dignity of nature," Benedict said this: "Man too has a nature that he must respect and that he cannot manipulate at will. Man is not merely self-creating freedom. Man does not create himself. He is intellect and will, but he is also nature, and his will is rightly ordered if he respects his nature, listens to it and accepts himself for who he is, as one who did not create himself."[40]

The difficult issue here is how far what is seen as human nature, deriving from classical sources, and the conclusions that have been drawn from these for the *Magisterium*, are themselves open to revision

[37] Entry on "essentialism," in Simon Blackburn, The Oxford Dictionary of Philosophy (Oxford: Oxford University Press, 2008), www.oxfordreference.com/views/ENTRY.html?subview=Main&entry=t98.e1139, accessed April 10, 2012.

[38] Tariq Modood, "Anti-Essentialism, Multiculturalism and the 'Recognition' of Religious Groups," The Journal of Political Philosophy, 6, 1998, 378.

[39] Pope Benedict XVI, Visit to the Bundestag, Reichstag Building, Berlin, September 22, 2011.

[40] Pope Benedict XVI, Meeting with the Members of the General Assembly of the United Nations Organization, New York, April 18, 2008.

on the basis of experience, which would include scientific and social science investigation, and the day-to-day experience of the laity. We have seen earlier how Benedict regarded these questions as profoundly difficult. So, too, do many other members of the Church. There is debate within the Church particularly as to the appropriate understanding of sexual "complementarity." The result is a sharp dispute over what is required to ensure human flourishing. Catholic theologians reflect a considerably greater plurality of viewpoints concerning the role of women, and the nature of sexual orientation, than those outside (and sometimes inside) the Church appear to recognize.[41] In particular, there are different understandings of the meaning and implications of human dignity for such issues.

How the Church engages with issues of "complementarity," and of human rights generally, can be seen as an example of the difficulty it faces in reacting to aspects of modernity more generally. In his 1967 essay,[42] Bernard Lonergan contrasts two modes of thinking about meaning, those characteristic of "classical" and those characteristic of "modern" culture, with the former being ahistorical and essentialist, secure in having a clear and accepted meaning, while the latter is more historical and inductive. Catholic moral theology, born in the former, is now confronted, according to Lonergan, with the latter world of meaning. Lonergan anticipated a split in Catholic theology in which "a scattered left" develops, "captivated by now this, now that new development, exploring now this and now that new possibility," in contrast with "a solid right that is determined to live in a world that no longer exists."[43]

In the passage from which this quotation is drawn, Lonergan criticizes both the "scattered left" (as being too relativistic and

[41] See Christopher McCrudden, "Reva Siegel and the Role of Religion in Constructing the Meaning of 'Human Dignity,'" in Hanoch Dagan, Shahar Lifshitz, and Yedidia Z. Stern (eds.), Religion and the Discourse of Human Rights (Israel Democracy Institute, 2014), 175, available at http://ssrn.com/abstract=2229832.

[42] Bernard Lonergan, "Dimensions of Meaning," in Collection: Papers by Bernard Lonergan, S.J., ed. Frederick E Crowe (New York: Herder and Herder, 1967), 252. I am grateful to James Hanvey S.J. for drawing this to my attention.

[43] Lonergan, "Dimensions of Meaning," 245.

uninterested in continuity) and the "solid right" (as reactionary and living in the past). In simply describing the debate within the Catholic Church in terms of scattered left versus solid right, one may lose sight of Lonergan's insight that both positions are open to criticism. Lonergan himself, crucially, proposes that "what will count is a perhaps not numerous center, big enough to be at home in both the old and the new, painstaking enough to work out one by one the transitions to be made, strong enough to refuse half-measures and insist on complete solutions even though it has to wait." One of the critical questions that Benedict worried away at in his speeches was the extent and nature of the Church's engagement with the external world, and how far change can occur within the Church, based on this engagement. In Lonergan's terms, he appears to want to locate himself, and the Church, in the "perhaps not numerous center," but is constantly in danger of straying too much to the solid right.

If a dialogue is encouraged, with whom should it take place? We saw earlier that Benedict rightly pointed out that human rights is not "exclusively" or "purely" the creation of law. In the United Nations speech, however, he went further, arguing that

> [e]xperience shows that legality often prevails over justice when the insistence upon rights makes them appear as the exclusive result of legislative enactments or normative decisions taken by the various agencies of those in power. When presented purely in terms of legality, rights risk becoming weak propositions divorced from the ethical and rational dimension which is their foundation and their goal.[44]

On one reading, this is simply a call for human rights not to be seen as the exclusive preserve of lawyers, and (perhaps especially for lawyers) that is a necessary corrective. A more complex reading is possible, however, which is interesting, but jurisprudentially challenging. What, for example, is the message that this meant to send to judges interpreting human rights standards? If, as I suspect, the message that Benedict intended to send is that human rights should be interpreted

[44] Pope Benedict XVI, Meeting with the Members of the General Assembly of the United Nations Organization, New York, April 18, 2008.

in light of their underlying normative underpinnings, then that is relatively uncontroversial, but it opens up the complex issue of how far legal interpretation is (and should be) relatively autonomous from politics and from religious belief.

There are indications in other speeches that a more radical approach, denying the autonomy of judicial interpretation, was finding its way into Benedict's speeches before he retired. In one particularly notable criticism of the decision of the Inter-American Court of Human Rights regarding in vitro fertilization,[45] Benedict described the court as "arbitrarily" redefining "the moment of conception" and weakening "the defence of unborn life," which he regarded as a "source of concern."[46] How should we read this criticism, in particular his description of the court as having acted "arbitrarily"? This is, of course, a very significant charge to level at a court and one that I assume was not made lightly. For Benedict to attack a major respected international human rights court for acting "arbitrarily" appears to strike at the legitimacy of the court more generally.

It is now commonplace for politicians in many countries to criticize judges for the human rights decisions they make, usually for populist advantage, but the precise basis of the criticism is seldom very clear; nor is it here. Is Benedict's criticism of the court that the judges made the "wrong" decision? And, if so, was the decision wrong legally, or wrong morally? If wrong legally, then (with the deepest respect) it is unclear why Benedict considers himself qualified to make that judgement. If, as is surely more likely, he means to say that it is wrong morally, then it is unclear what he would have wanted the judges to do. Should the judges have simply ignored the legal imperatives and imposed a moral judgment? That, surely, cannot have been Benedict's intention, given the very significant challenges this poses for the rule of law, which requires judges to act according to *law*. We are rightly concerned when judges act outside the law.

[45] *Caso Artavia Murillo y otros ("Fecundación in vitro") v Costa Rica*, Decision of 28 November, 2012, Series C, No. 257 (Inter-American Court of Human Rights).

[46] Address of His Holiness Pope Benedict XVI to the Members of the Diplomatic Corps Accredited to the Holy See, January 7, 2013.

The Inter-American Court of Human Rights is a court of *law*, not of *morals*, after all. If the sought-for dialogue is to include judges who interpret human rights law, and human rights lawyers more generally, a more carefully nuanced approach to the relationship between law and morals may be required.

In summary, there appear to be at least four interlinked problems emerging from Benedict's speeches that render a genuine dialogue with the secular human rights communities somewhat problematic: (i) adherence to prescriptive, dogmatic rules to regulate complex human problems; (ii) reducing the multidimensional nature of human dignity; (iii) appearing to resort to unchangeable understandings of what is natural as the basis for dogmatic assertion despite experience to the contrary; and (iv) the adoption of a problematic theory of judicial interpretation on issues of human rights law. Perhaps, above all, the opportunity that the concept of human dignity offers to critique rules, reason, authority, dogmatism, and natural law is not fully embraced.

* * *

Readers of these speeches are faced with an apparent paradox. On the one hand, we see clearly Benedict's enthusiasm for dialogue, for an engagement between faith and reason. On the other hand, we see many of the areas in which engagement might take place apparently closed off from questioning. How can this apparent paradox be resolved? It is time to reconsider what Benedict means by "dialogue."

Bradford Hinze contrasts two approaches to communication: "a dialogic mode of communication, in which messages oscillate between participants, and discursive modes, in which a message flows from sender to receiver."[47] In the latter, "[s]peakers are not required to listen and listeners are not required to speak. There is no open-ended mutuality, no chance for all parties to learn, for participants to be

[47] Bradford Hinze, Practices of Dialogue in the Roman Catholic Church: Aims and Obstacles, Lessons and Laments (New York: Continuum, 2006), 12. I am grateful to Timothy Radcliffe OP for bringing this to my attention.

influenced by each other leading to mutual growth." Benedict's speeches indicate that his preferred mode of communication is dialogic.

Hinze crucially distinguishes, however, between two different ways in which "dialogue" has come to be understood within the Church. One mode of dialogue "draws on classical Platonic, Augustinian, and personalist theories of dialogue," and is seen as "able to guarantee and safeguard the weight of truth in dialogue."[48] Another mode of dialogue is seen "risk[ing] placing the truth of tradition in jeopardy."[49] The former, according to Hinze, is a "medium for transmitting and conveying the truth of tradition already established" as opposed to the latter that advances "an approach to dialogue [that is] interested not only in handing on but also in generating, developing, or revising the truth of the living tradition of the Catholic faith."[50] It is of particular importance that he identifies Cardinal Ratzinger as having adopted the former mode of dialogue and rejecting the latter before becoming Pope Benedict. Though this rejection is not apparent in the speeches of Benedict we were asked to consider, it appears to be implicit, and resolves the apparent paradox I identified.

Hinze does not regard the former as constituting "true" dialogue, and I am equally sceptical. The interaction of reason and faith in shaping the Catholic understanding of dignity has been an historical process, leading to notable revisions. The Church is now and has always been deeply engaged with secular culture in developing its understanding of Church teaching, sometimes for the good and sometimes in unfortunate ways. To take just one example of current significance: Christianity began in the first century A.D. with a strong opposition to torture, but through the appropriation of Roman law, came not only to endorse torture, but to practice it. The Church eventually reversed its position on torture, influenced by developments in secular politics, and now declares that torture is one of the most fundamental violations of dignity of the person – an offense against God. This change in teaching, in both cases, was influenced by the complex interaction between the Church and secular culture that led to changing understandings of dignity and its implications.

[48] Id., 260. [49] Id., 260. [50] Id., 260–61.

Benedict appears to acknowledge positive interactions between the Church and modernity at Regensburg: 'The positive aspects of modernity," he says, "are to be acknowledged unreservedly: we are all grateful for the marvellous possibilities that it has opened up for mankind and for the progress in humanity that has been granted to us."[51] The implications of the acknowledgement of the potential value of aspects of modernity were not, perhaps, fully developed in the speeches we discuss here. One of the ways in which the Church has been called to account is by moral advances within secular culture, especially within the realm of human rights and dignity. The language of rights and dignity has increasingly become a moral (and not just a political) challenge to the Church itself.

The Church needs an understanding of dialogue that is open to change. As Benedict said at Westminster: "the world of reason and the world of faith – the world of secular rationality and the world of religious belief – need one another and should not be afraid to enter into a profound and ongoing dialogue, for the good of our civilization."[52] There is, in other words, a mutuality of need. A genuine conversation must allow the possibility of change on both sides; otherwise it is simply an occasion for teaching, and not learning, and risks becoming discursive rather than dialogic. Benedict's warm embrace of the need for a dialogue between faith and reason is, therefore, a critical legacy of his papacy, but the message he sent was not unambiguous. There is little apparent recognition of the ambiguity in the understanding of dialogue, and this risks misleading people of good will outside the Church. It is strongly to be hoped that the new papacy will continue Benedict's commitment to dialogue but encourage a mode of dialogue that is "interested not only in handing on but also in generating, developing, or revising the truth" of the tradition.

Vital to the self-critique that the Church must engage in are secular liberal understandings of dignity. The concept of human

[51] Pope Benedict XVI, Meeting with the representatives of science, Aula Magna of the University of Regensburg, Regensburg, September 12, 2006.

[52] Pope Benedict XVI, Meeting with the representatives of British society, Westminster Hall, Westminster, September 17, 2010.

dignity invites openness to the posing of the question of what it is to be human in our public and communal discourse. A dialogue with those who share that intuition, whether religious or not, is all the more important because there is something irreducible about the human person that cannot be fully captured. This means that there is always a need for discussion, the likelihood of disagreement, and a certain underdetermination. The very nature of what we are talking about – the human person – means that we should never presume to be able to specify dignity beyond contestation. Awful though the scandals have been and profound though the challenges are to the authority of the hierarchy of the Church, there is the opportunity for renewal. The Church must look inward to the laity, and outward to secular society, in seeking that renewal, through dialogue.

PART III Democracy in a Society of "Others"

12 CONCERNING THE DOCTRINE OF DEMOCRACY IN BENEDICT XVI

Massimo Luciani

DEMOCRACY IN THE CHURCH AND POLITICAL DEMOCRACY

I will address the following question: did Benedict XVI, in the course of his papacy, elaborate or consolidate[1] a doctrine of democracy? Since the question focuses on a Pope, such a doctrine could be either inward-looking, concerning democracy within the Church, or outward-looking, concerning democracy of the state or nonecclesiastical political communities in general. I will deal exclusively with the second kind of question, not only because the first is better suited to canonists or theologians, but also because it does not garnish much interest for concrete application.

Even before ascending to the throne of Peter, Joseph Ratzinger had already expressly rejected the idea that the Church could be considered a democratic order. If democracy is nothing more than the *kratos* (power) of the *démos* (people), then the Church is utterly lacking in prerequisites: the "people of God" is not the governing *démos* of a *polis* (political community or city); it is not the *laós* which forms itself into a political community.[2] Rather, as Ratzinger had already written in

[1] Because this inquiry involves a doctrine that may have been "elaborated" or merely "consolidated" in the course of his papacy, the following chapters will consider texts and speeches from both before and after his election, as signs of a single stream of thought, albeit one that was articulated differently over time.

[2] I find it significant that, in the text cited at the next footnote, not only is the idea of the faithful as *démos* rejected (it is not even mentioned), but that of *laós* is denied as well (which is the concept referred to). As per the reconstruction by

1970, when he was only a world-renowned professor of doctrine,[3] it is *ekklesía*, assembly, in which decision-making authority is not relegated to the majority – the *pléthos*[4] in the words of Herodotus – but to the magestierial authorities (those led by it can sometimes have an influence on its decisions, as happened in the early Church in the form of acclamation, but can never replace them).[5] Benedict was explicit in his critique of certain post-conciliar voices that sought to spur on a view of the "people of God" image as "the vehicle of an anti-hierarchical and anti-sacral idea of church."[6] He was explicit, too, in his defense of papal primacy,[7] even though the conclusions of the First Vatican Council were read as striking a balance between conciliarism and papism (not as a victory of the latter over the former)[8] and the Church was not

Benveniste (E. Benveniste, Le vocabulaire des institutions indo-européennes, II, Pouvoir, droit, réligion, Minuit, Paris 1969, trans. by E. Palmer, Indo-European Language and Society, Faber & Faber, London 1973), the *laós* is the warrior community which forms in following a leader.

3 "Demokratisierung der Kirche?," in J. Ratzinger e H. Maier, Demokratie in der Kirche. Möglichkeiten und Grenzen, 2nd ed. of the new ed. 2000, Lahn-Verlag, Limburg-Kevelaer 2005, Ital. trans. by C. Danna, "Democratizzazione della Chiesa?," in Democrazia nella Chiesa. Possibilità e limiti, Queriniana, Brescia 2005, 30 ff.

4 Herodotus, The Histories, III, 80, ad finem.

5 This relationship between the magisterium and the possibility for members of the Church community to have an influence on it through acclamation is singularly close to Schmitt's reconstruction of the plebiscite mechanisms of decision-making: see, in particular, C. Schmitt, Volksentscheid und Volksbegehren, de Gruyter, Berlin and Leipzig, 1927, 34.

6 "The Ecclesiology of the Second Vatican Council," in Joseph Ratzinger, Church, Ecumenism and Politics: New Endeavors in Ecclesiology, Ignatius Press, San Francisco, 2008, 29.

7 "Der Primat des Papstes und die Einheit des Gottesvolkes," in *Dienst an der Einheit. Zum Wesen und Auftrag des Petrusamtes*, Patmos, Düsseldorf 1978, pp. 165 et seq., trans. by M.J. Miller, J.R. Forster and A. Walker, "The Primacy of the Pope and the Unity of the People of God," in Fundamental Speeches from Five Decades, Ignatius Press, San Francisco, 2012; Joseph Ratzinger/Benedict XVI, La Chiesa: Una comunità sempre in cammino, San Paolo, Milan, 2008, 39 ff..

8 "Primato, episcopato e successio apostolica, in Catholica," 13 (1959), reproduced in K. Rahner and J. Ratzinger, Episkopat und Primat, Herder,

understood, as Karl Rahner put it, as a monarchy in the true sense (that is, absolute).[9] He even said relatively recently, in a well-known speech at the Meeting of Rimini in 1990, that "the Church is not a democracy" and could never be one, because "everything that a majority decides can be abrogated by another majority" and "a Church that rests on the decisions of a majority becomes a purely human Church" in which "opinion takes the place of faith."[10] It is also significant that in his first message as newly elected Pontiff, Benedict XVI recalled the Gospel passage "you are Peter, and upon this rock I will build my church" (Matthew 16:18) and said that "In choosing me as Bishop of Rome, the Lord wanted me to be his Vicar, he wanted me to be the 'rock' on which we can all safely stand."[11]

Basilea, trans. by K. Barker, *The Episcopate and the Primacy*, Herder and Herder, New York, 1962. It is important to note that Benedict XVI indirectly expressed similar ideas in his final general audience at St. Peter's Square (Feburary 27, 2013), when he said that: "The Pope is not alone in guiding the barque of Peter, even if it is his first responsibility."

9 K. Rahner, Der Bischof. Primat und Episkopat, in Sendung und Gnade, Tyrolia, Innsbruck 1959, 235 ff, Ital. trans., *Episcopato e primato*, reproduced in K. Rahner and J. Ratzinger, *Episcopato e primato*, 22, making the argument, which I admit to me seems very weak, that the Pontiff, even if he can give and take away as many powers as he wants from the individual bishops, still finds in the episcopate as an institution (of divine legitimization) an insurmountable legal limit on his own power. I call it weak because the paradigm we are considering is that of an absolute monarchy, of a pure, ideal type, whose historical existence is highly questionable (thus, it is difficult to find a "true" absolute monarchy among constitutional experiences).

10 The speech, entitled "Una compagnia sempre riformanda," can be found at www.meetingrimini.org. See also, from that time period, *Vent'anni della rivista Communio. Il coraggio cristiano di rischiare*, in "Communio," 124, 1992, 11 ff, reproduced in J. Ratzinger, *La vita di Dio per gli uomini. Scritti per "Communio"*, n. 208–210 (2006), p. 221.

11 Benedict XVI, First message of his Holiness Benedict XVI at the end of the Eucharistic concelebration with the members of the College of Cardinals in the Sistine Chapel, April 20, 2005 (in the same speech he referred to "divine Providence" which called him to this ministry "through the votes of the Venerable Father Cardinals"). It is interesting here to recall the different formulation used in his Declaration renouncing the Petrine ministry on February 11, 2013, in which he spoke of the "the ministry of Bishop of Rome,

This position makes clear the idea that the Church cannot be understood (or built) as a democratic structure – an idea supported by well-established theological grounds (that the Church claims that its authority is founded on truth)[12] far more than ideological ones,[13] and which have long been a part of Church doctrine (the following passage appears in *Lumen Gentium* at paragraph 22: "the college or body of bishops has no authority unless it is understood together with the Roman Pontiff, the successor of Peter as its head. The pope's power of primacy over all, both pastors and faithful, remains whole and intact"). Certainly the majority principle, which is central to democracy, has not had an easy life in the history of the Church and, as Edoardo Ruffini observed, for centuries the principle of the *majoritas* (greater part) ceded to that of the *sanioritas* (greater part with respect to wisdom of judgment).[14] But Benedict makes a different point: that a "democratic" Church would disown itself as Church.

RELATIVISM AND DEMOCRACY

Since an authentic doctrine of democracy has not gained ground *within* the Catholic Church, the question becomes whether one has been developed from an *outward-looking* perspective, which looks not

Successor of Saint Peter, entrusted to me by the Cardinals on 19 April 2005." The texts of these two speeches, as well as all the others provided without citations in this chapter, can be found at the Vatican website (www.vatican.va).

[12] L. Zannotti, La Chiesa e il principio di autorità. Una riflessione sugli elementi essenziali del diritto canonico, Giappichelli, Torino 2012, 133.

[13] In fact, the essential issue posed is that of the substantial illegitimacy of declining concepts that are considered theological (such as "people of God") in political terms (for more on this, see also G. Coccolini, "Alla ricerca di un ethos perduto. La relazione tra teologia e politica in Joseph Ratzinger," Il Pozzo di Giacobbe, Trapani 2011, 137).

[14] E. Ruffini, "Il principio maggioritario nella storia del diritto canonico," in Arch. giur., vol. XCIII (1925), 15, reprinted in *La ragione dei più*, Il Mulino, Bologna 1977, 23 ff., particularly pp. 63 ff.

at the Church, but rather at the state, the political community. It would be a doctrine calibrated to the secular and *extra Ecclesiam* life of human persons. Here too, there seems to be an insurmountable obstacle.

This obstacle is established by the famous premise of Hans Kelsen's theory of democracy: "*relativism* is the *Weltanschauung* that the *democratic idea* presumes"[15] Kelsen wrote (elsewhere he put it even more clearly: "democracy is philosophical relativism"),[16] while "One who claims *divine* inspiration, supernatural illumination for his political desires and actions may have the right to close his ears to human voices and impose his will, as the will of the absolute good."[17]

The trial of Jesus is paradigmatic of the clash between relativism and absolutism: the plebiscite demand to free Barrabas in place of Christ appears absurd and unjust to everyone and – Kelsen says – seems to make a strong argument against democracy. Nevertheless, this objection only holds "on one condition: of their political truth, which must, if necessary, be imposed by political force, the faithful be as sure as was the son of God."[18]

Benedict XVI has always been keenly aware of the obstacle posed by the Kelsenian premise, and has deliberately addressed it,[19]

[15] H. Kelsen, "On the Essence and Value of Democracy" (1929), trans. Belinda Cooper and Stephan Hemetsberger, in Arthur J. Jacobson and Bernhard Schlink (eds.), Weimar: A Jurisprudence of Crisis, University of California Press, Berkeley and Los Angeles, California, 2000, 84–109, 108.

[16] H. Kelsen, Absolutism and Relativism in Philosophy and Politics, in "Am. Pol. Sc. Rev.," XLII (1948).

[17] H. Kelsen, "On the Essence and Value," 108.

[18] Id., 109; See also H. Kelsen, "Foundations of Democracy," Ethics, 66, 1, Part 2, October 1955, 1–101, especially 39.

[19] Striking too is the fact that the criticism Benedict made of the naturalistic fallacy in his well-known speech before the Federal Parliament of Berlin on September 22, 2011, was aimed at Kelsen rather than at those thinkers who initially conceived it (D. Hume, *A Treatise of Human Nature*, III, I, 1, 469–470). This recognition of the greatness of Kelsen is appreciated as a proof of "particular intellectual probity" by N. Irti, in "Il diritto e il linguaggio della natura," in Vita e Pensiero, 1, 2012, 64.

picking up the issue of the "*risk of an alliance between democracy and ethical relativism*, which would remove any sure moral reference point from political and social life, and on a deeper level make the acknowledgement of truth impossible" already described by John Paul II, but going well beyond it in the depth of his analysis.[20] Kelsenian relativism is described as postulating truth as a product of politics, as opposed to the view that truth "is superior to it and therefore enlightens it."[21] Benedict does not share Kelsen's position, in keeping with certain general assumptions about the state and democracy that we examine later, because he does not consider the state to be an end in itself; rather it serves the function of protecting rights, either because it entails "denying the social importance of religion,"[22] or because it possesses "its own particular brand of dogmatism," that must be "imposed even upon those who do not share it."[23]

In short, a state cannot do without importing "from outside" the inheritance of truth which it cannot disregard, and this "outside" is not an abstract and pure reason, but rather the "historical forms of reason that matured in cultural expressions of religious faith."[24]

As I have already said, these positions are consistent with Benedict's general assumptions about state and democracy which we will now examine. These are also consistent with Benedict's attitude toward relativism, which he took on as a primary target of his critical thought. When he was still a cardinal, but only a few hours before ascending to the Chair of Peter, while presiding at the *Missa pro*

[20] Pope John Paul II, Veritatis splendor, Encyclical Letter, Libreria Editrice Vaticana, August 6, 1993, 101; see also John Paul II, Centesimus annus, Encyclical Letter to the Episcopate, Priests, and Deacons, Families of Men and Women Religious, all the Christian Faithful, and all Men and Women of Good Will on the Hundredth Anniversary of Rerum Novarum, Libreria Editrice Vaticana, May 1, 1991, paragraph 46.

[21] "Il significato dei valori religiosi e morali nella società pluralistica," in J. Ratzinger, *La vita di Dio per gli uomini*, 284.

[22] Pope Benedict XVI, Address to the members of the diplomatic corps for the traditional exchange of New Year Greetings, January 11, 2010.

[23] "Il significato dei valori religiosi," 289. [24] Id., 295.

eligendo Romano Pontefice on April 18, 2005, Joseph Ratzinger stated that "having a clear faith based on the Creed of the Church is often labeled as fundamentalism. Whereas relativism, that is, letting oneself be 'tossed here and there, carried about by every wind of doctrine,' seems the only attitude that can cope with modern times. We are building a dictatorship of relativism that does not recognize anything as definitive and whose ultimate goal consists solely of one's own ego and desires."[25] And he immediately continued: "We, however, have a different goal: the Son of God, the true man." He uses the term "however": he could not have made the contrast more clear. And this could not have been more significant, taking place in the context of the imminent and crucial decision of the Conclave.

In essence, the Kelsenian objection to the union of ethical absolutism and democracy is not only repelled, but completely overturned: not only *can* democracy coexist with ethical absolutism, but it *must* propose it as the necessary prerequisite for *itself* to be a real possibility.[26] From this perspective it is clear that the inquiry we started from can easily be given a positive response, because the person who accepts this premise would feel entirely justified in spelling out a theory of democracy that rests on the hypothesis of truth. But do the traces of such a theory appear concretely in the thought of Benedict XVI? It seems to me that here, too, the answer is yes.

[25] For more on the "tyranny of relativism combined with the dominating position of technique," see also Pope Benedict XVI, Meeting with the civil and political authorities and with the members of the diplomatic corps, held at the Presidential Palace of Prague on September 26, 2009, on the occasion of the apostolic visit to the Czech Republic.

[26] This still holds true when the issue is put in terms of individual freedom. Indeed, the principles that support individual freedom of conscience are considered "the 'bearing walls' of any society that wishes to be truly free and democratic" (Benedict XVI, Address to the members of the diplomatic corps accredited to the Holy See, January 7, 2013), and freedom of conscience is understood as an indicator of the "quality of democracy" (Speech given at the National Croatian Theatre of Zagreb, June 4, 2011, during the Apostolic Journey to Croatia).

DEMOCRACY AND THE STATE ACCORDING TO BENEDICT XVI

The general theoretical foundation seems highly traditional, in line with certain points already well established in Church teaching (formalized in 2004 in the eighth chapter of the *Compendium of the Social Doctrine of the Church*).[27] In short:

1. The all-encompassing claim of the state is flatly contested: "the state is not the whole of human existence and does not encompass all human hope"[28] instead it is bound by a "primary duty:" that of "protect[ing] its own population from grave and sustained violations of human rights, as well as from the consequences of humanitarian crises, whether natural or man-made."[29]
2. In keeping with this, "the development of other political players, of a cultural, social, territorial or religious nature, alongside the State"[30] is possible (and desirable). Among these, the international organizations charged with the protection of human rights stand out because "entrusting exclusively to individual states, with their laws and institutions, the final responsibility to meet the aspirations of persons, communities and entire peoples, can sometimes have consequences that exclude the possibility of a social order respectful of the dignity and rights of the person."[31]
3. The Church and the state are two distinct, interrelated communities and this dualism is founded on the principle "Render to

[27] See, particularly concerning the questions outlined in the text, nos. 384, 388, 389, 395, 407, 417, 418, 419, 421 ff.

[28] "The Biblical Aspects of the Theme of Faith and Politics," in Joseph Ratzinger, Church, Ecumenism and Politics: New Endeavors in Ecclessiology, Ignatius Press, San Francisco, 2008, 143.

[29] Pope Benedict XVI, Meeting with the Members of the General Assembly of the United Nations Organization, New York, April 18, 2008.

[30] Pope Benedict XVI, "Caritas in veritate, Encyclical Letter to the Bishops, Priests, and Deacons, Men and Women Religious, the Lay Faithful, and All People of Good Will on Integral Human Development in Charity and Truth," *Libreria Editrice Vaticana*, June 29, 2009, paragraph 41.

[31] Pope Benedict XVI, Meeting with the Members of the General Assembly of the United Nations Organization, New York, April 18, 2008.

Caesar the thing that are Caesar's and to God the things that are God's" (Matthew 22:21), which represents "the source and the abiding basis for the Western idea of freedom."[32]

4. Separation of powers is also essential for the protection of the rights of individuals (in particular, "the independence of the administration of justice from the organs of executive power"), because "what protects the citizen is not power but law."[33]
5. A merely formal idea of democracy is rejected ("the merely formal democratic system of limited power and the separation of powers does not function in and of itself") because "Democracy can not function in a values-free manner and, hence, can not be values-neutral, either"[34] and "If the moral principles underpinning the democratic process are themselves determined by nothing more solid than social consensus, then the fragility of the process becomes all too evident,"[35] while what is needed is

[32] "Teologia e politica della Chiesa," in *Communio*, 53 (1980), 60; "Das Gewissen der Zeit," in *Internat. kath. Zeitschrift*, 1 (1972), 432. See also the interview by Antonio Socci of "Il Giornale" from November 26, 2003. He is, on the contrary, critical of Islam, which "is quite obviously the exact antithesis of pluralistic democracy" (A Christian orientation in a pluralistic democracy?, in Joseph Ratzinger, Church, Ecumenism and Politics: New Endeavors in Ecclesiology, Ignatius Press, San Francisco, 2008, 203).
A different reading of the opposition between Caesar and God by the Gospel is possible, indeed. It could be noted that that statement had the result of "challenging the predominance of political reason over religious reason, which had gone uncontested until that moment" with clear protective and defensive effects for the newborn monotheistic cult (P. Bellini, Il diritto di essere se stessi: Discorrendo dell'idea di laicità, Giappichelli, Torino 2007, 34). And later on, in the fifth century, the separation was affirmed by the well-known Gelasian doctrine of two-fold government of the world ("Duo quippe sunt … quibus principaliter mundus hic regitur: auctoritas sacra pontificum et regalis potestas"). This was done with the aim of reclaiming the autonomy of the religious domain from that of politics and protecting the members of the Church from state power.

[33] "Freedom and Constraint in the Church", in Joseph Ratzinger, *Church, Ecumenism and Politics*, 178.

[34] Id., 179.

[35] Pope Benedict XVI, Meeting with the Representatives of British Society, London, Westminster Hall, September 17, 2010.

the "construction of a real democracy, founded on the ethical values rooted in human nature itself."[36]

6. As a result, in keeping with the well-known formula laid out for the secularized state by Ernst-Wolfgang Böckenförde (incidentally one of the most important representatives of Catholic constitutionalism),[37] we must acknowledge that democracy rests on preconditions that the state is not capable of guaranteeing.[38]

On this traditional theoretical foundation, which we have just briefly summarized, the Pope Emeritus develops original thoughts that are worthy of careful attention.[39] He has in mind a representative democracy, as stable as possible,[40] in which the Parliament and the parties play a central role. "Through elections individuals choose representatives who will make decisions on their behalf," but the mandate of the representatives is only free in theory, because "it is constrained by the framework of the party system, and encompasses only those areas of political action which are ascribed to state representative organs by the Constitution."[41]

Nevertheless, since "it is not always guaranteed that the representative I elect will really act and speak in the way I want," the

36 Pope Benedict XVI, General Audience on the topic of his apostolic journey to Croatia, June 8, 2011.

37 E.-W. Böckenförde, "Die Entstehung des Staates als Vorgang der Säkularisation," reproduced in Recht, Staat, Freiheit, Suhrkamp, Frankfurt am Main 2006, new ed., 112: "Der freiheitliche, säkularisierte Staat lebt von Voraussetzungen, dieer selbst nicht garantieren kann" (italics in original).

38 A Christian orientation, 191, 205. The importance of this text was exactly highlighted in G. Coccolini, *Alla ricerca di un ethos perduto*, 159.

39 Here too certain passages develop themes that have already been treated, especially in the aforementioned *Compendium of the Social Doctrine of the Church* (see, for example, nos. 414 ff. on information media and 441 on universal political authority).

40 Pope Benedict XVI, Address to H.E. Mr. George Robert Furness Troup Ambassador of New Zealand to the Holy See, Clementine Hall, June 9, 2011, in which the Pope invited the "the encouragement of mature and stable democratic institutions, and the fostering of authentic human rights and sustainable economic development."

41 Both passages cited here are found in Una compagnia sempre riformanda.

"victorious majority . . . cannot entirely consider itself to be the acting subject of political events."[42]

At any rate, the importance given to parliamentary debate is undeniable. Democracy is considered the "most appropriate form of political order" simply because it guarantees "a shared collaboration in the elaboration of law,"[43] a collaboration that is considered indispensable in light of the idea that "Not the uncompromising stance, but compromise is the true morality in the political matters"[44] As Benedict stated in the well-known speech at Westminster Hall, the parliamentary tradition, so deeply rooted in England, "owes much to the national instinct for moderation, to the desire to achieve a genuine balance between the legitimate claims of government and the rights of those subject to it."[45] The parliamentary *method* is, in short, that of dialogical and discussionary interaction among different people and groups, the outcome of which can be (and preferably should be) a compromise decision.

Although it may seem paradoxical, here we find the maximum overlap with Kelsen, who repeatedly insisted on the fact that "the entire *parliamentary process* is geared toward reaching a middle way between contrasting interests, a result of social forces in opposition."[46] Representative democracy, moreover, requires a pluralistic environment in which to develop. Indeed, the language of pluralistic democracy, Benedict points out, is very similar to that of Catholic social doctrine;[47] and if it is true that the state cannot be an end in itself, "Christian faith respects the nature of the State itself, *especially* of the state of a pluralist society."[48]

42 Id.

43 In Jürgen Habermas and Joseph Ratzinger, The Dialectics of Secularization: On Reason and Religion, Ignatius Press, San Francisco, 2006, 59.

44 The biblical aspects, 145.

45 Pope Benedict XVI, Meeting with the Representatives of British Society

46 H. Kelsen, Das Problem des Parlamentarismus, Braumüller, Wien u. Leipzig 1925, trans. It. by C. Geraci, "Il problema del parlamentarismo," in Il primato del Parlamento, Giuffrè, Milano, 1982, 195.

47 Pope Benedict XVI, Meeting with the Representatives of British Society.

48 Pope Benedict XVI, Address on the occasion of being awarded the degree of Doctor Honoris Causa by the LUMSA Department of Jurisprudence, Rome, November 10, 1999, the English text of which may be found at https://www.ewtn.com/library/theology/lawmeta.htm (emphasis added).

Social media play a central role in the construction of this environment, but here once again the form without the substance is not enough: "Just because social communications increase the possibilities of interconnection and the dissemination of ideas, it does not follow that they promote freedom or internationalize development and democracy for all"; this only occurs when they "focus on promoting the dignity of persons and peoples, [and are] clearly inspired by charity and placed at the service of truth, of the good, and of natural and supernatural fraternity."[49]

In line with this, even the material conditions for human life are an indispensable precondition for the system to function well: not by accident the Pope Emeritus, on May 1, 2005 – feast of St. Joseph the Worker – expressed the wish that "I hope that work will be available, especially for young people, and that working conditions may be ever more respectful of the dignity of the human person."[50]

Pluralism, then, and pluralism in a substantial sense. Furthermore, it is not enough that a pluralistic expression be affirmed only on the state level, because it must be replicated at every level of political power: "The articulation of political authority at the local, national and international levels is one of the best ways of giving direction to the process of economic globalization. It is also the way to ensure that it does not actually undermine the foundations of democracy."[51] The "positive partnerships between markets, civil society and states," which marked the economic development of the twentieth century, can play an important role in this,[52] but the political power of these states should not be undermined "in an epoch

[49] Pope Benedict XVI, Caritas in Veritate, 73.

[50] Pope Benedict XVI, Regina Caeli, St. Peter's Square, May 1, 2005. He addressed the issue of work from a different angle in his important (particularly for its profound examination of the relationship between the word of God and human word) Meeting with representatives from the world of culture at the Collège des Bernardins, Paris, September 12, 2008, in which he described how the "culture of work" grew out of the European tradition after the advent of Christianity.

[51] Pope Benedict XVI, Caritas in Veritate, 41.

[52] Pope Benedict XVI, Message for the Celebration of the World Day of Peace, January 1, 2009.

in which limitations to their sovereignty de facto exist because of the new international economic, commercial and financial context,"[53] at least until "the need for a world political authority, regulated by law, which would abide by the aforementioned principles of subsidiarity and solidarity" has been satisfied.[54]

This conclusion too, upon reflection, is not far from the one reached by Kelsen, who, aside from his formulation of the relationship between international law and state law (as a believer in the primacy of the former),[55] shared the idea that a worldly political authority is necessary.[56]

RELATIVISM AND ETHICAL ABSOLUTISM: HOW OPPOSED ARE THEIR PERSPECTIVES ON DEMOCRACY?

The frequent intersection between a conception of democracy to which Benedict deliberately counterposes his own leads to certain systemic considerations. The impression is that radical differences among *theoretical* assumptions will not impede alignment on certain important, *practical* outcomes that can greatly reduce the distance between the positions. Benedict's well-known speech before the Bundestag on September 22, 2011, confirms this impression as a certainty.

In a particularly meaningful passage, he says that, "[f]or most of the matters that need to be regulated by law, the support of the majority can serve as a sufficient criterion. Yet it is evident that for the fundamental issues of law, in which the dignity of man and of humanity is at stake, the majority principle is not enough: everyone

[53] Pope Benedict XVI, General audience, July 8, 2009. [54] Id.

[55] H. Kelsen, Das Problem der Souveränität und die Theorie des Völkerrechts. Beitrag zu einer reinen Rechtslehre, Mohr, Tübingen 1920, It. trans. by A. Carrino, Il problema della sovranità e la teoria del diritto internazionale. Contributo per una teoria pura del diritto, Giuffrè, Milano 1989, particularly 302.

[56] Id., particularly 469.

in a position of responsibility must personally seek out the criteria to be followed when framing laws." This is the heart of the matter. The majority principle is not rejected *in toto* as an instrument of rational public decision-making, but it is proclaimed inadequate "for the fundamental issues of law."[57]

This acceptance under ordinary circumstances explains the points of contact between ideas of democracy that are opposed in their premises. In essence, the majority principle gives way when two issues are in play: freedom of conscience and the right of active resistance.

For a positivist, freedom of conscience can (and must) be guaranteed, but subject to the conditions set by the positive legal order, which is otherwise threatened by collapse. A consistent positivist, then, does not see the right of active resistance as an authentic right (positively protectable), but brings it back into the dimentions of the facts. And the same goes for the situation in which the majority of citizens decide to give themselves a new constitutional order: this transition, too, must be reconstructed as a "fact" (from which – if it is accepted – the legitimacy of the new constitution derives), rather than as a "right" in the natural law sense (as imagined in the French revolutionary Constitution of 1793, which says at article 28 that: "Un peuple a toujours le droit de revoir, de réformer et de changer sa Constitution. Une génération ne peut assujettir à ses lois les générations futures").

Benedict's position is, obviously, opposed to this one. But this opposition on the basis of underlying principles does not impede agreement on the day-to-day aspects of the life of the social order, making it possible in most cases to reach the compromises that both

[57] According to N. Irti, Nichilismo giuridico, 3a ed., Laterza, Roma-Bari, 2005, 22, the distinctive characteristic of modern law is the fact of being "by now consigned to the solitude of the human will," even including the choice of the fundamental norm of the legal order. The opposite, but substantially unsupported (Irti correctly observes) position is taken by P. Häberle, Wahrheitsprobleme im Verfassungsstaat, Nomos, Baden-Baden, 1995, Ital. trans. by F. Fiore, Diritto e verità, Einaudi, Torino 2000, 86. As the quotation in the text shows, this characteristic is repudiated in principle, but not totally set aside from the perspective of practical activity.

sides consider essential to the proper working of a pluralistic democracy founded on political representation.

Is it not possible that this partial, but nevertheless important, overlap is due to the fact that the theoretical underpinnings of the two positions are less opposed than they appear? This is the widespread opinion of those who think that supporters of a necessary connection between relativism and democracy are themselves putting forward absolute ethical claims, that is, "values" (or "truths" as Benedict would say). I, however, would be more cautious.

I would begin by pointing out that this is a slippery slope because the very definition of relativism is debatable.[58] I would then reject the idea that the comparison can be made when relativism is understood as a belief in the nonexistence or unknowability of absolute truths: as a "belief," this seems to be wholly at odds with its own underlying assumptions. In my view it would be more accurate to establish, if anything, a relationship between democracy and a certain *noncognitivism*, understood as a culture of doubt concerning the effective substance of the truth of one's own moral judgments,[59] or better, as the basic conviction that moral propositions cannot be rationally proven as true or false (and therefore that absolute truths could *potentially* exist).

This being said, I venture to propose the following hypothesis (which will require further development): that the democratic principle (and with it the majority principle, which is its functional manifestation) is the *logical* consequence of a noncognitivist approach, and not the result of acceptance of (undisclosed) *axiological* assumptions. The noncognitivist does not consider the qualitative judgments underlying the idea that all persons are not equal to be rationally demonstrable – an idea that indeed presupposes that some people have a higher value than others. Moreover, in the absence of *qualitative*

[58] Truly, there is not only one single form of relativism: A. Coliva, I modi del relativismo, Laterza, Roma-Bari, 2009.

[59] This seems to be the position taken by G. Zagrebelsky in Il "Crucifige!" e la democrazia, Einaudi, Torino, 1995, 6 ff., when he ties democracy to the "concept of possibility," as a third way between skepticism and dogmatism. See also G. Zagrebelsky, Contro l'etica della verità, Laterza, Roma-Bari, 2008, viii.

determinations, only *quantitative* ones can serve as the basis for a non-cognitivist theory of political community. This means the heads have to be counted, not weighed, and therefore noncognitivism entails the principle of political equality (and the related majority principle) by mere logical reasoning, and without any appeal to an axiological premise. This can only be rejected if one accepts the noncognitivist option as a value choice. But this widespread view,[60] in my humble opinion, amounts to a paralogism, because the option is chosen not because it is "good," but rather because it is the only one compatible with the position that the absolute (ethical) "truth" can never be rationally demonstrated (which the consistent noncognitivist must first have tried). Contrary to Böckenförde's belief, therefore, it seems to me that the democratic state is itself capable of guaranteeing the underlying preconditions on which it is founded.[61]

It is always a matter of logical consequence, then, that from the principle of equality derives that of liberty, because the *aequales* are such that none of them can vaunt an unequal claim of supremacy over the others (which would negate the liberty of others). This opens up the vast field of *substantive* determinations of equality and liberty, but the logical principle of noncontradiction does not fail here either: people are only equal and free if these two adjectives have a meaning (already Cicero had said that liberty, "*si aequa non est, ne libertas*

[60] That implies diverse corollaries, such as that in which the very conviction where one cannot predict whether legal norms be true or false is itself the fruit of a choice (see, for example, A. Pintore, Il diritto senza verità, Giappichelli, Torino, 1996, 8).

[61] A different, well-known response to Böckenförde's critique is found in the Habermasian communicative worldview, which sees in democratic debate a process that validates the presumption of acceptable expected results and attempts to remove modern law from the fate of being abandoned to the whim of volition by positing that: (a) legislative power must act within a scope fixed by the constitution; (b) the constitution is not the law produced by an arbitrary political power, but it is the very mode of being of political power, which is born already juridicized, as "It is the specific task of politics to apply the criterion of law to the power, thereby structuring the use of power in a meaningful manner" in Jürgen Habermas and Joseph Ratzinger, The Dialectics of Secularization: On Reason and Religion, Ignatius Press, San Francisco, 2006, 43 ff. and especially 59.

quidem est"):[62] if equality is not merely formal, but also substantive (as the Italian Constitution specifies at Article 3, paragraph 2), and freedom of self-determination is authentic (this is only possible if we build the *enlightened citizenship* that Robert Dahl has described for years).[63]

In sum, the contrast between these two perspectives be neither diminished nor denied. The question of the majority principle (and of the limits of democratic consensus) remains. For the noncognitivist, working within a legal-positivist framework, that question is insurmountable. On the other hand, Benedict XVI treats it as one of the present-day risks of the law (the other risk being "the dissolution of law through the spirit of utopia"), which, in fact, cannot be left to the changeable whims of the majority.[64]

And yet, the points of contact between the two positions are real and make the future of dialogue between them less uncertain.[65] Dialogue not only favors, but dictates the historical development of constitutionalism, which in the postwar period gave us democracies regulated by "value-oriented constitutions"[66] that cannot be modified with the passage of ordinary laws and are not ethically neutral (even though it must be clear that even the constitutions are always law, voluntaristically "established").[67]

62 Cicerone, De re publica, I, XXXI.

63 R.A. Dahl, Democracy and its Critics, Yale University Press, 1989.

64 Pope Benedict XVI, Address on the occasion of being awarded the degree of Doctor Honoris Causa by the LUMSA Department of Jurisprudence, Rome, November 10, 1999, 11. See also Pope Benedict XVI, Message for the Celebration of the World Day of Peace, January 1, 2009.

65 Benedict's view itself resolves in a proposal of dialogue, as seen in A. Travi, "Un criterio di giustizia per l'azione politica," in Vita e Pensiero, n. 1, 2012, 72.

66 The expression "value-oriented constitution" means a constitution deeply rooted in fundamental values affecting the human dimension. Such a constitution is not simply devoted to the definition of the relations between the powers of the state (as Kelsen wished), but tries to indicate the essential lines of human social activity.

67 The observation (of A. Nicolussi, *Un'ecologia giuridica per il futuro*, in *Vita e Pensiero*, 1, 2012, 67) is not correct in saying that contemporary constitutions cannot recognize the absolute value of the person if they deny the "possibility

To be sure there remains intact a disagreement as to whether the foundation of these values is human and legal-positivistic, as it is for some, or divine and legal-natural, as it is for others. Nonetheless, the debate remains open for human action that will actualize these values in the ordering of daily life.

of absolute truths." Since there is no constitutional value that cannot be balanced, the "absoluteness" of that recognition is unproven: therefore, the voluntaristic foundation of the constitutions remains intact no matter what the content of the will that was positivized in it.

13 ACTING CONTRARY TO REASON IS CONTRARY TO GOD'S NATURE

Andrés Ollero

For a professor such as myself, it is a true gift to read and listen to Pope Benedict XVI who, after being intellectually formed as an educator, thought it logical to go on being one, and never stopped adding to his long list of academic works. It is also reassuring for a lay person that he spent years orienting his thought toward academics of widely diverse beliefs and mentalities, and not to a specialized audience that was already convinced a priori. And for a person who has served as an elected representative during the last two decades, gratitude is owed to Benedict for the careful attention he paid to the issues of law and politics that are crucial to democratic life. Therefore, I was honored to receive this invitation to comment on some of his speeches, as I have done elsewhere on other occasions, and it was only logical for me to accept.[1] This time I will focus on his speech at the historic University of Regensburg, which – for reasons which today seem purely anecdotal – has been a constant source of controversy. In order to do so, it is important for me to acknowledge the significant intellectual debt that I owe to Benedict XVI, even at the risk of seeming vain in my use of self-citations.

What struck me most in all of these speeches was the fact that Benedict was constantly concerned with the dialogue between "faith and reason," which he addressed at Regensburg in such a risky way. The Pope Emeritus strove to discredit two points of view. First, the

[1] "Hacer entrar en razón al Estado de Derecho. Benedicto XVI aborda los fundamentos del Estado," in *Acta Philosophica* (Pontificia Universitá della Santa Croce) 2012 (21-II), 386–390, which discusses: Pope Benedict XVI, Visit to the Bundestag, Reichstag Building, Berlin, September 22, 2011.

view that places God beyond any possible logic, and ends up justifying the use of violence in the name of certain sacrosanct rights to truth: "To convince a reasonable soul, one does not need a strong arm."[2] Second, the view that, consciously or unconsciously, fails to free itself from the "modern self-limitation of reason" that prevents one from finding rational responses to important "specifically human" questions.

Figurative speech aside, it would be unfair to attribute the barely rational premises of the first view to Muslim culture alone. While it is certainly true that theirs is an "absolutely transcendent" God whose "will is not bound up with any of our categories, even that of rationality," I fear that this fideistic approach is widespread even in culturally Christian circles, which are as in need of a new evangelization as are nonbelievers.

In my opinion, the medieval voluntarism of William of Okham[3] or Duns Scotus is not a thing of the past, but continues to present us even today with an arbitrary God, who is "not even bound to truth and goodness." How many Christians believe that we should not kill another human being because God wills it, and how many because this kind of behavior expresses an inhuman irrationality? Is the natural law true because God wills it to be, or does God teach that we should follow it because it is true? And do we say that marriage is indissoluble because God wills it, or are there reasons – reasons not derived from some supernatural knowledge – which explain why indissolubility is an essential characteristic of this natural institution? It is a shame that the natural law has become a doctrine for Catholics, but it is even more serious that they are unable to justify it without fideistic references to a supernatural foundation, perhaps believing that by eliminating reason the glory of God is increased.

[2] This and the following quotations are from Benedict XVI, Meeting with the representatives of science, Aula Magna of the University of Regensburg, Regensburg, September 12, 2006.

[3] This would fit smoothly with Ibn Hazm's assertion that God "is not bound even by his own word, and that nothing would oblige him to reveal the truth to us. Were it God's will, we would even have to practise idolatry" (id.).

THE SECULARISM OF BENEDICT XVI

I am happy to note that Benedict takes an intellectual approach as he points to a God who delights in interacting with human beings and reasoning with them: "the truly divine God is the God who has revealed himself as logos and, as logos, has acted and continues to act lovingly on our behalf." Repeatedly faced with the experience of a God who loves us, a natural enough response is to love him back. If – in order to be more human – we must imitate him, we must begin by insisting that we ourselves act with rationality. Indeed, as one can infer from the dialogue presented in the speech at Regensburg, "'[n]ot to act reasonably ... is contrary to the nature of God.'"[4]

It is important to clarify what is meant here by "rational." If some Christians subscribe to a form of fideism similar to that of many Muslims, then it is not unlike the moral issues to which positivism refers. We live in a civilization that ends up subscribing by default to scientific positivism, with its dogmatic idea of reason, science, and experimental methodology; the absence of reflection and weak effort to reason have allowed legal positivism to flourish where rationality has never been cultivated. We pass our days discussing the rule of law, but in the end we must always acknowledge that the law is a tool of the state. Our legal order is presumably founded on respect for certain fundamental rights, but we rarely acknowledge the existence of an objective ethical foundation that is purely assumed.

Perhaps the most obvious proof of the fact that, tied as we are to this rigid, pseudoscientific concept of rationality, "we are faced with a reduction" that carries negative practical consequences. Fundamental needs – respected in many premodern cultures – such as the respect for human life, are met with serious resistance in the context of the very young and very old; provided that no racial or gender connotations are involved.

This *unconscious positivism*, no stranger to Catholic circles, illustrates a curious connection between law and morality. The tendency

[4] Benedict was forced to clarify that "It was purely for the sake of this statement that I quoted the dialogue between Manuel and his Persian interlocutor" after an explosion of controversy.

to misunderstand law as a helpful reinforcement for particularly important moral demands does not, in my view, generate favorable consequcnces. Much more sensible is the understanding of law as a *minimum ethical standard*, to which must be added a character of indispensability in order to make truly human coexistence possible.

Certainly the *minimum* character puts it at risk for being transposed to highly moral demands. Pope Benedict XVI himself had to face this problem in a speech that focused on marriage, but which can ostensibly be applied to the tragedies brought about by the occurrences of pedophilia that rocked the Church in several different countries. Despite being minimal, its *necessary* character means that it does not make sense to propose the minimal demands of charity which, rather than respecting it, contend to be its alternative.[5]

Moral demands lead a Christian to strive for behaviors that transcend any logic: to love one's enemies and turn the other cheek (thus the danger of considering them to be exaggerations relegated to experts). Natural law, on the contrary, does not claim to go beyond the elucidation of certain ethical standards that prevent our societal life from falling below minimally acceptable levels. It is not that we reject the love of neighbor; but we begin with a basis of respect and equal treatment.

LAW AND MORALITY

In large part, the Ten Commandments, despite being minimal, are more juridical than moral. The commandment *do not kill* is more convincing if, rather than considering it a moral requirement – one that is so important as to deserve back-up from the law – it is

[5] "Justice, which the Church pursues through the contentious-administrative process, can be considered as a beginning, a minimal requirement and at the same time an expectation of charity, at once indispensable and yet insufficient, if it is compared with the charity on which the Church lives. Nevertheless the pilgrim People of God on earth will be unable to realize its identity as a community of love unless it takes into consideration the demands of justice." Pope Benedict XVI, Address to members of the Supreme Tribunal of the Apostolic Signatura, February 4, 2011.

recognized as a legal requirement without which human coexistence would fall below minimally acceptable levels. Precisely because of its minimal, indispensable nature it generates a moral obligation, inverting the usual order.[6]

The well-intended subordination of law to morality can paradoxically undermine the strength of its demands, in a cultural context in which – as Benedict points out – "the subjective 'conscience' becomes the sole arbiter of what is ethical. In this way, though, ethics and religion lose their power to create a community and become a completely personal matter."[7] Abandoning the objectivity of the *logos*, because of a tendency toward pious sentimentality, leads to a wrong understanding of the expression *act according to conscience* as an invitation to a well-intended arbitrariness. The result is rejection of the need for a well-established foundation of ethical criteria, based on the careful interpretation of objective norms.

The difficulty of admitting that law – in the sense of the indispensable minimums described earlier – has priority over the minimal demands of morality is tied to the *unconscious positivism* referred to earlier, which overlooks the natural law. If law refers to what is imposed by those in power, then clearly it makes little sense to suggest that moral obligations derive therefrom; even the most inflexible positivists acknowledge this.[8] If, on the contrary, law is considered an ensemble of ethical demands derived from the nature of humanity itself (as it must be, since we consider certain human rights to be capable of affecting the laws in force), it comes as little surprise that they generate a moral obligation to obey. Ultimately, the moral virtue of justice is in giving each his just due; this implies an a priori awareness of what is or is not legally due.

[6] I gave a more detailed account of this idea in *Derecho y moral. Una relación desnaturalizada, Fundación Coloquio Jurídico Europeo*, Madrid, 2012, 11–51, 117–131, 133–162 and 265–311.

[7] This and the following citations are once again from Benedict XVI, Meeting with the representatives of science, Regensburg.

[8] Norberto Bobbio, for example, writes it off as an expression of ideological positivism. Cfr. N. Bobbio, Giusnaturalismo e positivismo giuridico, Laterza, Roma-Bari 2011, 92–94.

Unconscious positivism, which results from a dearth of reflection and reasoning, leads to a misunderstanding of conscientious objection, as though a conflict existed between legal demands and moral convictions. This understanding leaves it defenseless because it makes little sense to suggest that adherence to legal norms comes second to each person's moral code, let alone that we all have a right to such a code. If the objection appears in international declarations of rights and in democratic constitutions, it is because it is understood as a legal discrepancy between two concepts of justice. It follows that, in a liberal system, a place must be carved out for the legal demands of the minority such that they are not crushed by those of the majority, to the extent that the exception is compatible with social stability. At play here are two different concepts of law, not the juxtaposition of law and morality.

Few worldviews illustrate the consequences of a restrictive approach to rationality better than legal positivism, intentional or not. Therefore, it is appropriate to propose not a rejection of positive science, but an invitation to "broaden ... our concept of reason and its application," without implying any intention to "retrenchment" or "negative criticism." Unsurprisingly, this is one of the points of complete agreement between then-Cardinal Ratzinger and his compatriot Jürgen Habermas[9] in one of the most important cultural debates of the turn of the century.[10] What they propose is "courage to engage the whole breadth of reason, and not the denial of its grandeur." The two thinkers concur in suggesting a resetting of modern reason, without calling into question its positive contributions. This has to do with facing "a critique of modern reason from within [which] has nothing to do with putting the clock back to the time before the Enlightenment and rejecting the insights of the modern age." For Benedict XVI, *Aufklärung* (enlightenment) began on Mount Sinai. We find ourselves before a "process which started

[9] I explored this debate in "La crítica de la razón tecnológica. Benedicto XVI y Habermas, un paralelismo sostenido," *Anales de la Real Academia de Ciencias Morales y Políticas* 2010 (LXII-87), 435–451.

[10] J. Habermas and J. Ratzinger, The Dialectics of Secularization: On Reason and Religion, San Francisco: Ignatius Press, 2006.

at the burning bush," then before the possibility of a "new understanding of God" which is "accompanied by a kind of enlightenment." "A profound encounter of faith and reason is taking place here, an encounter between genuine enlightenment and religion," that makes it possible to say: "Not to act 'with logos' is contrary to God's nature."

BIBLICAL MESSAGE AND GREEK THOUGHT

In response to a frivolously liberal belief that the rejection of the past is enough to bring about positive consequences, and that the natural law should be consigned to some obscure altar, Benedict XVI suggests that "[t]he encounter between the Biblical message and Greek thought did not happen by chance," but that "[t]his inner rapprochement between Biblical faith and Greek philosophical inquiry was an event of decisive importance" that marks "world history."

Here again we see the parallel with Habermas, who no longer sees in "modern science a practice that is completely understandable in its own terms, establishing the measure of all truths and falsehoods," but rather the result of "a history of reason that includes the world religions."[11] For Benedict XVI, respect for the *logos* and the resulting conviction that "not acting reasonably (σὺν λόγω) is contrary to God's nature," are not "merely a Greek idea," but is "always and intrinsically true." Therefore what we are faced with is not an occasional "initial inculturation which ought not to be binding on other cultures" and which would give us the "right to return." We must continue to nurture an ambitious process of rational unveiling of the truth.

The consequences of this are obvious, and call into question the secularists' attempt, made in the name of neutrality, to seize for themselves alone the ability to offer reasons in public debate. The result of transforming the historical ties between religious traditions and certain rational ideas into a reason to disqualify them has been that: "[t]he West has long been endangered by this aversion to the questions which underlie its rationality, and can only suffer great harm thereby."

[11] J. Habermas, "Religion in the Public Sphere", European Journal of Philosophy, **14**, 1, 2006, 20.

Aware of the ethical impoverishment of our society and convinced that the mere economic rationality of the market is incapable of resolving the situation, Habermas' agnosticism would not prevent him from recognizing that religions are capable of offering reasons in public debate. Benedict, too, would affirm that "listening to the great experiences and insights of the religious traditions of humanity, and those of the Christian faith in particular, is a source of knowledge, and to ignore it would be an unacceptable restriction of our listening and responding."

At Regensburg he suggested that Muslim culture's lack of acceptance of a reasonably accessible natural law would inevitably slow its prospects of broaching a dialogue with modernity. Only a rationally shareable natural law can open up a "dialogue of cultures," inviting the potential interlocutors to have access "to this great *logos*, to this breadth of reason." Equally far from being capable of dialogue, according to Habermas,[12] are those secular people who forget that the liberal state "must not discourage religious persons and communities from also expressing themselves politically as such, for it cannot know whether secular society would not otherwise cut itself off from key resources for the creation of meaning and identity."[13] Essentially, he is suggesting at once that "the world's profoundly religious cultures see this exclusion of the divine from the universality of reason as an attack on their most profound convictions. A reason which is deaf to the divine and which relegates religion into the realm of subcultures is incapable of entering into the dialogue of cultures."

The disinclination of many religious people toward reflection and rational argument may turn out to be just as bad as the lack faith of those who claim to have a monopoly on reason. Therefore, it is a real gift to be able to rely on the teachings of a Pope who truly exercised his role as *Defensor rationis*.

[12] I explored this topic in "Poder o racionalidad. La religión en el ámbito público (En diálogo con la "sociedad postsecular" de Jürgen Habermas)," *Anales de la Real Academia de Ciencias Morales y Políticas* 2012 (LXIV-89), 147–156.

[13] J. Habermas, "Religion in the Public Sphere," 10.

14 A LISTENING HEART

Where Democracy Begins

Andrea Pin

INTRODUCTION

The speeches of Pope Benedict XVI that inspired this book interweave reason, truth, justice, and religious and political experience with what is, in my view, a single, fundamental concern.[1] As he himself said when he addressed the Bundestag, it is necessary to leave behind a narrow understanding of human experience, like "a concrete bunker with no windows.... The windows must be flung open again, we must see the wide world, the sky and the earth once more and learn to make proper use of all this."

I intend to reflect on Pope Benedict's legal ideas, and see how they resonate with key elements of the contemporary debate on the relationship between religion, politics, and law. I will first examine the Pope Emeritus' thought on this relationship, which he describes as marked by *transcendence*. With the help of contemporary scholarship, I will then consider the implications of this idea, and ponder how this affects both the way law and politics should deal with the hottest topics, and the ways that religions can express themselves in the public square.

It is important to note that the Pope Emeritus does not simply carve out a role for religious experience, but intends to restore value to political and legal experience as well. This is made particularly clear by his reference to Saint Augustine's well-known passage in

[1] I wish to thank Marta Cartabia, Mario Cucca, Tomaso Epidendio, Moshe Goldfeder, Paolo Gomarasca, Antonino Scalone, Andrea Simoncini, and Valentina Zappulli for the debates, the comments, and the observations.

which he wonders about the difference between political authority and brute force.[2] But Benedict also considers the same issue in other contexts, dealing with themes more closely related to Christianity. In his second book on Christ, he asks "what happens when truth counts for nothing? What kind of justice is then possible?" In doing so, he highlights that this question not only applies to religion and morality, but is rather "the question that is also asked by modern political theory."[3] Indeed, his observations have been recently shared by quite famous secular philosophers.[4]

Benedict's proposal is not to create a Catholic foundation for the postmodern state, of which the state has no need, but rather to contribute to an understanding of the role of law and politics at a time when both face challenges. Speaking from his unique perspective, he suggests that the fate of religion in the democratic state is shared by both justice and truth: the struggle to decipher the relationship between democracy and religion is merely one aspect of the troubled relationship between law, democracy, and justice.[5]

POPE BENEDICT'S PERSPECTIVE: THE HEART OF THE MATTER

In addressing the role of religion in public life, Benedict points directly to the meaning of religious experience in the public square, without lingering on specific arguments at the heart of the political debate. Not one of the words one might expect – such as "abortion," "gay marriage," or "euthanasia" – appears anywhere in any of his speeches. His points do not lean toward Catholic – or

[2] Pope Benedict XVI, Address at the Bundestag, Berlin, September 22, 2011.

[3] Pope Benedict XVI, Jesus of Nazareth: Holy Week: From the Entrance into Jerusalem to the Resurrection, San Francisco: Ignatius Press, 2011, 191.

[4] See, among many, G. Agamben, Homo sacer: Sovereign Power and Bare Life, Stanford: Stanford University Press, 1998, 31, and *Il mistero del male. Benedetto XVI e la fine dei tempi*, (*The Mystery of Evil: Benedict XVI and the End of Times*), Roma-Bari: Laterza, 2013.

[5] See Pope Francis's first Encyclical *Lumen Fidei*, 2013, par. 25.

conservative – apology. What concerns Benedict, and the goal of his reflections, is something else entirely.

Benedict starts with a unitary vision of the human being, signaling that the human capacity to build a truly open political environment and legal experience is closely tied to the internal dynamism each person feels that pulls toward the infinite and his or her own fulfillment.

For Benedict, this vision is not a theory, but a fact. In the speech he delivered to the Collège des Bernardins of Paris[6] he reminds us with particular intensity that the reconstruction of Europe took place in the monasteries. These gradually changed the face of history and the world with a dynamism that passed through and transcended the particular without avoiding it, but, on the contrary, causing it to flourish. *Quaerere Deum* (searching for God) is a formula Benedict used repeatedly on that occasion, to describe how human industriousness rebuilds the community when and because human beings reach toward the *beyond*, toward God.

The Pope Emeritus highlights the fact that political and legal experience is open to transcendence: this opening – Benedict's address at the Bundestag reminds us[7] – even Kelsen could not ignore, and, toward the end of his life, he considered the idea of a legal order open to transcendence.

Benedict places heavy emphasis on this point; the words "transcendence" and "transcendent" appear nine times in these texts: four times in the speech he gave at Regensburg, three in his United Nations address,[8] and two in his talk at Paris.[9]

The transcendence Pope Benedict describes[10] expresses the dynamism of politics and of human experience to emerge from themselves,

[6] Address at the Collège des Bernardins, Paris, September 12, 2008.

[7] Address at the Bundestag.

[8] Address at the United Nations Organization's General Assembly, New York, Friday, 18 April 2008.

[9] Address at the Collège des Bernardins.

[10] See also Pope Benedict's talk at the general assembly of the Italian Bishops' Conference, Rome, 24 May 2012: "The heart of the crisis that is damaging Europe – a spiritual and moral crisis – can be identified in this neglect; this

without, however, pushing too far from material realities. Earthly societies remain autonomous from the religious sphere, despite a bond that links the two.[11] If the bond is broken in the name of the absolute transcendence of a God who is inaccessible to humanity and human reason, then any chance of communication between political or human experience and religion will vanish. Human dignity will be debased: "God's transcendence and otherness are so exalted that our reason, our sense of the true and good, are no longer an authentic mirror of God, whose deepest possibilities remain eternally unattainable and hidden behind his actual decisions."[12]

On the other hand, if the bond were broken by separating human or political experience from religious experience, and the legal-political dimension from the dimension *beyond*, as many thinkers propose,[13] the result would be the same: human dignity would be threatened. In the speech he gave at the United Nations, Benedict pointed out that such a split did, in fact, occur in the first part of the twentieth century, and was fortunately healed thereafter: "The founding of the United Nations, as we know, coincided with the profound upheavals that humanity experienced when reference to the meaning of transcendence and natural reason was abandoned, and in consequence, freedom and human dignity were grossly violated."[14]

For Benedict, therefore, recognizing the transcendental dimension of human and political experience is the first line of defense for freedom and human dignity. In Benedict's speeches, transcendence

lack of openness to the Transcendent, since man claims to have a complete identity simply in himself."

11 Analogies can be traced in M.W. McConnell, "'God Is Dead and We Have Killed Him!': Freedom of Religion in the Post-modern Age," Brigham Young University Law Review, 1993, 172.

12 Pope Benedict XVI, Meeting with the representatives of science, Aula Magna of the University of Regensburg, Regensburg, 12 September 2006.

13 A. Sajó, "Preliminaries to a Concept of Constitutional Secularism," International Journal of Constitutional Law, 6, 2008, 618: "Constitutionalism exists only where the society does not take into public consideration transcendental concerns."

14 Address at the United Nation Organization's General Assembly.

describes the relationship between law and justice, and is therefore the first political and legal good to be preserved.

Now that we have understood transcendence to represent the possibility of a relationship between politics and religion, and between law and justice, we can move to consider what, in Benedict's thought, allows mankind to experience transcendence.[15]

THE HEART OF THE SOLUTION

Benedict, linking the capacity to build and better oneself to the *Quaerere Deum*, centers this idea on the human heart. "[S]earching for God," the engine behind all human action, is an attitude found in the heart of the person. Benedict speaks about the "heart" ten times in these speeches,[16] placing special emphasis on the "listening heart," the ability of the heart to grasp the truth. As he reminds us at the close of his speech to the Bundestag, this listening heart was what Solomon asked for from God as a gift. Interestingly, in the original Hebrew these words of the Bible read as a "wise and discerning heart," that is, an ability to distinguish and determine.

Benedict's protagonist is the human heart, presented as the true counterweight and antidote to tyranny. Lawmakers, and voters even before them, are uniquely called to carry out this discernment, in search of what is good and just. Benedict commends the democratic structure for the fact that it distributes the duty to engage in a "wise and discerning" way among all its citizens. Speaking of the current relevance of the prayer in which King Solomon asked God to give him such a heart, Benedict does not make a general reference to the "law-makers of today," but instead refers to "we, the law-makers of today." All citizens are implicated in the right-duty to engage the heart in choosing good rather than evil. In the words of contemporary political philosophy, which has frequently, and not by accident

[15] On the topic of transcendence, see *Lumen Fidei*, para. 33.

[16] Three times in the Paris speech, two in the UN speech, five in the Bundestag speech. The term is also used in other places, but in a figurative way, to refer to the nucleus of certain cultures or of institutions.

referred to biblical texts, "Evil ... is a *historical* drama in which each person's decisions are at issue at every turn."[17] This is why democracy is, as Benedict points out, echoing Habermas, a system that is sensitive to the truth:[18] because in a democracy, every person is called to put the criteria inscribed on their human nature to use. We might add that all this also makes democracy a particularly demanding system,[19] in which both citizens and those in power are equally called upon to practice the virtue of justice.[20]

THE GIFT OF BENEDICT: FROM LAW TO RELIGION

The Pope Emeritus paints a munificently favorable picture of democracy, highlights its methods and goals, and introduces important points of reflection for contemporary thinkers. On the one hand, he draws out the fact that democracy rises up from the people and therefore is the most appropriate way to involve each person in the right and responsibility of judgment. On the other hand, and precisely for this reason, democracy is more open to transcendence than any other system, and represents the place in which the greatest number of people can wonder reciprocally about their own origins and ultimate destiny.[21]

17 Agamben, *Il mistero del male*, 39.

18 Lecture intended to be delivered at the University of Rome "La Sapienza," January 17, 2008, where Benedict XVI mentions Habermas talking about the "sensibility to the truth as a necessary element in the process of political argument."

19 As R. Niebuhr has already pointed out with regard to American history in *The Irony of American History*, Charles Scribner's Sons (1952), Italian and English version from Turin: Bompiani, 251, "Our difficulty as a nation is that we must now learn that prosperity is not simply coordinated to virtue, that virtue is not simply coordinated to historic destiny and that happiness is no simple possibility of human existence."

20 A. MacIntyre, Whose Justice? Which Rationality?, Notre Dame: Notre Dame University Press, 1988, 103.

21 J. Stout, Democracy and Tradition, Princeton: Princeton University Press, 2004, 23.

Democracy provides the place where narratives about human destiny, origins, and ideals can intertwine.[22]

Ideas of democracy such as that offered by Benedict are especially necessary at our particular moment in history. Science and technology have provided us with tools and capabilities that are intimately tied to humanity's ultimate questions:[23] the questions that deal with the origin and the ultimate meaning of existence, honing in on issues such as conception and death, have assumed a practical relevance involving law and politics.

It is not religion which invades the political-legal realm, but rather politics and law which inevitably ask religious questions. The modernist, liberal distinction between "secular" and "religious" fades away,[24] and not because the religious overflows into the secular,[25] but because the political and legal realm thickens over time, as it draws into itself the most fundamental questions of existence.

The relationships between religion, politics, and law must, therefore, be reconsidered: the political sphere itself, together with its law, evokes ultimate questions, interrogating spiritual and religious experience. Along these lines, Ronald Dworkin recognized the connection between law and ultimate questions, concluding that: "lawyers and judges are working political philosophers of a democratic state."[26]

The Pope Emeritus' speeches provide us with useful tools for facing the yet unwritten pages of the present age. Together with Benedict, we can begin by remembering that points of contact between religion and law are not accidental. The relationship between the political-legal and religious spheres is not that of occasional

[22] Id., 6: "[t]he democratic practice of giving and asking for ethical reasons, I argue, is where the life of democracy principally resides. Democracy isn't all talk."

[23] A. Finkielkraut, Nous autres, modernes: Quatre leçons, Paris: Ellipses, 2005.

[24] A. Shachar, "State, Religion, and the Family: The New Dilemmas of Multicultural Accommodation," in R. Ahdar, N. Aroney (eds.), Shari'a in the West, Oxford: Oxford University Press, 2010, 120.

[25] See M. Cacciari, Il potere che frena (The Power that Resists), Milan: Adelphi, 2013, 12.

[26] R. Dworkin, Justice for Hedgehogs, Cambridge: Belknap Press of Harvard Press, 2011, 414.

interference (as when policies and religious beliefs collide) or coincidence (when policies and religious beliefs get along well): it is rather human coexistence that is structurally open to what is beyond itself. And only through this openness can it respond adequately to the challenges ahead, especially in any methodological way: "the religious dimension can help to achieve this, since recognition of the transcendent value of every man and woman favours conversion of heart, which then leads to a commitment to resist violence, terrorism and war, and to promote justice and peace."[27]

The Pope Emeritus' reflections even cast the religious dimension in a new light. Religious traditions are not simply the reservoir from which constitutionalism and the culture of rights emerged. Tradition and law do not inhabit a universe in which concepts may only exit the religious realm and become secularized[28] – the opposite process can also occur: technological and scientific advancement poses questions, through the heart of each individual, to both religion and politics, forcing people to reflect on themselves and to interact with one another. Indeed, the Catholic Church has historically learned from human experience: think, for example, of the doctrinal changes on the topic of slavery.[29] Contemporary reflections of religious traditions, in fields such as biotechnology[30] or economics,[31] confirm that policies that make the fruits of scientific advancement available through welfare systems incentivize theological reflection.[32]

[27] Speech before the United Nations.

[28] See, for all, C. Schmitt, Political Theology: Four Chapters on the Concept of Sovereignty, Chicago: University of Chicago Press, 2006.

[29] J.T. Noonan, Jr., A Church that Can and Cannot Change: The Development of Catholic Moral Teaching, Notre Dame: University of Notre Dame Press, 2005, 210.

[30] Among myriad works, see, for example, F. Rosner, D. Bleich, (eds.) Jewish Bioethics, Chicago: KTAV, 2000; D. Atighetchi, Islamic Bioethics: Problems and Perspectives, Dordrecht: Springer, 2007.

[31] M.A. El-Gamal, Islamic Finance: Law, Economics and Practice, New York: Cambridge University Press, 2006.

[32] K. Greenawalt, Law and Objectivity, New York: Oxford University Press, 1992, 167: "cultural morality is responsive to legal change."

Religion's contribution to political experience needs, therefore, to be understood from a fresh perspective. It is not simply religions that wish to participate in the world of politics; it is the political dimension itself, in its natural openness to transcendence (which has increased particularly over the last several decades) that involves itself in topics touching on ultimate issues.

This contiguity between politics, law, and religion does not blur their respective spheres. These remain distinct, for reasons that go back to the transcendental relationship between the levels of political and religious experience.

LISTENING TO THE RELIGIONS

As Benedict provides an interesting portrait of the relationship between law, politics, and religion, we are faced with the question of how the religious traditions can interact with the sphere of law and politics in a concrete way: how should religions speak out in the secular sphere.

Some have conceded, as one British court pointed out, that in religion "[i]ndividuals cannot always be expected to express themselves with cogency or precision:"[33] Where this does happen, it is not necessarily because religious belief is not "always susceptible to lucid exposition or, still less, rational justification,"[34] as that court believed, as though it belongs to some lower class than politics.

It is just as possible that the rationality of religious experience *exceeds* that of politics, because of its transcendental character. The gap between the political and legal spheres, on the one hand, and the religious one on the other may also come from the transcendental nature of human experience. Politics and law carry one toward a depth that surpasses them but does not necessarily contradict them, and of which religions traditions are the predominant historical manifestation.

[33] *Regina (Williamson and Others) v. Secretary of State for Education and Employment* [2005] UKHL 15, quoted in ECtHR, *Eweida & Others v. UK*, (app. nos. 48420/10, 59842/10, 51671/10, 36516/10), judgment January 15, 2013, para. 45.

[34] Id.

Permitting religious expressions, in their specificity, means permitting transcendence, in the forms in which it has traditionally – but not exclusively – expressed itself. To cite an often-discussed statement by the American Supreme Court Justice Antonin Scalia, "If religion in the public forum had to be entirely nondenominational, there could be no religion in the public forum at all."[35] Allowing a religious expression only insofar as it is nondenominational and distilled into secular terms, on the basis of a form of logic described as *neutrality*, particularly in Europe,[36] is tantamount to disallowing it in its nature and origins. In short, it is disallowing it completely.

The asymmetry between religion, on the one hand, and law and politics, on the other, does not render communication between them impossible, but rather requires that the political-legal dimension recognize the religious dimension, even in its language, for the valuable contributions it can make to topics of mutual interest. David Novak has pointed out that religious experience offers a contribution with particular traits, which derive from the characteristics of religious experience itself. For example, God's will may be expressed through commandments, some of which are not separable from the divinity that establishes them, while others are easily understood and gain independence from divine provenance. Fasting on Ash Wednesday, observing a day of rest on the Sabbath, or changing the ordinary schedule of meals during Ramadan are not comprehensible outside of a relationship with a divinity who demands adoration in these forms. But the commandment "thou shalt not kill," while it is well-known and embraced by people within a certain religious experience, also assumes an independence that renders it comprehensible to anyone.[37] In other words, although the religious traditions have a capacity for reflection and discussion that follows their own track, this is not a reason to sustain that their reflections and discussions are less rational, shareable, and objective: "There are powerful traditions

[35] *McCreary Cty. v ACLU*, 545 U.S. 844, 893 (2005).

[36] A. Scola, Let's not Forget God: Faith, Culture, and Politics, New York: Random House, 2014, 80.

[37] D. Novak, Natural Law in Judaism, New York: Cambridge University Press, 1998, 16.

of reasoned argument, rather than reliance of faith and unreasoned convictions, in India's intellectual past," Amartya Sen points out, reminding us of how deep, albeit sometimes hidden, is the bond between the rational, religious, and traditional dimensions.[38] This leads to the recognition of a much more realistic role for religion, rather than simply as the historical antecedent of the contemporary, legal civilization. Even today, religious education transmits contents that are embraced prior to full theoretical comprehension, without requiring a demonstrative or experimental procedure. It is also possible that a demonstrative procedure, through its concepts or lines of reasoning, is incapable of encompassing the whole, rich experience that brought an individual to a specific conclusion.[39]

Religious experience is not necessarily a shortcut. It can also offer better, richer, and more accessible reasons for fundamental truths.[40] Vladimir Solovyov, faced with an epoch in which rationalism was groping to find rational support for universal brotherhood, warned that it would be impossible to substitute the immediately accessible idea that we were all loved by God and therefore should love one another with the syllogism that "Man descends from the apes, therefore we must love each other."[41]

We cannot expect to substitute rich arguments drawing from religious traditions with poor arguments that deprive our customs and values of sense and meaning. For instance, concerning the custom of burying dead, which has been widespread throughout history and the globe, it may be possible to maintain that "people are buried in cemeteries not because it facilitates resurrection," but it is certainly not suitable to assert that this practice is based solely upon "public health reasons,"[42] which have nothing to do with the

[38] A. Sen, The Idea of Justice, London, New York: Allen Lane & Harvard University Press, 2009, 25.

[39] See J.H. Newman, An Essay in Aid of a Grammar of Assent, London: Burns, Oates & Co., 1874, passim

[40] H. Putnam, Reason, Truth and History, Cambridge: Cambridge University Press, 1981, 158.

[41] Quoted in C. Taylor, A Secular Age, Cambridge, London: Harvard University Press, 2007, 596.

[42] Sajó, 618.

deep vein of a culture. Peoples have buried their dear ones with honor for much richer and often more anguishing reasons since long before Sophocles wrote his Antigone. Respecting the language and modes of expression of each religion means respecting the way in which many people continue to this day to learn values, principles, and truths,[43] as well as the contexts in which they are often introduced to the search for truth and justice.[44] Denying religions the possibility to participate with their own lexicon means denying citizenship to arguments that still play a role in society, as well as denying self-expression to the many people educated with a lexicon and a sensibility that are inseparably tied to the religious dimension. It also means denying room to journeys of personal growth, which, for many people, wind their way through, or in relation to, the religious community they belong to.[45] Finally, it means condemning democracy to a reductive vision of political and legal rationality and procedures.[46]

Moreover, the lexicon a religious tradition uses to express itself is inevitably a mix of experiences: it merges the religious dimension with the rational and cultural ones.[47] Claiming to separate the religious element from the rational one means imposing a "radical separation between the domain of faith or of the religious and the domain of reason,"[48] which, as described earlier, does not consist either with religious experience or with political experiences open to transcendence. To place preconditions on the experiences that will be allowed to play a role in public debate means forcibly separating aspects that have been interwoven for centuries, and which uniquely characterize

[43] G.F. McLean, "Hermeneutics of Tolerance in a Multicultural Society," in E. Alam (ed.), God in Multicultural Society: Religion, Politics and Globalization, Louaize: Notre Dame University Press, 2006, 15.

[44] Novak, 13. In *Lumen Fidei*, Pope Francis, too, reflects on the ability of the Christian faith to "provide a service to the common good with regard to the right way of understanding truth" (par. 32).

[45] MacIntyre, 390.

[46] C. Schmitt, Roman Catholicism and Political Form, Westport: Greenwood Press, 1996.

[47] A. Scola, "Faith and Culture: The Insuperable Circularity," Oasis, 10, 2009.

[48] G. Richi Alberti, "Looking for Good, Looking for the Truth," Oasis, 10, 2009.

religious traditions as well as their evolutions. If the Catholic Church permitted slavery for hundreds of years, secular thought did likewise. Both eventually reached the same, opposite conclusion; nevertheless, this did not mean that the Church became more secular, or that it lost its religious nature.[49]

It is crucial to respect religious traditions for *how they express themselves*, even more so than for *what they say*, which may indeed be distasteful. A selective logic, which fractures the languages people may use to express themselves, does damage to the most fundamental way that many religious traditions express their beliefs while still respecting the freedom of others: that is, giving witness.[50] A filter that only allows communication in the rationalistic, discursive form threatens the method of giving witness. Benedict also developed the idea that truth, justice, and goodness can be reached through witness, and not exclusively through discursive procedures. See for example, his comment on Abraham's prayer to save Sodom and Gomorrah from destruction, which culminates in God's promise to spare the cities if even ten upright inhabitants live there. Benedict points out that, in God's teaching, all that is necessary is "a tiny particle of goodness with which to start in order to save the rest from a great evil."[51] What are needed are a "few innocents from whom to start in order to turn evil into good." A political coexistence able to accommodate religious experiences must also make room for this notion of justice and the role that witnessing plays in it.

CONCLUSIONS

In the final analysis, to purify reason with religious experience, as Benedict suggests, means enriching its contents and even its vocabulary – not weakening and simplifying it. As Robert Cover

[49] Noonan, 94–95.

[50] J. Prades, "Knowing the Truth through Witness: The Christian Faith in the Context of Interreligious Dialogue," A. Lopez & J. Prades, (ed.), *Retrieving Origins and the Claim of Multiculturalism*, Grand Rapids: Eerdmans, 181.

[51] General Audience, May 18, 2011.

wrote, already thirty years ago, it is not possible to absorb the richness of a people's *nomos* in a circumscribed legal experience, since this experience comes into being through religious and cultural experiences, and needs them deeply. He concluded by urging that "[w]e ought to stop circumscribing the *nomos*; we ought to invite new worlds."[52]

Benedict's thought on democracy and religion supports Cover's intuition. But the principle does not only apply to democracy, and the attention it should be paying religion. The opposite also holds true. Since the religious dimension transcends the political one, by its nature, it is impossible that religion find politics to be large enough to house it entirely: religious experience can enter into relationship with that of the secular law, but it can never completely exhaust itself within it. It exceeds it. A culture's narratives on its origins and destiny can never be entirely played out within the secular legal order: "the very patterns of meaning that give rise to effective or ineffective social control are to be left to the domain of Babel."[53] Therefore, the heart of democracy resides in the tension that exists between human coexistence and the object toward which it naturally turns, and from which it is nourished. Any attempt to unify these planes cannot avoid losing something, be it part of legal-political experience, or part of the religious one.

Pope Benedict XVI offered a defense of religion in the public square and an *apologia* for democracy rich with implications for the contemporary legal-philosophical culture: a democracy that requires a "listening heart"; a political and legal order open to transcendence; and an idea of reason that would allow people and communities to bear reciprocal witness to one another.

[52] R. Cover, "Foreword: Nomos and Narrative," Harvard Law Review 97, 1983–1984, 68.

[53] Id., 17.

CONTRIBUTORS

Giuliano Amato, Emeritus of Constitutional Law, European University Institute, Florence; currently Judge of the Italian Constitutional Court

Armin von Bogdandy, Director at the Max Planck Institute for Comparative Public Law and International Law, Heidelberg; currently Chairman of the European Tribunal for Nuclear Energy

Marta Cartabia, Full Professor of Constitutional Law; currently Judge of the Italian Constitutional Court

Sergio Dellavalle, Associate Professor of Public Law, University of Turin; Associate Director of Project at the Max Planck Institute for Comparative Public Law and International Law, Heidelberg

Rafael Domingo, Professor of Law and ICS Research Professor at the University of Navarra; Francisco de Vitoria Senor Fellow at the Center for the Study of Law and Religion at Emory University

Wael Farouq, Lecturer at the American University in Cairo

Mary Ann Glendon, Learned Hand Professor of Law, Harvard University

Christoph Grabenwarter, Christoph Grabenwarter, Full Professor of Public and International Law, Vienna University of Business; Judge of the Austrian Constitutional Court and member of the Venice Commission

Massimo Luciani, Full Professor of Public Law, University of Rome "La Sapienza"

Chistopher McCrudden, Professor of Human Rights and Equality Law, Queen's University Belfast; William W Cook Global Professor of Law, University of Michigan Law School; Fellow, Wissenschaftskolleg zu Berlin (2014–15)

Giorgio Napolitano, President of the Italian Republic

Andrés Ollero, Full Professor of Legal Philosophy, Rey Juan Carlos University, Madrid; currently Judge of the Spanish Constitutional Court

Andrea Pin, Senior Lecturer in Comparative Law, University of Padua

Martin Rhonheimer, Professor of Ethics and Political Philosophy, Pontifical University of the Holy Cross, Rome

Andrea Simoncini, Full Professor of Constitutional Law, University of Florence

Joseph H.H. Weiler, President of the European University Institute in Florence

John Witte, Jr., Jonas Robitscher Professor of Law and Director of the Center for the Study of Law and Religion, Emory University

INDEX